T0245994

Praise for
Hometown Betrayal

"*Hometown Betrayal* is a powerful book that exposes child sexual abuse at its worst. Some may think this story is an exception, but the national and global data tell us otherwise. We must break the silence and do more to stop both the horrific acts and cover-ups that negatively impact survivors, their families, and even the generations that follow. Thanks to the Millers for their perseverance and courage to share their tragic story so that we can all be moved into action."

—**Susan Madsen,** EdD, Founding Director, Utah Women & Leadership Project, Utah State University; Karen Haight Huntsman Endowed Professor of Leadership, Jon M. Huntsman School of Business, Utah State University

"*Hometown Betrayal* recounts the remarkable story of a family's quest for justice for terrible crimes committed decades earlier. All too often, such stories recount nothing but frustration, dead ends, and legal barriers. But in this case, the family was able to obtain some measure of justice. It is a powerful story of how, at least sometimes, the truth can ultimately be uncovered."

—**Paul G. Cassell,** JD, Ronald N. Boyce Presidential Professor of Criminal Law and University Distinguished Professor of Law, S. J. Quinney College of Law, University of Utah

"The devastating and long-lasting impacts of child sexual abuse cannot be ignored. Valarie Miller's story is a stark reminder to acknowledge the systemic failures many survivors encounter and a call to action to prevent such injustices from occurring in the future."

—**Betsy Kanarowski,** PhD, LCSW, chief clinical officer, Saprea

HOMETOWN
BETRAYAL

HOMETOWN BETRAYAL

A TRAGIC STORY *of* SECRECY *and* SEXUAL ABUSE *in* MORMON COUNTRY

EMILY BENEDEK

GREENLEAF
BOOK GROUP PRESS

Any full name in this book represents a real person. On a few occasions,
the author has used a first name alone, and acknowledged it as a pseudonym,
to protect that individual's privacy.

Published by Greenleaf Book Group Press
Austin, Texas
www.gbgpress.com

Distributed by Greenleaf Book Group

For ordering information or special discounts for bulk purchases, please contact
Greenleaf Book Group at PO Box 91869, Austin, TX 78709, 512.891.6100.

Design and composition by Greenleaf Book Group
Cover design by Greenleaf Book Group

Publisher's Cataloging-in-Publication data is available.

Print ISBN: 979-8-88645-248-8

eBook ISBN: 979-8-88645-249-5

To offset the number of trees consumed in the printing of our books, Greenleaf
donates a portion of the proceeds from each printing to the Arbor Day
Foundation. Greenleaf Book Group has replaced over 50,000 trees since 2007.

Printed in the United States of America on acid-free paper

24 25 26 27 28 29 30 31   10 9 8 7 6 5 4 3 2 1

First Edition

Dedicated to the memory of Valarie Clark Miller
and all others who suffer the unspeakable
harm of childhood sexual abuse.

Content Note

This book was written to shed light on a painful reality, that many people can be victims of abuse and not know how to seek help or may struggle to be believed if they do. In addition to child sexual abuse, *Hometown Betrayal* also discusses challenging topics related to mental health and suicide.

If you or someone you know is struggling with thoughts of suicide or is in emotional distress, you can access free and confidential emotional support by calling 988, the National Lifeline. If it is a life-threatening situation, call 911.

RAINN (Rape, Abuse & Incest National Network) provides a free, confidential national sexual assault hotline that you can access 24/7 by calling 1-800-656-HOPE (4673).

You can also contact the Substance Abuse and Mental Health Services Administration (SAMHSA) National Helpline at 1-800-622-HELP (4357) to access free, confidential referral and information services for individuals and families facing mental health and/or substance use challenges.

Foreword

AS I PREPARED TO WRITE this foreword, so many thoughts and emotions spun around in my head. While my story and Valarie's story are different, there are also many similarities. Both Valarie and I grew up in Utah, we both loved riding horses, and we both had families and friends who loved us and took care of us. We also both experienced horrific sexual violence at the hands of grown men.

My name is Elizabeth Smart. I was kidnapped back in June of 2002 when I was 14 years old and held captive for nine months. I experienced sexual violence, rape, and abuse, to name a few.

Though I never had a chance to meet Valarie Clark Miller, the first thing I would have said to her is, "I believe you!"

All the time, people ask me questions like "Why do you seem so normal despite what you endured?" or "What therapy did you use?" or "I know someone who was sexually abused. What can I share with them to help them heal?" While there is no one-size-fits-all solution for healing, there is one way we can make a huge difference together. The first thing is to believe the survivor's story!

For that to happen, we need to create spaces and procedures where survivors feel safe and confident enough to share what has happened to them without being questioned, doubted, or blamed. We should decide, as a society, to vocally state our belief and support for survivors, both individually and on a large scale.

I wholeheartedly understand the terror that silenced Valarie as a child.

It grew from both the vicious beatings and sexual assaults to which she was repeatedly subjected and the true fear that if she told on the men who were abusing her, they would hurt her family.

And then, almost 20 years later, after she was finally ready to tell what had happened to her, she was dismissed by law enforcement and a community that lied and collaborated to protect her attackers. This devastated her, destroyed her health and her family, and ultimately took her life. My heart aches for the pain that Valarie and every other victim in this book experienced.

Valarie's story shows vividly why victims of sexual abuse do not share the abuse they have suffered, let alone report it to authorities. It also helps us understand the complex challenges of PTSD and how trauma finds many unique ways to undermine lives, health, and peace of mind.

John Miller and his family have been heroic in their efforts to pursue justice and share the unfathomable details of Valarie's tragedy. When I first met John, he said Valarie frequently spoke about wanting to write a book about her experiences in the hope it could help other women and girls share their stories and get well. This book is not easy to read, and it leaves you with so many maddening questions: How could so many bad things happen to one person? How was it possible that the people who could have stopped her torment all looked away? But that is what makes this book so important. It reveals the unspeakable reality that affects tens of millions of people in our country.

For the past 20 years, I have met survivors from around the world and all 50 states. I can confidently say the reason why survivors don't share what happens to them is because they are afraid they won't be believed. Any time a victim comes forward, they are immediately put on trial in the court of public opinion. We, as a society, tend to judge everything about them—their appearance, their behavior, their occupation, and so on. Without saying it out loud, we essentially question whether they are worthy of our belief. As Valarie's story shows us, we judge them more quickly and more harshly than we judge those who have hurt them.

I grew up thinking it was so noble of us as a nation to believe "innocent until proven guilty," but my experience as a victim, survivor, and advocate has shown me that in pursuit of that goal, our legal system does a grave disservice to our most vulnerable victims—child victims of sexual abuse.

Because sexual crimes tend to take place behind closed doors where there are no witnesses, predators and rapists have traditionally hidden behind the argument: "It's a case of he said/she said." This formulation has protected many guilty men. But I ask: How can it possibly be right to examine and then cross-examine a child about the worst moments of their lives, when their attacker sits within feet of them, staring at them, effectively victimizing them all over again in court? A courtroom does not level the power dynamics at play. When someone has been hurt, manipulated, and silenced, even as they "freely" walk about, those invisible chains do not suddenly disappear in the courtroom. They are always there: What if I'm not believed? What if they release him? What will happen next?

My story is famous because it has a happier ending than those of most survivors. Despite being held hostage for nine months and raped daily, once I was rescued, I was immediately safe, and I was immediately believed. My perpetrators were placed behind bars, and very few people ever questioned my story because it had taken place in real time in full view of the world.

Because I was attacked by a stranger, survivors often compare their story to mine, diminishing their own experiences by saying theirs was "not as bad" as my story because they were abused by someone close to them—a family member, neighbor, or teacher. This talk of comparing experiences needs to end. Sexual abuse of children is a sadistic, sometimes deadly crime. Personally, I cannot imagine trying to live my life each day in a state of constant fear like Valarie did. I would not be the person I am today if I had to show up somewhere at any moment to serve myself up to be raped and abused, be scared to come home after school not knowing if my perpetrator would be there, or go to bed at night afraid I wouldn't be safe there.

If you want to know why I am the way I am, it is because from the first time I opened my mouth after I was rescued, I was believed and supported.

We should all want that for every survivor. We need this for every survivor. Based on the high incidence of childhood sexual abuse and sexual violence in our society, and its outsized contribution to rates of mental illness and substance abuse, we have to continue to be advocates for change. There are too many who don't make it back alive, even if they are still breathing.

It has now been more than 60 years since Valarie's abuse. As heartbreaking as it is, we should use her story as a spark for change. Her reality is the norm for so many survivors. We must read these stories, not look away, even if it's hard. We need to become the safe spaces in which to create healing.

I am excited for you to read this book, and I hope you will allow yourself to feel the same feelings I did—anger, sadness, empathy, hunger for justice, and passion for change. And then let's go into the world and work to make a difference, together.

Elizabeth Smart
Salt Lake City
March 2024

PART I

A Little Bird, Lying There Broken

MAY 21, 1983, DAWNED SUNNY and warm in Hyrum, Utah, a rural town of about 5,000 souls named after the brother of Joseph Smith, founder of Mormonism. The tiny, white trumpet flowers of the catalpa trees had already burst open in bunches, and the bark of the tall ponderosa pines oozed its butterscotch-scented sap. John Miller, who had gone to his office that Saturday at E. A. Miller & Sons, the family meatpacking plant, for a few hours, realized the spring day was too beautiful to waste inside, so around noon he headed home. He pulled into his driveway and ran into the house to ask his wife, Valarie, if she'd go for a drive with him. He'd just imported a Mercedes-Benz 280SL, and he wanted to take her for a spin. After checking that the neighbors would keep an eye on the Miller's six-year-old daughter, Annie, Valarie jumped in the Mercedes beside him, her long, brown hair loose. John put down the top. Valarie was 28 years old, and John was 30.

After a pleasant drive, they returned home. Valarie went into the house, and John struck up a conversation with a neighbor. "I remember what happened next like it was yesterday," said their son, Ryan, then three and a half, who had remained at home with his toddler sister, Erin, and their nanny while their parents were out and was then walking atop a wall at the end of the driveway. "My mom suddenly ran out of the garage, frantic. She said my sister, Annie, had been in an accident. I remember my dad jumping into the car, and them racing down the street."

John and Valarie sped to the center of town where they saw a group of people "gathered around a little lump in the middle of the street."[1] Their daughter, John recalled, "looked like a little bird fallen from its nest, lying there, broken." She was on her back, gasping for air. Blood dripped from both her ears, and her pupils were rolled back into her head. No emergency responders were yet on the scene, but John remembered someone saying, "Give her a blessing, and let's pray." As an elder in the Church of Jesus Christ of Latter-day Saints, John had the authority to offer a prayer for healing, so he placed his hands on his daughter's head and "blessed her to live," all the while realizing the terrifying indications that his first-born was grievously injured and likely near death.

John's boss, uncle, and mentor, Junior, materialized beside him. Someone placed a coat over Annie to keep her warm, and a couple of men came out of the local pool hall and propped up her feet on a six-pack of Budweiser.

Finally, the paramedics arrived and went to work. Valarie kept reaching for her daughter, trying to gather her into her arms, but the EMTs restrained her. She finally was able to get ahold of the little girl's limp hand. "Oh, Annie," she kept saying. "It's okay, it's all right."

John sketched out a picture of what had happened from information offered by onlookers. Annie, a "pretty, capricious, little blonde" in his words, "verbal and full of life," had decided with her friend Holly and Julie, Holly's 14-year-old sister, to bike into town, although Annie knew the family rules allowed her to ride her bike on only the quiet street in front of their house. The girls took off, three in a row, Annie in the rear, a bit wobbly on her beloved pink two-wheeler. Reaching Main Street, they pedaled along the sidewalk under a canopy of trees, stopped at the drug store to buy candy, then decided to cross the street to go to the library. Riding carefully inside the lines of the crosswalk, Annie and Holly made it across the busy thoroughfare, but Annie abruptly reversed course and, without looking left or right, re-entered the crosswalk to head back to Julie, who was still on the other side. Annie was immediately struck by a truck going 40 miles per hour and thrown more than 20 feet.

The EMTs loaded Annie into the ambulance and notified Logan Regional Hospital they were bringing in the injured girl. Annie's pediatrician, Dr. Stowell, was paged at home. Before leaving the scene, Valarie passed by the young, desolate truck driver who had struck her daughter. She stopped and told him in her soft voice, "It's not your fault." An onlooker was stunned "by Valarie's ability to be so kind and forgiving."

The ride to the hospital took only 15 minutes, and Dr. Stowell, who had also taken care of Valarie when she was a child, wasted no time in examining her daughter. He was alarmed that she was still unconscious and unresponsive. Her pupils were dilated and fixed, and blood and spinal fluid dripped from her right ear. He ordered her into the operating room.

As John paced in a waiting area outside, his uncle Junior and his wife, Norma, arrived, as did John's mother and his four brothers, one after the other. They all cried and prayed, silently and out loud.

After about 20 minutes, John saw Dr. Stowell walking toward him. "I'm sorry," he said. "She's very seriously injured."

The doctor told John and Valarie that Annie had been put on a ventilator. The medical team had tried to lower her blood pressure with steroids and other means, but she had not responded. Because Logan Hospital did not have a CT scanner, they were unable to establish the extent of the brain injury.

"We need to get her to a neurosurgeon," he said, "and the nearest is Ogden. I don't know if she'll make it there, but I think we should try."

"She isn't going to die," Valarie said quietly.

McKay-Dee Hospital was 45 miles to the south, and Annie was readied for another ambulance ride. Peggy Wolfley, one of the nurses who had worked to stabilize the struggling child, said she would accompany her in the ambulance and try to keep her alive. Valarie stepped toward Wolfley in the corridor and said, with a calm certainty, "I trust you to do this. I know that you can save her."

Annie remained stable throughout the 45-minute trip. At McKay-Dee, the neurologist, Dr. Glen Church, met the Millers at the emergency entrance. Annie was sent for a CT scan and readied for surgery immediately. "I felt as though my heart was in my hands," John recalled. He looked over at Valarie and saw she was "praying furiously that somehow Annie would survive. She refused to believe Annie might not make it."

After an hour or so, Dr. Church approached Valarie and John and told them that their daughter had suffered an injury to her brain stem and three fractures in her basilar skull. She also had indications of trauma to her abdomen and a possible pelvic fracture. He explained that they had inserted a tube into their daughter's head to relieve the pressure and that he was worried about the continued leak of cerebrospinal fluid into her right ear canal; he'd been unable to determine the location of the wound and feared an untreated tear might allow bacteria entry into her brain, which might then lead to meningitis. He repeated Dr. Stowell's fear that she might not survive. "But kids can surprise us," he added. "They can be quite resilient."

John and Valarie asked to see their daughter, and the doctor prepared them by explaining that a tracheotomy had been performed to help her breathe and that she'd been placed in an induced coma. "Annie was engulfed in a large hospital bed," John recalled, "her little head wrapped up, and a tube protruding from it, leading to the brain monitoring machine that was measuring the internal pressure." Later, the nurses explained that Annie's life might be in danger if the number on the dial reached 10.

As John and Valarie sat vigil beside their daughter, they were informed that the waiting room had filled with relatives and friends. The boy who had been driving the truck was there, along with his parents, all of whom were employed at E. A. Miller. John's mother, Emma, left at midnight to go to John's house (which he'd recently built next door to hers) to stay with Ryan and Erin.

"Valarie and I stayed on, consoling each other," John said. They also kept speaking to Annie, hoping she could hear them. "We need you to come back," they told her. But Annie's condition remained perilous. One night, John witnessed the pressure in his daughter's head spike to 24, and the neurologist on call discussed with them the possibility of unhooking her from the breathing machine. John and Valarie dismissed the suggestion out of hand. They knew that Annie was fighting for her life, and they were committed to fight alongside her. Indeed, she rallied, and the pressure went down.

Ten days later, John's mother and Valarie's parents spent the night at the hospital so John and Valarie could go home and rest. The next morning, John stopped by E. A. Miller for the first time since the accident. He was struck by how differently he felt there. As he walked down the hall toward his office, he remembered how important work had always been for him, but "now none of it seemed important anymore." He was proud of his efforts to modernize the company, acknowledging that his work "was an integral part of who I was." Or so he thought. "Now, all that mattered was family, my children, and little Annie laying in the hospital bed."

In the following days, they took turns staying with Annie. At work, John found it difficult to refocus, but he realized being at the plant gave him an opportunity "to feel productive" and to take his thoughts, even for just a brief moment, "away from the helplessness of worrying about Annie." It occurred to him that Valarie didn't have such an outlet. "She would sit in her rocking chair in a daze. I believe she felt it was up to her to save her daughter by exhibiting faith. She had convinced herself that if she possessed enough faith, Annie would live. For hours, Valarie would rock back and forth, with no expression on her face. Just staring emptily and rocking. I grew very concerned about her."

When Annie surprised the doctors by making it to two weeks, the neurologist began to think she might survive. John then wondered what her life might be like if she did pull through. He became very angry when one of the nurses said, "She won't be the same. This girl here is not the same girl that you knew before."

Eventually, Annie was weaned from the drugs that kept her unconscious and, later, unhooked from the ventilator. The tube in her head was removed. After some weeks, she seemed to begin moving her hands, though it didn't seem to be purposeful. "Finally, her eyes opened," John said, "but she stared with more of a glaze, and then stared into space." After that, "her eyes moved from side to side, but she still wouldn't make eye contact with anyone." It never occurred to him that she might be blind. At this point, though she was breathing on her own and coming closer to consciousness, Annie had no body control and was in a diaper. "I would talk to her and ask her to squeeze my hand, but nothing."

Annie had been in the hospital for about a month when her pediatrician came to visit. He told John he felt Annie was aware of him when he entered the room. "His years of experience had taught him that brain damage in children was unpredictable," recalled John. "He had seen children recover from very severe injuries, even though, on a statistical basis, their chances had been slim."

After five weeks, Annie was transferred from the ICU to the pediatric ward, where she was visited by a variety of therapists every day. Annie was belted into a wheelchair with her head stabilized by a head strap "because she couldn't control anything, and her neck would droop." The following week, she was moved to a rehabilitation center.

On August 15, almost three months after the accident, Annie went home for the weekend. Although the family was jubilant over Anne's progress, the strain of the ordeal had taken its toll on Valarie. John had kept a daily journal since his Mormon mission as a young man, and that day he wrote, "Valarie is having a hard time thru all of the problems with Annie. She has lost a lot of weight and emotionally is very exhausted. I am very concerned about her."

At the end of August, the rehab center said its staff had done all it could for the girl. She was still in a diaper, her eyes were open but sightless, and she couldn't communicate except, as John put it, "for an odd scream she would make to express discomfort." She remained in a partial coma, and she couldn't move her arms or legs. The doctors said further improvement depended on the "regeneration of neural connections," which John hoped would come with time and "the prayers of friends and family." Valarie's father, Denzel Clark, said that Valarie was very upset by a hospital staffer who told her that Annie would remain a vegetable.

A few days after Annie's return home, Debbie Clark Cooper, Valarie's older sister, came to pick up Ryan to stay with her family for a few days. She remembered seeing an emaciated Valarie rocking in her chair, dark circles under her eyes, still beseeching God to help her child get well. Debbie overheard Valarie tell someone, "I know a place where I can go where I can't feel any of this pain."

Debbie had an eerie sense that Valarie was not new to that place.

Nevertheless, small signs of improvement "brought enormous hope and happiness," John told a writer who prepared a narrative about Annie's accident and recovery. He continued:

> *I vividly remember one day when she gave us one of these little signs. We had to feed her by using a syringe, which we would place in her mouth and squeeze liquid nourishment into the back of her throat. About a month after Annie had been home, I was clowning around and loaded a syringe with water and squirted it playfully at the other kids. Not being a particularly good shot, I missed and landed a direct strike on the bridge of Anne's nose.*
>
> *A tear came to her eye and trickled down her cheek. It was the first sign of emotion we had seen from her since the accident, and I was overcome with joy. It might seem heartless to feel so elated that my daughter was crying, but to me it signified that she was registering feeling, and that she could convey emotion. I apologized to Annie for squirting her with water, but each time I said I was sorry, her*

*bottom lip and chin curled up. This single tear and the subtle facial
movements were major milestones. This meant she was waking up. We
all shed tears together as hope was renewed.*

Not long after, Annie laughed for the first time since the accident.
She also seemed to be moving her right hand with some intention. Then
she slowly formed the word *mommy*. A few weeks later, John said she was
mouthing the ABC's—not in her formerly sweet, high voice but rather with
a rough, throaty sound. Gradually, her sight returned; the doctors theorized
that the extreme pressure in her head may have damaged her optic nerves,
which repaired themselves over time.

"Dr. Church told us Annie was one of the greatest miracles he had seen,"
said John. "My heart was filled with gratitude."

Valarie continued with her nonstop praying. Her friend Sue Saunders
said, "I feel like she prayed Annie awake." Without that, Sue sometimes
wondered "if God would have taken her."

John threw himself into Annie's rehabilitation. Most evenings, he carried
Annie down into their basement gym for physical therapy. First, he focused
on helping her relearn how to sit. "Again and again, I would prop her up,
only to see her tip and fall to one side or the other."

John felt that Annie hated these physical therapy sessions because she
"would make a frightened whining sound," but she eventually learned to
hold herself in a seated position, supported by her arms, legs splayed on the
floor. The next task he set for her was crawling. "Day after day I sat behind
her and helped her lift one arm and then a leg, slowly teaching her how to
crawl. It was tedious and at times discouraging, but the slightest bit of progress would give all of us the courage to push on."

Just as Annie was scrabbling her way back to health, Valarie's strength
seemed to be ebbing away. For five months she had prayed incessantly for
her daughter's recovery, believing her daughter's future rested completely on
the power of her faith. But now, with victory close, Valarie couldn't seem to

shift gears and come out of her fixation. And it was weakening her. During those long months praying for Annie's recovery, Sue Saunders learned that Valarie had been tortured by frightening flashbacks. "I remember going to her home in Hyrum, and she was pacing the floor and just saying, 'These thoughts in my head, I feel like I'm going crazy.' And she kept praying and pacing and fretting," said Sue.

When Sue asked her to describe what she saw, Valarie said, "I don't know. It's just scary and hard."

Sue said, "That's when things started to really crumble."

The morning of September 19, when Valarie woke up, she was frightened to realize that the skin on the left side of her torso had gone numb. From her belly button around to the middle of her back, from her hip bone up to her neck, in a perfect rectangle, she had no feeling.

Then on September 30, Valarie discovered she was pregnant with her fourth child.

Three days later, John noted in his journal that Valarie had suffered frightening seizures that were "extremely painful," made "her head hurt," and then brought on great fatigue. The doctor suspected Valarie might have multiple sclerosis (MS), an immune system disorder in which the body's natural defenses mistakenly attack the body itself—in this case the white matter of the brain and the spine, the material that protects the neurons so that they can transmit signals properly. MS has highly variable courses, but it can lead to trouble with vision and movement, and in the worst cases, paralysis.

On October 10, Valarie's MS diagnosis was confirmed. Two weeks after that, her father, an engineer for the Union Pacific Railroad, was struck by a train in a switching accident and almost killed. It took him weeks to recover in the hospital.

People like to say that God allows only the challenges people are capable of handling, but an observer might reasonably think this was all just too much to bear. In the span of five months, Valarie had endured her daughter's almost fatal accident, her father's train collision, and now a frightening diagnosis and a new pregnancy, which carried its own debilitating prognosis for Valarie because throughout her previous pregnancies, she had suffered extreme morning sickness, causing nausea and vomiting and leaving her unable to eat. Most women, if they experience morning sickness at all, find relief after three months. Not Valarie. And she was starting this new pregnancy already at a diminished weight.

Something was desperately wrong.

There is home movie that was shot in the Millers' backyard a year before Annie's accident. In it, Valarie is flirtatious and coy. Her hair is styled in the fashion of Diana Spencer and she exudes a shy insouciance reminiscent of the famous princess. She picks up Annie and flips her through the air—a weightless puff of shiny blonde hair and a poufy red plaid dress.

In a rough-cut typical of home movies before the era of iPhones, the action skips forward almost a year, to months after Annie's accident, when she is doing exercises with her father at home. There seems nothing therapeutically sophisticated about it—rather more like a cowboy breaking a wild horse. Standing behind her, John holds Annie up on her feet. She is smiling and excited. Then John lets go of her, and she falls toward the floor like a rag doll until John catches her. He lifts her again to her feet, steadies her, then lets her go, and she once again falls in a heap. The camera pans to Valarie, lying on her back on the rug in the same room, near a wall. Her hair is blown out and her makeup carefully done, but her eyes, terrifyingly, are vacant orbs.

CHAPTER ONE

"A Choice and Special Spirit"

JOHN MILLER WILL TELL YOU with a sheepish chuckle that he made his fortune by "murdering 38 million cows." That sounds brutal and coldhearted, but it's an unusual butcher who hires Temple Grandin, the autistic savant and animal rights activist made famous by a 2010 movie starring Claire Danes, to crawl around the kill floor of his meat processing plants, eye-level with the livestock, to identify which areas contained visual elements that might cause them undue stress.

E. A. Miller & Sons had long been a fixture in the Cache Valley community and helped support a constellation of related businesses, including a rendering plant, cattle feed yards, farms, and a trucking company. John Miller's ability to see the future in spite of the entrenched ways of the past allowed him to turn an important yet floundering family business into a huge moneymaker through improved technology, modern management, and creative financing.

The personal qualities he used to his advantage—respect for tradition and family history, but with an ambitious eye tuned to the wider world— were apparent in his youth. In some ways, he was a stereotypical Mormon boy from the West, a three-sport athlete and leader in student government, but he also put together a rock 'n' roll band that titillated his peers and distressed his parents. Though mindful of the rules and strict Mormon tenets that governed his family's world, his curiosity and talent, coupled with a healthy tolerance for risk-taking, propelled him past his peers. As a teenager, his musical talents allowed him to travel abroad with the United Services Organization (USO) as lead guitarist in several bands, where he learned about rank and power. "I came to the conclusion after the tours, that if I was to go into the army—or any branch of the service—it would have to be as an officer. During both tours we had officer rights and privileges, which I quickly discovered was a big advantage on base," he said.

His growing appreciation for the females of the species, and their evident appreciation of him, led him into a few high jinks, but he always managed to turn back from the brink in the nick of time—or concoct a convincing enough story to avoid punishment. He wanted to know the world, but he also sensed his safe boundaries.

John clearly remembered the first time he laid eyes on Valarie Clark in the fall of 1969—his junior year of high school, her sophomore year—not long after her arrival at Sky View, a consolidated county high school whose students hailed from towns separated by as many as 30 miles. John's hometown, Hyrum, was on the southern end of Cache Valley while Valarie's, Clarkston, was far to the north, a few minutes from the Idaho border.

One day, in a school hallway, John's friend Ralph Barson introduced him to Valarie. She was 15 years old.

"I was, wow! She was really, *really* pretty," John recalled, his voice rising with enthusiasm at the memory. "I'll never forget it."

Among the ubiquitous blondes of Cache Valley, Valarie Clark was an exotic beauty. Like her Norwegian forebears, the Carlsons on her father's side, she had dark hair. Her eyes, wide set, almond shaped, the color of juniper, conveyed a vivacious allure. Her sister Debbie remembered feeling so jealous one day when they were both out sunning in the backyard—Debbie's fair skin growing redder and redder as Valarie's browned into a delicious dark tan—that she rose up and shouted "you have shit-brindle green eyes" in frustration, an outburst Valarie found endlessly amusing and a reliable font of teasing for years to come.

She was also "whip smart" according to her brother, Zane, and earned straight As in high school and college. She was clearly a catch, but John was not the first in line. By the time he was introduced to her, Valarie was already dating Kim Oliverson, the quarterback of the Sky View football team. John was a football player, a starting running back, and he had a girlfriend, a cheerleader whom he quite liked, so he kept a respectful distance. But they all moved in the same circles—Valarie was a member of the drill team, the Vistauns, which performed at halftime for the football games. But when Kim was offered a scholarship to the University of Colorado, John sensed his opening. He and Valarie continued to flirt and talk, but he waited until the next fall to ask her out. At first, she demurred, telling him she was still attached to Kim. John said he understood and to let him know if she ever changed her mind. Valarie made him wait a couple of months. Around Christmas 1970, she called him, and they were instantly "*the* couple of Sky View High," said one friend. "Beauty and the Successor."

They skied, rode horses, and once took a five-hour ride to Jackson Hole, Wyoming, on John's Honda 450 motorcycle. The Miller family had use of a ranch in the mountains above Cache Valley, which John and Valarie visited for some "camp-overs." Valarie even spent the night at his family home in Hyrum—in a separate bedroom, of course. Looking back, John was amazed her parents allowed this, but he concluded they must have liked him and trusted them both. They dated for the second half of John's senior year and continued their relationship the next year, after he had gone as a freshman to Utah State University (USU), which was 10 miles from Hyrum (and 19 miles from Clarkston).

Although Valarie received an offer for a full track scholarship at Brigham Young University (BYU), she decided to follow John to USU, where she had also been offered a track scholarship. "I think I kind of talked her out of

BYU, to the chagrin of her parents," said John. Valarie's father wanted her to go to BYU, as its women's track program was far superior, but as he put it, "she was busy romancing John."

And so, in the pattern set by her mother and reinforced by the customs and mores of her community, Valarie gave up opportunities of her own for the sake of future marriage and family. Valarie still ran the 100- and 220-yard dashes for four years at USU, but the women's sports program was low-profile. In spite of this, she was a clear standout. One of the professors who knew Valarie said she was "a beautiful, very athletic, talented person who had the world in her hands." In high school she had spoken of becoming a lawyer, but in college she picked a major more suited to a traditional Mormon girl of the time: education.

In May 1973, John's sophomore year at USU, his father died of a heart attack at age 57, throwing John into a period of soul-searching. "It shook me up pretty good," he said. The changes in family dynamics led him to become a Mormon missionary, which meant being sent somewhere by the church to proselytize for two years. "My dad went on a mission, and he always spoke positively about it," he explained. It had been an important time in his father's life, leading to a 1937 trip to Europe, where he was pleased to have observed a parade in which Adolf Hitler drove past in an open car. He snapped a photo, which was placed in the family album. Going off into the world had tested his father, John said, "and he told me it made him a man." John knew his mother wanted him to go on a mission, particularly since his two elder brothers had declined this important rite of passage. And Valarie supported the idea. "I wasn't sure if it was that she wanted to get rid of me, or she thought it would be a good thing," he said, only half-joking. They spoke about it a lot. "Truth be said, I think the reason I didn't go right away [as a 19-year-old], when most Mormon boys then went on their missions, was I was afraid she wouldn't be there for me when I got back." But he also knew that the devout Valarie wanted "to be married to a returned missionary, because that's what her parents had been teaching her to want for her whole life."

So, in the summer of 1973, John embarked on his journey. He had requested he be posted to Australia, where his father had served, and was granted his wish. The life of a young Mormon missionary is strict and spartan—up at 6 a.m. six days a week for hours of study and prayer with his companion, followed by full days of proselytizing, in shirt and tie, facing rejection and occasional danger—until 10 p.m. The missionaries lived with few creature comforts and, of course, no alcohol, caffeine, cigarettes, or dating, a regimen designed to push the young men to focus on spiritual matters.

In time, John settled into the routine, made lasting friendships, and deepened his faith. However, he was homesick and "deeply missed Valarie." Early on, her letters sustained him, cryptic though Valarie could sometimes be. In one note, after writing out two stanzas' worth of lyrics from The Carpenters' saccharine 1971 song "Sometimes," she hinted at an anguished, secretive, and fearful past at odds with her status as a straight-A student, champion sprinter, and beauty queen. The lyrics, she explained, reminded her "of so many times I have 'almost' told you about things in my heart. But always some barrier stops me." Thanks to John's love, however, Valarie could feel that barrier dissolving. "All my life I've been alone, never having close friends, staying in a world by myself," she wrote. "It seemed like I had so many things locked up within myself, and I wanted to free them, I wanted someone who I was not afraid of to touch my soul."

Valarie did, however, date other boys while John was on his mission, as they had agreed. Her letters then waned, and at a few depressing moments, he received more letters from her parents, Denzel and Shirleen, than from Valarie.

When his two years had passed and he prepared to return, he wasn't sure he still had possession of her heart. She had been dating Nolan Johnson, the head of student government at USU. Her dear friend Sue Saunders said that

Nolan and Valarie loved each other very much and that Valarie was conflicted about what to do as John's return approached, so she asked Sue for advice. Sue didn't hesitate: "You've known John since high school. You have to at least give him a chance when he comes back."

The night before John returned, Nolan told Valarie he predicted she would go back to her old love.

When John arrived at the airport in Salt Lake City in September 1975 and he saw Valarie waiting for him with a handmade sign adorned with a yellow happy face, he was elated. Valarie's beauty flooded him with the same disoriented feelings he had experienced when he first saw her. On the drive home, they sat together in the back seat of someone's car, their conversation so giddily happy that he forgot who drove them.

Passionate and impatient, John gave Valarie a ring a month after he got home, on October 15. It was her 21st birthday, and he noted in his journal: "Given stewardship over Valarie, protect, honor, responsible for her salvation. Will give accounting to God." Though his love for her had been unwavering since he'd first set eyes on her, his deepened Mormon faith helped him push aside vague worries of a delicacy or vulnerability about her. He adored Valarie and couldn't wait to cleave to her in a full sharing of body and soul, a marriage made on earth and destined for heaven. Mormons believe that once a marriage has been sealed in one of their temples, husband and wife will enjoy eternal life together, surrounded by their children. John's two years of missionary work had fueled his zeal for a perfect union with a partner in life and love.

They married in the Logan, Utah, temple during Christmas break. On December 12, 1975, John noted the following in his journal: "I must always be kind and thoughtful to Valarie. She is a choice and special spirit." After a short honeymoon skiing in Vail—Valarie was a natural athlete and avid skier—they moved into an apartment in Logan that John rented from his mother. The next entry he made was neither a paean to marriage nor an outpouring of love or desire about his new bride. Rather, on December 21 he wrote, "I've felt kind of lost the last few days. I think because of the lack of pressure due to school being out. When I'm not busy working, I don't feel at peace with myself." He didn't write again until February 8, when he noted that he took Valarie to Salt Lake City "to see a doctor about her neck and back troubles." He noted that the doctor "could not see anything serious."

Both were enrolled in school—Valarie finishing up her last two quarters of classes and her student-teaching requirements before graduating from USU in the spring of 1976. She had also worked throughout college, first doing water testing in the canyons for a USU lab, then working in the university student center and later at the front desk of a hotel. And in addition to pursuing his degree at USU, John worked at E. A. Miller in the afternoons, on weekends, and during the summers, as he had since he was a youngster, to learn more about the meat-processing business.

From an early age, he rotated through the departments, learning every aspect of the business, from purchasing cattle to the gory details of the kill floor. John collected the dirty meat hooks, stacked them in carts, and brought them to be washed and boiled in oil, then hauled them back to the slaughterhouse floor to be reused. He shoveled out manure from under the scale house, where the livestock was weighed, scoured dirty meat barrels, and even scooped out kidneys from hardened fat. He took a turn as a meat boner on the assembly line, cutting meat off the bones with a razor-sharp knife. He finally scored a delivery truck route that got him away from the suffocating smells of the plant and into the beautiful country of Cache Valley and Salt Lake City. Then he switched gears again, working in the back office with a gruff CPA who taught him the importance of managing the books with precision, getting accounts paid up, and cutting costs.

An article in the local *Herald Journal* in the winter of 1975, Valarie's senior year, included her on its list of students on USU's honor roll. She was a natural student, unlike John, who had to work hard for his grades. As part of her degree program in education, where she was majoring in communications with a minor in theater arts, she worked as a student teacher. But she had been assigned to a middle school, which she didn't like. "That's when she said she wished she'd have gone on to law school," recalled her sister Debbie.

John was majoring in history, with a minor in accounting, and had accelerated his graduation by taking on 23 credits each quarter. After less than a year, he and Valarie moved from their apartment to a pretty little white house with lacy Victorian trim directly across the street from the rendering plant owned by Junior.

"This was a step up!" John said. "We had a house and a yard. I mean, it was tiny, and we caught like 30 mice the first night, but . . . my uncle had kind of redone it, it wasn't rundown or anything. It was just tiny."

John called Valarie "Thumper," after the lovable rabbit from the Disney movie *Bambi*. Said her friend Sue Saunders: "She was silly like Thumper. And sweet and adorable." Since nature is an irresistible force for both rabbits and humans, Valarie became pregnant in May, a month before her college graduation. John noted in his journal on June 6, 1976: "Valarie graduates from university. I love her and appreciate her philosophy of life. She lifts me, and makes me a better person."

On September 19, he happily noted the pregnancy was visible. "I love her. I am lucky to have someone like her." Unceasing morning sickness had been rough on her, though. "I need to demonstrate more love and respect to Valarie. I would be lost without her love and support."

Valarie was sensitive to smells, and the rendering plant across the street from their home, constantly spewing an odor of wet animal hides and the putrid, steaky smell of burning fat, tormented her. She had to ask John to shed his clothes immediately upon arriving home, throw them in the washing machine, and then take a shower. Nine months of nausea. Nine months of not being able to eat more than a few bites here and there.

That September and October were difficult, and John wrote in his journal that he felt sorry for his wife. She came down with the flu in early December, and on December 19, he again noted in his journal that she was not feeling well.

For the birth of their first child, they had chosen to try Lamaze instead of an epidural to manage the pain, but the ordeal was almost more than Valarie could bear. At one point, she screamed at John to throw her out the window to stop the pain. But she got through it, and on January 16, 1977, Valarie gave birth to a beautiful blonde baby girl, six pounds, eight ounces, whom she and John named Anne Marie. Valarie's sister remembered that as soon as she gave birth, Valarie asked for food. She particularly loved her mother's Sunday night roast beef dinner.

On February 20, John wrote: "Valarie is a good mother. I am proud and thankful." He graduated from USU in the spring and agreed to work full-time for E. A. Miller while studying for the Graduate Record Examinations (GRE). The small family thrived and their prospects grew. But, as their ancestors had learned through the decades as pioneers in the untamed West, Nature wields Her mighty power in unpredictable and often cruel ways.

On April 1, 1977, E. A. Miller's company plane, a twin-engine Cessna 411, went down in heavy rain while returning to Cache Valley from a truckers' convention in California. On board were Junior's son, Ernie, and five of the company's truckers, chosen by lottery, whom Ernie had treated with a special opportunity to look over the latest vehicles and gadgets.

Ernie—the heir apparent of E. A. Miller—was killed along with the five drivers and the pilot. The tragedy shook the family to its roots. Ernie and John were close friends as well as relatives, and Valarie was friendly with Ernie's wife, Teri Benson, who was also her cousin. The entire company of 400 people, of which the truckers made up an important part, operated as an extended family; everyone was crushed by the news.

Within hours of the accident, John accompanied his Uncle Junior on condolence calls to the families who had lost loved ones, even though Junior was mourning himself. "I can remember holding Junior when he came out of those homes—he was so shaken and so emotionally broken," said John.

The tragedy changed John's life overnight. Though the secret wish he'd nourished for years was to attend Harvard Business School and get as far away from meatpacking as he could, he would no longer dream about a life on the banks of the Charles River. He had to step up and try to turn around an aging, unprofitable, but vital business in Cache Valley at a time of great change in the meatpacking business. "Now, I had a job to do," said John. "It was my duty. It was no longer about what I wanted for my life. It was about my responsibility to my family and to the memory of Ernie."

The tragedy had a profound impact on Valarie as well. It unnerved her, upset her equanimity. Debbie remembered going up to visit her sister at the little white house during this time. As an infant, Annie suffered from colic, as many babies do, but like her mother's nausea during her pregnancy, the infant's distress never seemed to let up. Debbie recalled that "Valarie just walked the floor with her constantly crying. Valarie told me, 'I couldn't get her to sleep, night or day.'"

Valarie sought help in the one place she had confidence she could find it: prayer. "I just went into the bedroom and kneeled down and I said, 'Heavenly Father, I can't do this anymore,'" she told Debbie. "You've got to help me. I can't, I can't do this." And after that, Debbie said Annie started doing better. "Valarie was amazing that way," she said. "It just seemed like she had such faith that Heavenly Father was going to help her. And He did—a lot of times."

On their third wedding anniversary, in December of 1978, John noted that he and Valarie "had lots of fun." She was soon pregnant again, and after almost a year of good health, it was time once again for her to soldier through the interminable nausea that marked her pregnancies. This one, however, was easier on her, and by March she was able to gain weight. She felt pretty good, but tired, through the summer and up to the birth of their son, Ryan, on October 11, 1979. John wrote: "I am grateful for a wonderful wife. I am blessed by her spirit." Soon after, the family moved to a new house that John built next to his mother's in Hyrum, far away from the smelly rendering plant and close to Grandma Emma's loving ministrations.

Life was happening very fast for both of them, and more demands were being placed on Valarie. She returned to church work, serving in her ward's Young Women's program as camp director and taking groups of girls on week-long excursions in the summertime.

On a positive note, for the first time in a long time, Valarie was able to resume many of the activities that had given her life meaning as a younger woman and to display some of her many natural gifts. Freed from the nausea that marred her pregnancies, she was able to expand her activities, though all were aimed at fulfilling her obligations as wife, mother, daughter, and devout Mormon.

Meanwhile, John was, with great effort, remaking E. A. Miller & Sons into a modern, efficiently run beef production plant. He had pushed the firm to change with the times from a community slaughterhouse that invited neighbors and local stores to choose and mark the cuts of meat they wanted on the hanging carcasses to an operation that produced prefabricated cuts of meat packed into CRYOVAC bags that were boxed and dispatched to their destinations. He also served, with his uncle Junior, as a leader in an LDS ward for students at Utah State.

When he was just 28, two years after stepping into his first management role, John was named general manager. He had his own ideas about how to continue improving the company, but he also sought advice from mentors, including Steven Covey, a fellow Mormon and the author of the megabestseller *The 7 Habits of Highly Effective People*, whose brother had been John's mission president in Australia. Despite all John's early success, he couldn't help but wonder what his life might have been like had he gone to business school, had he been allowed to explore other paths. But his regrets were dismissed by a friend, a Harvard MBA himself, who told him, "Who cares about going to Harvard? *You're* the case study they now teach at Harvard."

CHAPTER TWO

"Like a Weird Faulkner Novel"

CLARKSTON, TUCKED INTO Utah's Cache Valley, sits on a grassy plateau hugged by two mountain ranges—the Wellsville–Malad range to the west, and the Wasatch Mountains to the east. About 50 miles long, an average 12 miles wide, and reaching up into Idaho, Cache Valley is a verdant wonder in an otherwise arid chunk of the American West—a rich grassland irrigated by rivers and streams fed by melting snowfall from peaks as far away as Wyoming. In 1840, one early visitor called it "one of the most extensive and beautiful vales of the Rocky Mountain range."

The area's Shoshone, who had inhabited the area since 3000 BCE, never set down permanent camps in the valley, probably because of its harsh winters and punishing snow. However, white arrivals in the 19th century were aware of a traditional Shoshone winter camp at the confluence of the Bear River and the Little Bear River in Battle Creek, Idaho. Rather, every year, when the green shoots of grass appeared in the spring, they traveled south from Idaho or Wyoming to camp along the banks of the rivers of Cache Valley, to fish, hunt, and gather food and skins for clothing and shelter. The then free-flowing rivers supported abundant trout, and the mountains were filled with deer, elk, coyote, and bears. The valley even had a few large buffalo herds. After acquiring horses about 1750, the Shoshone became better hunters and were less dependent on gathering food. Come winter, they headed back up north.

The area's first European explorers, who arrived as early as 1818, were mountain men, explorers, and beaver trappers who trafficked in the silky pelts prized for the manufacture of men's top hats back East. One of those trappers was the frontiersman Kit Carson, who later gained fame as a guide for John C. Frémont's explorations of the Oregon Trail, and later still notoriety as a US Army officer who helped subjugate the Navajo, Mescalero Apache, Kiowa, and Comanche by destroying their food supplies. The area was named Cache Valley for the subterranean vaults and natural redoubts in which trappers stashed their valuable pelts and skins. It has long been a place where people buried their treasures, their secrets, and even their pasts.

In the first decades after contact, the mountain men generally coexisted peacefully with the Shoshone. However, the white men's decimation of the beaver population would have critical effects on the area's ecology and, along with other changes, eventually the ability of the Shoshone to feed themselves.

The settlers were another matter entirely. The first Mormon pioneers arrived in the Great Salt Lake Basin of Utah in 1847, led by Brigham Young, Joseph Smith's successor as head of the Church of Jesus Christ of Latter-day Saints. This was three years after a mob had murdered Smith and his brother Hyrum in Illinois. There were 148 Mormons in the first party, including three women, and over the next two decades, thousands of Mormons followed Young's path out West. They believed they had found their promised land of Zion in the Salt Lake region, which was sparsely populated, minimally supervised by Mexico, and safely situated between the customary use areas of the Shoshone to the north and the Ute to the south. Mormon settlers began to flow northward into Cache Valley in the fall of 1856, and for the next six years, they established settlements wherever streams ran down the slopes of the Wellsville and Wasatch mountains.

The Mormons' path into the northern reaches of Cache Valley was cleared only after murderous violence against its Native population. During the Civil War, Colonel Patrick Edward Connor and the Third California

Volunteers were dispatched to Salt Lake City for two purposes: to "watch the Mormons," whose loyalty to the Union remained unclear, and to protect the overland routes between the Pacific Ocean and the East. Suffering the diminution of their traditional hunting grounds and obstruction of freedom of movement by white settlers, the Bannock and Shoshone had begun to attack freight trains for foodstuffs they could no longer acquire by their traditional ways. In January 1863, as the Shoshone and white interlopers were still working out the rules of coexistence, Connor precipitously marched 400 soldiers into Cache Valley and, after being informed by Mormon settlers where the Shoshone were, headed north to their encampment (near what is now Preston, Idaho) and ambushed them in the dead of winter with cannon and small-arms fire. Known thereafter as the Bear River Massacre, the assault killed nearly 350 Shoshone, mostly women and children, making it the deadliest attack on a Native tribe in the history of the United States military. The traumatized Shoshone survivors fled to the north, while the Mormons concluded "that the entire valley was now theirs to secure."[1]

In 1864, 12 Mormon families were sent north by church leaders to found a new homestead. They were led by Israel Justus Clark, whose name would be given to the new town of Clarkston. He would serve as its first religious leader, known as a bishop. The area met all the needs of the pioneers: water, arable land, and wildlife to hunt. But Clarkston enjoyed another advantage that would influence its future identity as closed, provincial, and suspicious. It was not only located within the confines of Cache Valley but also nestled in a valley within a valley—protected on its western flank by the foothills of Gunsight Peak, from the east by the gentle rise of Little Mountain, and from the south by the meandering Bear River.

Clarkston's families put up hay and built dugout homes to protect themselves from the expected heavy snow of the first winter. Natural springs provided water for home use. Snow runoff that charged Clarkston Creek was first collected in a reservoir in 1872 by the building of an earthen dam, which was washed away and rebuilt numerous times. The so-called Newton

Reservoir is a winding lake of almost 300 acres, surrounded by cottonwoods and willows, that offers summer swimming and fishing, as well as limited irrigation for neighboring Newton. Though relatively green, Cache Valley is still part of the Great Basin Desert, where rainfall is limited—only 18 inches a year, compared with the US average of 38.1.[2] Beginning in the late 1870s, Clarkston's early residents experimented with various techniques of mulching and tilling to retain moisture in the soil and eventually found special wheat seeds that would mature in dry ground. Not long after the settlers' plows touched the soil, Cache Valley bloomed with wheat and quickly became Utah's breadbasket.

For the people of Clarkston, this past is vivid and close at hand. In May 1869, the joining of the Central Pacific and Union Pacific railroads and the completion of the Transcontinental Railroad was commemorated at Promontory Summit, 50 miles from Clarkston. The event still figures in the town's conception of itself, in part because many of the community's men have supplemented their income as small farmers with more remunerative employment on the railroad. Yet in spite of the constant stream of technological, economic, medical, and social advances brought by new arrivals from the East, Clarkston residents clung to a stubborn self-reliance, reinforced by varying measures of defensiveness, pride, and religious belief. Some followed the pioneer practices of avoiding doctors and undertakers deep into the 20th century, believing they could take care of such matters themselves.

Local midwives guided women through pregnancy. "Birth was a natural process that worried no one," a Clarkston native wrote, "and if complications ever set in, it was not known. These women were on call night and day for the sum of $8 or less if you could not afford it." Dentistry fell to Thomas Godfrey, who "pulled our teeth while his wife retired to the cellar so as not to hear." When injuries happened, Jack Thompson "set the broken bones, and always told jokes during the painful process." If the homespun medical care didn't work as expected, Jim Thompson constructed caskets of native lumber. He lined them with velvet, black or white, depending on what was available, but the dead "never wanted for a neat, substantial coffin." Of course, a fiddler was essential, and Joe Myler filled in—both leading the choir and fiddling at the dances.[3]

It was a tiny town—reaching a population of 464 in 1880, settling around 500 when Valarie was born, then back down to 420 in 1970. Few who know them would dispute the statement that the people of Clarkston remain clannish and wary of outsiders. Historian Ross Peterson, a faculty member at Utah State and longtime friend of the Miller family, has lived in and written about Cache Valley for more than 50 years. In *A History of Cache County*, Peterson highlighted the "parochial views" and "genuine fear of the outside world and its influences" that continue to shape local culture; the residents of Clarkston in particular, he wrote, embrace a "polarized view of the world— them versus us, outside versus inside, Mormon versus non-Mormon."[4]

This is the reclusive and often violent world of midwifery, homeschooling, and doomsday prepping evoked by Tara Westover's 2018 bestseller *Educated*, which details the author's childhood in Clifton and Weston, Idaho, both just a few miles across the state line from Clarkston.

Though they appreciate their isolation, the residents of Clarkston still must live together on their one square mile of land. To neutralize the power of gossip, the oxygen of every small town, they try not to speak ill of each other. It's surprisingly common to hear the phrase "well that's just hearsay" in Clarkston, though it's not attorneys saying it. They seem primed to protect their reputations from the judgment of outsiders—and each other. Because of the Mormon emphasis on the family, which is bound up with the concept of eternal life, residents are protective of the reputations of kin—and everyone, it seems, is related. "They're cousins, and second cousins," said Peterson. "And when you throw the [history of] polygamy in the mix, it's just really a complicated village. . . . It's a little bit like a weird Faulkner novel."[5]

Part of the weirdness, said Dwight Pearce, Valarie's first cousin, is that many people, including his mother and her brother, Denzel Clark, refuse even to consider the possibility that wickedness might reside in their town.

"Denzel and Shirleen could not think anything bad about anyone," Dwight said. "My mother couldn't either, that's just a family trait. That's just the way it was. Everything was rosy and perfect. My mother would never say anything negative about anything, whether it was that way or not. My dad would always say, 'Oh, he was really a good guy. I don't know what made him do such a terrible [thing].' If somebody did something wrong, he'd say, 'Yeah, I know they wronged me, but he's really a good guy.'"

But there were quite a few characters in town who attracted attention for their odd ways. One was Jack Thompson, the bonesetter, whom Denzel called a "prankster." He "pulled tricks on everybody." But sometimes his humor morphed toward the cruel or bizarre, as it did one day when his wife observed someone who she didn't want to see approaching the house. Jack told her to wrap herself up in the floor-length drapes that were hung behind the dining room table, and he'd "tell this person she wasn't at home," said Denzel. But when Jack answered the door and the unwanted visitor asked for his wife, he promptly led him over to the curtains and said, "Trala! Lift up the drape; she's under the table," much to his wife's humiliation. Denzel also said Jack Thompson once created an uncomfortable situation for a church leader who came to town from Salt Lake City by handing him a gift of a basket of apples, later revealing that they had come from his neighbor's tree. The general authority was afraid he'd be mistaken for a thief.

Jack the Bonesetter was the father of Earl Thompson and the grandfather of Gary Thompson, Denzel's first cousin who lived across the street, and whose repugnant sexual proclivities, once they were revealed, would turn Denzel's world upside down. There was also Burke Godfrey, who against the town's Mormon prohibitions against liquor, drank alcohol with other local men in a shed behind his house. And the local law enforcement officer, Robert Dahle—known by all as Bob—who drove his prized green-and-white 1965 Ford pickup through town, a snarling Doberman in the back, with his pals Gary Thompson or Sterling Jardine riding shotgun. Women in town knew to stay away from those men, especially if they were drinking.

They were known as womanizers whose activities many knew about but few acknowledged publicly. Shockingly, for an austere Mormon town whose inhabitants had foresworn coffee, tea, and all sexual relations outside of marriage, "they would just drive around and they would try to pick up girls and then they'd go to the bars and try to pick up women there too," recalled Jann Pugmire, a neighbor of Valarie's who grew up in Clarkson.

—

Valarie Clark was a true daughter of Clarkston. Her lineage—Clarks on her father's side, Thompsons on her mother's—reached back to the town's founding families. The descendants of those first families—Thompsons, Clarks, Jardines, Godfreys, Goodeys, and Dahles—were Valarie's relatives and neighbors. They were the people she played with as a toddler, went to school with as a child, worshipped with every Sunday, and depended on for love, fellowship, and protection all her life.

Since the survival of farmers is to a great degree dependent on the goodwill of Mother Nature, and her bounties are ever unpredictable, it was critical that neighbor help neighbor in Clarkston. Leaders of the LDS church encouraged communal cooperation, and mutual dependence became a habit as well as a revered value. In fact, the Mormon religion considers cooperation to be "the Lord's way."[6]

"There was no need for locks or bars on the doors of our little town," explained local writer Ann Godfrey Hansen. "Neighbors shared freely. At butchering time, meat was exchanged, and starts of yeast went from house to house, as well as bread and fresh honey."[7] The entire town was mobilized during the wheat harvest and the hay-cutting and gathering. Valarie's mother, Shirleen Thompson Clark, even when she was 91 years old, vividly recalled every step in the process, including her job as a little girl: stomping down the hay after it had been gathered by her father and a "hired man." In the communal spirit of the town, as soon as her family's hay was put up, her father and his kin helped the hired man put up his hay as well.

The town had everything the families needed. In the late 19th and early 20th centuries, the dugouts were soon replaced with simple houses. Hansen wrote:

> *The architecture of the homes was very similar. People first built a two-room house and as their family and finances increased, they added a kitchen and dining room and connected them with a large, L-shaped porch. In every backyard was a well with a bucket tied to a rope. There was a chopping block sprinkled with chicken blood and in the chips glazed rooster heads with half-open eyes bore mute evidence of many a fine dinner. In the corner stood a whitewashed privy with the convenience of a can of ashes and a Sears Roebuck catalog, and sometimes some old newspapers. Here one could retire with impunity and rest or read. Every lot had a row of plum trees. Under them sat a few farm implements profusely sprinkled with droppings of chickens and birds. Close by, the straw-covered stable provided shelter for a team and a scrub cow or two, and near this was a log henhouse without windows. Five or six sleek porkers peeked up over a crude pen, and these, with the dog, a few cats and the roosters, completed each barnyard orchestra. We didn't always have plenty of money, but we always had enough food and a warm home, and love and kindness.[8]*

Life for a child in early 20th-century Clarkston was full of the simple pleasures provided by nature. Shirleen remembered on Easter carrying woven baskets up to a place they called Long Hill, where the wildflowers were abundant. "They had Johnny jump-ups and buttercups, and we'd take our lunch out there and roll eggs down the hill and then pick the curlicues and the buttercups," she said. She also remembered that in the old days there were white sego lilies whose bulbs the pioneers dug up and ate in the tough early years in Clarkston. Like much of the wildlife that was once plentiful in Cache Valley, it was overpicked and is now gone.

Shirleen's father had beef cattle, horses, and milk cows on 160 acres, both grassland and agricultural plots. It took him a month to plow his fields. When they were through with the plow horses for the season—Shirleen calls them "harses," using the distinctive accent of her mother's generation of Utahns—Shirleen would ride over to the pastureland and leave the horses there to graze. "We had Bess and Dolly, Dutch, and Dinah," she recalled. "Dad'd put me a sack on the back of the horse and push me up there and hand me the halters of two others. And I'd lead 'em until we got them into the pasture." She'd then walk the five miles back home.

Like their neighbors, Shirleen's family had a large vegetable garden, and her mother put up vegetables and fruits—apples from their trees and raspberries. They made jam, too, and her aunt later used the preserved fruit to make pies. Her father kept pigs and chickens, and they made their own bacon. They rented a refrigerated locker at the grocery in which they hung their meat. When they needed anything, they'd just walk over to the store, open their locker with a key, and cut off what they needed.

Shirleen possessed a beautiful singing voice, and she was offered a music scholarship to Utah State University, but life and duty intervened. She had fallen in love with Denzel Clark, who lived a few blocks down from her on Main Street, and they got married. Denzel was dreamy and kind; she was tough and practical. When they were courting, he attended a dance one night with friends who, without telling him, spiked his Coke with whiskey. After the dance, they delivered the slightly tipsy Denzel to Shirleen's house, thinking his sweetheart might treat him with a bit more charity than his parents. Shirleen walked him around the block a few times, listening to him chatter giddily, and then deposited him at his parents' house. "He's drunk," she told them.

It was the first and only time he found himself in such a condition.

Their life together was not easy. Shirleen was pregnant seven times, but only had three live births. She suffered two miscarriages and delivered a seven-month stillborn boy and a full-term stillborn boy. Debbie, the eldest, who was three years older than Valarie, remembered that "they never let [Shirleen] see or hold these babies even though Dad said they were perfectly formed. It must have been so traumatic and heartbreaking for her to carry these babies to seven and nine months and then lose them. Her deliveries and labors were long and difficult. There was no counseling back then. You were just supposed to go on with your life." Confined to the hospital for two weeks after the loss of each child, Shirleen missed both funerals.

Valarie was born in 1954, and she was three years old when her mother lost the first baby boy. She was six years old when her mother gave birth to her brother, Zane, and eight when she delivered the full-term stillborn. Shirleen bore the sorrow of these losses without much outward fuss, but they took a deep toll. "I wasn't destined to raise those boys in this life," she said in her matter-of-fact way a few months before her death. "Maybe in the next, if I'm worthy." Her religion gave her hope of being rejoined with her entire family—including the children who did not live—in the afterlife, but the grief in this life left a ragged edge in their home. Valarie's first years were full of sadness and loss.

"Mom never complained," said Debbie, "just kept everything inside. After the babies were born, I would see her sitting and quietly crying."

Adding to Shirleen's distraction, Zane was born with two club feet. Rejecting newer and less invasive treatments, Zane's doctors opted for surgical reconstruction, which required multiple operations on both feet and lengthy immobilizations of both ankles. The procedures failed, leaving Zane permanently injured and in constant pain. Once the operations began, Shirleen was very much caught up in Zane's care while Denzel was often away working on the railroad. The emotional needs of the girls were filled by grandparents and aunts who lived nearby.

Today, Clarkston is still an insular, closely knit community of 762. People whose Clarkston roots don't reach all the way back to the 19th century are considered outsiders; the rare newcomer, even if he or she has been resident for 30 years, is referred to as a "move-in." In Clarkston, people are identified by their first and last names—and then by the name of their mother's family, as in "she's a Thompson" or "she's a Jardine." In this way, it's made clear how everyone is stitched into the fabric, which can help avoid cousin marriages, a source of shame now in these parts and an obvious concern when it comes to the gene pool.

A few weeks before her passing in August 2021, Shirleen said that Clarkson was "a lovely place to live. I've always thought so." Her husband, Denzel, 92, broke in, shaking his head. "Well, we *thought* it was . . ."

—

"Valarie was gorgeous. I mean, shockingly beautiful," said Sue Sanders, Valarie's college roommate and best friend. Valarie was also a straight-A student and involved in a dizzying array of activities. As a high school sophomore, she served as a class officer, then became a member of the high school executive council. She sang in the a cappella choir, was a trophy-winning debater, and earned a place on the vaunted drill team, the Vistauns. She was also crowned Cache Valley Dairy Princess in 1972, and later finished as runner-up in the Miss Utah contest. "Every girl envied her," said her cousin Dwight, "and every boy was in love with her."

There were no athletic teams for high school girls at Sky View High School until the 1980s; Title IX was adopted slowly. But Valarie was a gifted sprinter, and she ran in Amateur Athletic Union (AAU) sponsored track meets. In her senior year, her parents brought her to an AAU meet at Idaho State University in Pocatello so college coaches could see her run. She was offered three full scholarships.

Valarie was determined and accomplished, but what people most remember about her was a sweet disposition and a personal appeal that seemed both intensely innocent and mysterious. Debbie said, "I still run into boys who were her age in high school. They'll say to me, 'One of my only goals in high school was to marry Valarie Clark.'" On the other hand, some boys said their goal was more prosaic: to beat her in a footrace.

She made people feel special. She listened to them in a way that made them feel understood. She was a good Mormon, a faithful follower of the Church of Jesus Christ of Latter-day Saints. Dwight said she had "a strong testimony," meaning she had a powerful belief in Jesus Christ and the tenets of her church. Sue, who met Valarie as an undergraduate at Utah State University, was drawn to her extraordinary spiritual power. When Valarie led group prayer, Sue felt the presence of God about her. At 23, Sue was already a widow—she had gone back to school after her young husband died of diabetes-related kidney failure, and her brother had died of ALS. "I was going through some hard stuff," said Sue. "Valarie taught me how to survive it because of her closeness to God. When she prayed, I always thought that if I opened my eyes, I would see the Savior standing here. That's how it felt to me. The Spirit in the room. It was like she had this direct conduit to God."

When Valarie was in college, she was asked by the Mormon artist Bill Hill from nearby Mendon if she would serve as his model for a painting and sculpture he planned to make of the Virgin Mary at the moment of her visitation by the Angel Gabriel—referred to by Christians as the Annunciation. The New Testament (Luke 1:26–38) describes Gabriel's appearance in Nazareth to tell Mary, who was then betrothed to Joseph, that she would conceive and give birth to a baby boy who would be named Jesus. Mary asked the angel how this could be true since she was still a virgin. The angel answered: "The Holy Spirit will come on you, and God's power will rest on you." Mary replied, "I am the Lord's servant."

Valarie told Zane that she prepared for the sitting with two weeks of fasting and prayer so that she might be able to "know Mary's countenance."

It would turn out that she was uniquely qualified to represent Mary and the wrenching sacrifices that would be required of her.

———

The Clark girls, like all the children in Clarkston, were free to roam far and wide. The town itself was tiny, only a little more than a dozen square blocks, and they were surrounded by relatives. Their base was the family home on Main Street; next door were their Thompson grandparents, and four blocks north were their Clark grandparents. They explored town and walked into the hills as far as their little legs would carry them. When they were very young, Debbie and Valarie dammed up the trickle of Big Creek with rocks to make miniature lakes, and sometimes they ventured into the culvert that ran under Main Street. When first Debbie and then Valarie reached the age of seven, Grandpa Clark let them ride his horses, which he kept in a corral behind his house. He'd saddle them up for the girls, but Valarie soon learned to do it herself. She was a "daredevil" and "fearless," said her sister. She once jumped off the roof of a chicken coop at her Clark grandparents' house and landed on a piece of wood that had a nail protruding from it. The wound didn't seem to faze her.

Denzel recalled an electrifying moment during a family camping trip to Yellowstone National Park. A bear lumbered up to their car, inside of which Valarie was sitting. She stared at the beast through the open window, without fear. The bear lifted its snout to sniff the air a few times, whereupon practical-minded Shirleen grabbed a couple of cooking pots and banged them together. The grizzly eventually turned and walked slowly away from Valarie, who remained unperturbed.

When Dwight was a teenager, he liked team roping, so he bought an Appaloosa gelding named Leo, which he kept in Grandpa Clark's paddock. Turns out Leo wasn't a great roping horse, but he was "gorgeous," according to Dwight, a flashy mount with a black body, white face, and four white stockings. "I liked to get into the rodeo arena, and let people watch how good looking my horse was."

Valarie was a few years younger than Dwight, and when she noticed her cousin was too busy at college and working on the railroad to spend much time with Leo, she asked if she could ride him. Dwight said yes, and in no time, she fell in love with the horse. Apparently, the feeling was mutual. Though with other riders he was skittish and sometimes hard to handle,

Leo was completely at ease with Valarie. When Denzel or Dwight took the horse out hunting and tied him up to a tree, he would rub off his bridle in no time and run home. But never with Valarie. "She could leave the reins draped over a bush and he'd stay put," said her mother. When Valarie whistled for him, Leo responded with a whinny, and he followed her around the corral with his head pressed into her back.

"Boy, she'd ride all the time," recalled Dwight. "She'd come over and she'd feed him and brush him. She loved that horse. Roping horses, they're not really gentle, but he was for her."

Though Valarie didn't need to argue with Leo, she was a great debater. Debbie recalled that neither she nor her mother liked to get into it with Valarie because she always won. "She'd argue you to the floor," said Shirleen. Valarie did everything to the max, and she wore herself out. And then she'd take herself to bed. Once it was 9 p.m., it was lights out for Valarie. "All the time, growing up, even as she got older," said Debbie, "at nine o'clock she'd disappear. And you'd think, 'Where's Valarie?' She wouldn't say goodnight or goodbye. She'd go to bed. Nine o'clock."

When Valarie was almost 14, her sleeping habits were suddenly, and without explanation, altered. Debbie remembered waking up in the middle of the night and finding her sister wasn't in bed, and when Debbie walked around the house looking for her, she couldn't find her anywhere. The next day, when she asked Valarie where she'd been, Valarie was vague, saying only that she liked to ride her horse at night.

This wasn't the only odd behavior Debbie noticed. Around the same time, long after the girls had settled on their knees beside their beds to pray before going to sleep, Debbie would awaken and find her sister still praying, hands clasped, sobbing, and "quietly and inaudibly almost pleading with Heavenly Father about something." Debbie witnessed this distressing scene a few times but never asked her sister what was wrong. At the time, she assumed Valarie was "having a private conversation with Heavenly Father," and it was none of her business.

Later she would wonder, "Why didn't I ask her?"

One night when Debbie was getting ready for bed, there was another disturbing incident. As she was brushing her teeth at the bathroom sink, she saw in the mirror the face of a man peering in through the window. She screamed, ran into the bedroom, and told Valarie. Debbie was dumbfounded when Valarie reached under her bed for a BB gun. She then dropped to the floor and crawled commando-style toward her mother's bedroom. Valarie told Shirleen that Debbie had seen "a peeper," and Shirleen walked right out the door to look around. "Mom was not afraid of anything," said Debbie. She didn't see anyone, but later they learned that the peeper was Mike Henderson, a cousin. Although Debbie was surprised by Valarie's response—she had no idea her sister had a BB gun, let alone that she had ever learned to army crawl—again, she didn't ask Valarie about it. "I didn't even know she had a BB gun. Here she is my little sister, and she is trying to protect me!"

Don Tarbet saw something even stranger. A little younger than Valarie, Don lived with his grandparents in Clarkston for two years in the late 1960s while his parents worked in another state. He rode the school bus with Valarie and attended church services with her—both the Sunday morning sacrament meeting and the weeknight meetings for young men and women known as Mutual. One night, as Don left Clarkston's chapel after Mutual, he saw Valarie get into a police car driven by Bob Dahle, a Utah Highway Patrol officer. She hardly needed a ride home; her house was a block and a half away.

"Everyone knew," Don said.

A female town gossip told friends that "Bob Dahle used to take Valarie up around the Loop"—a dirt path to the northwest of town—"by the washboards"—an area of undulating grassland—"and right under the mountain, then back down around and home." The road through the washboards was known in the 19th century as "The Thrill Bumps," according to a locally written history.[9]

As the people who loved Valarie looked back, they all recalled an inexplicable void in her life, in her stories, in her countenance. "I've been thinking about this a lot lately," said John. "I remember sitting behind Valarie's house at a picnic table, when we were first dating, just looking at her. She had this contemplative look on her face, like she was lost in deep thought. And I thought to myself there was something really mysterious about her. I was certainly affected by her beauty, but I wondered if there was something she was hiding."

CHAPTER THREE

"He Never Saw Her Run"

IN MARCH OF 1984, although Annie was making unexpected gains in her recovery, the strain on the Miller family from the accident was impossible to ignore. John wrote in his journal, "I seem kind of restless the past few months. I can't seem to get ahold of myself. Maybe with the family problems I've had I'm discouraged. Valarie is sick, her legs hurting her. I think these problems have made me apprehensive about what may happen in the future. Maybe with Valarie not being very well and unable to do much together I'm a little lonely."

In the previous year, Valarie had endured numerous blows: Annie's almost fatal accident and the ensuing six-month coma, her beloved father's near-fatal train accident, her first symptoms of multiple sclerosis, the physical and emotional strains of caring for a suddenly handicapped child, and an unplanned new pregnancy. All the while, she was expected to look good, keep a neat house, cook, clean, raise the children, and be a responsive wife.

Debbie said that her sister underwent a profound change after her marriage to John—and not for the better. "She became submissive. And that was not how she was. She was outgoing and independent, and I just could not believe the change after she married him."

Sue Saunders also recalled that at the beginning of the marriage, "she would go toe to toe with John," but she observed that for Mormons, female self-assertion was "hard in a marriage." Sue wondered if John had forgotten about the characteristics of the girl he had fallen in love with. To her mind, Valarie's independence was "a reason John fell for her in the first place."

"She could be a little impulsive and maybe not super-organized all the time," recalled Sue. She was dreamy, like her father, caught up in the mystery and magic of her intense religious upbringing. Even early in her marriage, she may also have been silently confronting the beginnings of the psychological crisis that would ultimately consume her. "Valarie was a strong woman, feisty," Sue said, "but life kept beating her down."

Even John admitted it was a tall order—"taking care of four children and dealing with a type-A husband." But John was more than a type-A husband. He was a man with an imperative to succeed, and he carried with him a frontier toughness and a confidence that his way should prevail.

John was raised in a household of four boys and a single girl. "Between my father and church, there was a very heavy emphasis on the value of work," he said. "You've got to earn your way through life." But the emphasis on work had a neurotic quality. "No matter how much you tried," he explained, "no matter how much you worked, no matter how productive you were, there was an implied sense that it was never enough." As an adult, John maintained this expectation of high performance for himself and everyone around him—including his wife and children. But, as he himself observed, it was not always clear: What effort was good enough?

John came from tough stock. After converting to Mormonism in 1840, his twice-widowed great-great-grandmother, Elizabeth Haigh, defied the wishes of her wealthy family and left England for Utah in 1856. For the final leg of Elizabeth's migration, she and her children joined the Martin handcart company—a group of Mormon converts who headed west from Florence, Nebraska, on August 27, 1856, their meager possessions piled into poorly built hand-pulled carts rather than wagons pulled by oxen. Low on food, the company was caught in an early season blizzard in what is now Wyoming.

By the time rescuers arrived and guided the Martin company into Salt Lake City, nearly 150 of its 500 or so members had died of starvation or exposure while dozens of survivors had endured amputations due to frostbite.

Elizabeth Haigh's 19-year-old daughter Sarah Ann became a Mormon hero during the ordeal, carrying 16 people across the frigid North Platte River as the handcarts bogged down in the snow. Sarah Ann later married a former soldier named Louis Frederick Miller; their son, Louis Thomas Miller, married a Hyrum girl, Martha Marinda Anderson, whose ancestors were also handcart pioneers. Together the Millers bought a meat market, thus starting the business that would make their family wealthy. Each passing generation retold the stories of Mormon faith and industry that defined their legacy.

These values surely contributed to the family's fortunes, but the constant pressure inevitably had their less salutary effects. John's mother, Emma, became so miserable when her children were growing up that she would retreat to the garage alone to weep, and she was briefly hospitalized for depression that her father, not a doctor, attributed to a vitamin B_{12} deficiency. The rambunctious boys occasionally misbehaved and got whuppings. But John usually avoided the harrowing punishments occasionally offered up to his older brothers. He was too savvy—and generally well behaved—to provoke his father, Lynn.

Little was said about the lack of approval or affection from Lynn. "Mom and Dad's relationship seemed a bit emotionally detached," John observed. "I believe Mom resented the fact that he was working long hours and then wanted to fish after work to relieve the stress." But go fishing Lynn did. At first, he wanted his bride to accompany him, but being left alone in the truck while Lynn was on the water gave Emma plenty of time to reconsider. Eventually she refused to go.

The Clark forebears, on the other hand, had not endured the handcart pioneers' brutalities, but after their journeys west had settled into the regular cycles of dry farming in Cache Valley, providing the wheat that made their fellow Mormons' bread. If the rains came, the harvest would be better than if they didn't; beyond that, there wasn't much to do but pray. And pray they did, every Sunday at church, and at home via family prayer.

There were three separate Clark families in Clarkston, and Denzel said his branch of the family carried its special burden: a "cloud over their heads." He said when he was a boy, his parents told him their family was not well liked, and there was nothing he could do about it. "As a youth, a tiny, tiny boy," Denzel told a Mormon historian, "I was taught by my grandparents, uncles, and father that I could never amount to anything in life—especially here in Clarkston. I could never contribute. I would never be accepted. I could not achieve the things in life that a young man would like to achieve."[1]

Denzel said the belief in this curse originated with some bolts of fabric that the family had carried with them from Europe when they moved to Utah to join their Mormon brethren. The family gave this fabric to the church but were never paid for it. Why they thought they would be recompensed for a donation to the church is unclear. However, family lore held that the lack of payment reflected something about the family rather than the church. They believed they were not well liked, and the idea of a curse upon them was handed down, generation after generation, until Denzel decided he would prove it wrong by becoming a beloved member of the community and an exemplar of Mormon virtues. He first began to think the curse was lifting after high school when he had the opportunity to play and coach basketball. He was able to "prove to [himself] and to those who thought [he] was inferior that [he] could achieve as much as they could." One of the boys he coached was Bob Dahle.

When Denzel was called to be bishop of his LDS ward in Clarkston, one of his cousins told him jubilantly, "We've broken the string. We've gotten out from under the cloud!" Denzel was respected throughout Cache Valley for his piety and good works, serving his town and the church for a full five-year term as bishop. He was a cheerful, loving person. "If you ever have a bad day, you just want to run into Denzel Clark," declared one neighbor.

"He'll make you feel like a million bucks." Jann Pugmire said her daughter thought Denzel was Heavenly Father Himself.

Denzel was later elected mayor of Clarkston and served in that role for 12 years. He helped the town strengthen its water supply, purchased the gravel pit, and created the annual Pony Express Day parade, among other civic improvements. He also served on a Boy Scouts council in Cache Valley. He participated in the writing of an encyclopedic history of Clarkston, and he established—and for many years ran—an annual pageant to honor Martin Harris, one of the three witnesses who testified that he had seen the golden plates Joseph Smith was given by an angel, according to the tenets of the LDS church.

In the early 1990s, Denzel turned the pageant's operation over to the LDS church and became president of the Pageant Committee. At Denzel's initiative, an amphitheater was built to house the pageant beside the Clarkston cemetery, where Harris is buried. In 2018, the LDS church voted to discontinue the pageant, along with three others.[2] Denzel told me he thought the church preferred to build more temples.

———

Denzel and Shirleen were intensely proud of Valarie, but John's father was not quite sure she was a good match for his son. He sensed there was something weak or distracted about her. Shirleen recalled, with all the indignation a woman of her generation could allow herself to muster against a man—just a whiff above zero—that John's father called Valarie "Pokey."

"I guess he never saw her run," she said drily.

Although Valarie was a popular beauty queen and sports star known to everyone in Clarkston, she described herself as a loner. Growing up, she loved above all to ride her horse Leo into the canyons around "their mountain," Gunsight Peak, which was the touchstone for Clarkston residents, the peak they could always seek out for orientation, the mountain into whose flanks their roots had grown strong. It was out in nature, on her horse, where Valarie found peace.

But one day Valarie showed up at the corral and Leo wasn't there. Shock gave way to grief when she found out her cousin Dwight had sold him. "Dwight didn't even ask her if she wanted to buy him!" a neighbor later lamented. "It broke her heart." Today, Dwight Pearce explains that Leo was, after all, *his* horse; Valarie was just borrowing him. And when he was approached by yet another cousin offering to buy him, he didn't really take him seriously until a couple of days later, when the cousin handed Dwight $800 minus a small commission he'd taken for himself and loaded up the horse to take to his new owner.

It seemed never to have occurred to Dwight or Denzel to mend Valarie's aching heart by offering to buy the horse back for a small premium above $800. Valarie certainly didn't lobby for it; she probably never would have thought of it. Her fate, like that of most of the women around her, was to suffer the decisions of others. Although her religious and social duties were clear, her power to chart the course of her own life was diminishing year after year. Even the people closest to her didn't occupy themselves with how she felt. It probably didn't even occur to her that they should.

Denzel tried to find her another horse. One was a wild mustang that couldn't be broken; the next didn't interest her. By then it might not have mattered anymore.

—

Valarie married John during her senior year of college, and she was pregnant before graduation. In the first eight years of their marriage, she was with child nearly half of the time, and because she suffered from hyperemesis gravidarum—extreme nausea and vomiting throughout the pregnancy—she was gravely ill for almost four total years. She also suffered from sinus, lung, and bronchial infections that frequently put her in the hospital, as well as pain that didn't seem to have any physical cause at all.

John had long worried about her hardiness. Just two weeks after their engagement, John had written in his journal, "Valarie is sick. I comment that Valarie has not had good health. I often worry about her and how her health will affect our future and family."

In March 1984, when she was pregnant with the couple's fourth child, John wrote that Valarie was "miserable" with congested lungs for a few weeks. But she pulled through, and on May 19, 1984, she gave birth to a baby girl they named Donna Brooke, whom they called Brooke. At long last, the nausea was over, and Valarie could finally eat without provoking a rebellion in her stomach. The doctor told Valarie that she could not risk another pregnancy, and he recommended she get her tubes tied. She did so.

As soon as she was on her feet, she was back home with four children to feed, clothe, bathe, and love. She was caring for a newborn, a brain-damaged almost-eight-year-old, a very active five-year-old son, and two-year-old Erin, energetic and fearless. Notwithstanding help from Grandma Emma, nannies, babysitters, and well-meaning family members, the gathering storms in Valarie's mind rendered the task overwhelming.

Both Valarie and John were standout athletes, and their children were beneficiaries of their superior genetic gifts. A home movie shows the kids riding bikes in what appears to be a youthful war drill, pushing and shoving each other like demolition derby contestants, true hellions. Sister Debbie said, "Annie, Ryan, and Erin were the busiest, most active children I've ever seen. It was a handful to take care of them. I just thought that one day, one of them was going to be president of the United States."

John's mother, Emma, had been a widow since the early 1970s, and after John built their house next door to hers in Hyrum, the kids were in and out of their grandma's house all the time. Emma offered generous help and emotional support while Valarie tried to get back into the family routine. "Grandma Emma was awesome," said Ryan. "I always felt like if I was with my grandma, everything was going to be okay."

Ryan often climbed in the tall ponderosa pines planted on the boundary line between the two houses. He remembered that Valarie walked out of their house one day looking for him, and he was "30 or 40 feet up" in a tree.

When he realized she had seen him, he said, "*Shhhhhh!* There's a peacock in the next tree, and I am going to jump over and catch him." Valarie watched quietly for a few seconds, then in her soft, whispery voice, asked if he might not want to come on down instead, which he did. Another time, his father came out of the house and heard Ryan in the top of a tree swearing at the top of his lungs, spitting out every bad word he knew.

Sometimes, though, Ryan fell out of the trees. "I was always having concussions as a kid," he said. Once, he toppled off a huge snow pile, fell into a hole, and couldn't get out. "I was there for hours, screaming for help." Finally, the bus dropped off kids from school, and as they walked home, they heard him and pulled him to safety. Valarie used to tell him she'd get calls from neighbors saying he was outside without any clothes on.

He was an adventurous child, and he often wandered off. Home movies show him trying to attract attention by making grotesque faces and hurling his body through space in desperate attempts to gain the attention of his distracted parents.

Valarie was happy about at least one thing after Brooke's birth. She was having an easy time nursing the new baby—much different from her experiences with her older children. "Brooke was doing so good, and Valarie was so excited," recalled Debbie. But Debbie remembered that when Brooke was six weeks old, John wanted to go on a vacation to the Caribbean to give both himself and Valarie a much-needed break, and he planned to leave the kids at home with a nanny and his mother Emma. Valarie protested. She didn't want to leave her infant at such a delicate time. "Valarie cried and cried," her sister recalled. Some Mormon women of Valarie's age believed the wants of the husband trumped the needs of the children, so Valarie lost that battle. But it also affected her—abruptly ceasing breastfeeding led to full and leaky breasts, as well as rapid and dramatic hormone changes that can trigger MS flare-ups.

And so it was. When she and John returned from that vacation, Valarie suffered an MS exacerbation: the terrifying arrival overnight of a symptom, such as numbness or difficulty walking or seeing, that might take weeks or months to resolve, if it did at all. For that Caribbean trip, both Valarie and Brooke paid a high price.

·······

In November 1984, Valarie expressed a perplexing fear that there was a Doberman pinscher in the basement and repeatedly asked John to go down to check. He never found a dog. Disjointed memories flashed into her mind's eye and terrified her; she couldn't differentiate between images of past events and real, imminent threats. She cried a lot and began to stay up very late at night cleaning the house. She pulled out anything plugged into an electrical outlet, an old habit of her father's to reduce the chance of fire. John noted in his journal that she became uncharacteristically impatient and was often angry with the children—"she is quite abusive verbally with the kids."

The pressure kept building. Just before Christmas, Valarie was admitted to the University of Utah Medical Center and diagnosed with "severe depression," according to John's notes. She was hospitalized for 10 days, then sent home. On January 3, 1985, John wrote that she checked herself into the mental ward of Logan Hospital: "Valarie continues her struggle with intense depression. I am very frightened. She tried to commit suicide."

On January 14, she was still hospitalized. "Her racing thoughts and the constant need to move and run are wearing her down. My heart is heavy," John noted. He couldn't fathom what had become of her. "I don't think she even recognizes me sometimes. I am really frightened." She lost a lot of weight and "regressed to the state of a little child"—retreating, as many people in the grip of a psychological crisis do, to an earlier, safer stage of life in which a parent would have saved them from harm.[3]

Seeing her so lost shook John, and he wondered if he'd made mistakes in his marriage for her to have sunk so low. "I feel like so much could have been prevented if I had only tried to be more sensitive over the past 8 years," he wrote.

One of the nurses caring for Valarie told her psychiatrist, Dr. Milo Andrus, that she feared Valarie may have been sexually abused. After discussing the nurse's suspicions with John, Dr. Andrus decided to use sodium amytal, a barbiturate known as "truth serum," to help Valarie get past the resistance that may have been blocking her memory.

Dr. Andrus conducted his first session with Valarie on March 17, 1985. John went to the hospital to await the results. After Dr. Andrus exited the session, he told John that Valarie had recalled a harrowing event from her teenage years: being gang-raped at knifepoint by two older men, both members of the community. The first was her father's first cousin Gary Thompson, the second a Utah Highway Patrol officer, former town marshal, and neighbor named Bob Dahle. Valarie said a third Clarkston resident, Lloyd Clark, watched.

"I remember feeling two things," said John. "Anger about what had happened to her, and also relief." Relief, he explained, that there was finally a possible explanation for the cyclone of afflictions battering her.

Later that day he wrote in his journal: "For the first time in eight years I am beginning to understand her. She is very mentally distressed. I love her so much and pray she can heal."

Not long after, John called Helen Godfrey, a woman he knew from high school who still lived in Clarkston. "I just had a feeling she might be sensitive to Valarie's experience," he said in an interview. He asked if he could visit her the following Sunday, and she quickly agreed. Sitting in Helen's living room, he told her about Valarie's depression, fears, and regression. And then Helen made a stunning revelation. "I remember her face exactly as she sat on her sofa," he recalled. "Leaving out any details of who was involved, I told her about what happened to Valarie, and she said, 'I know who did it. . . . It was Bob Dahle and Gary Thompson,'" both of whom, she said, "drove around town in Dahle's truck with a large, mean dog."

John was shocked. He asked Helen if she had also been assaulted by the two men. She demurred but said she just always knew they "were to be avoided at all costs."

CHAPTER FOUR

Crawling through Broken Glass

ONLY A FEW WEEKS AFTER Valarie's recollection of the rape, she was out of the hospital and back home with her four children, all clamoring for her care. They were hard to manage under ideal circumstances, but Valarie was a friable shell of her former self, terrified by long-repressed intrusive memories of a violent sexual assault when she was a prepubescent teen.

Bessel van der Kolk, MD, a leading researcher in trauma, first learned about post-traumatic stress disorder (PTSD) while working with combat veterans in the early 1970s. He was surprised to see similar patterns of behavior in women who had been sexually abused as children. "In many ways," he writes in *The Body Keeps the Score: Brain, Mind, and Body in the Healing of Trauma*, "these patients were not so different from the veterans. . . . They also had nightmares and flashbacks. They also alternated between occasional bouts of explosive rage and long periods of being emotionally shut down."[1]

Childhood sexual abuse, he discovered to his shock, was not rare. He wrote in 2014 that "twelve million women in the United States have been victims of rape [and] more than half of all rapes occur in girls below age 15." The scale of this trauma appalled him. For "every soldier who serves in a war zone abroad, there are ten children who are endangered in their own homes." We now know, he wrote, that "more than half of the people who seek psychiatric care have been assaulted, abandoned, neglected, or even raped as children, or have witnessed violence in their families."[2]

Like a combat soldier suffering from PTSD, Valarie's daily functioning was jolted by the sudden, random intrusion of frightening images and the emotional and physical reactions they produced—rage, helplessness, and fear. This caused her trouble managing her children and keeping up her adult relationships.

According to van der Kolk, "You can get along with other people only if you can accurately gauge whether their intentions are benign or dangerous. Even a slight misreading can lead to painful misunderstandings in relationships at home and at work. Functioning effectively in a complex work environment or a household filled with rambunctious kids requires the ability to quickly assess how people are feeling and continuously adjusting your behavior accordingly. Faulty alarm systems lead to blowups or shutdowns in response to innocuous comments or facial expressions."[3]

Today, we would cringe at the idea of an Iraq combat veteran crippled by PTSD placed back into her home to care for four children. When Valarie was first able to speak to Dr. Andrus about what had happened to her, it was only five years after the American Psychiatric Association had acknowledged PTSD as a diagnosis. In rural Utah, the syndrome was probably little known or understood. John doesn't remember it being mentioned at all.

On April 21, 1985, John wrote: "Valarie is still struggling under the weight of her problems." Hard to imagine how it could have been any other way. After all, only a month had passed since her recollection of a gang rape at knifepoint that was so shocking and unacceptable to her that she had repressed its memory for 17 years.

After returning home from work, he noticed she was "acting a little strange," and he suspected she "was high on some drug," but he felt obligated that evening to work on a church welfare project, so he left her alone with the children, thinking "she would probably be okay for a while."

He later wrote of that night: "I left around 4:30 p.m., and around 7:00 p.m. I became a little uneasy and decided to return home."

When he opened the front door of their house, he found his Uncle Don and Aunt Mardel Wimmer there, "very upset." An hour earlier, they had dropped by to say hello to Annie, and Valarie had met them at the door, invited them in, and then passed out in the hallway. While tending to her, they heard children crying and walked to the kitchen where they found Brooke, 10 months old, crawling through "broken dishes and glasses and food." The other children were huddled in the corner of the family room, crying. Apparently, Valarie had gone into a terrible rage and had thrown whatever glasses, plates, pots, and pans she could get her hands on against the walls and the floor.

John rushed Valarie to the hospital, where they pumped her stomach and admitted her once again.

—

John did not understand the extent of Valarie's psychic wounds. Always action-oriented, he urged Valarie to tell her parents that she had been raped. Valarie was horrified at the prospect and tried desperately to put it off. In the Clark home, the children felt it was incumbent on them to keep any sadness or upset from their parents in the service of protecting their view of the world, in which bad things did not happen. Debbie recalled that one day, while she was a young teen, she went to a sleepover at her friend Ruth Ann Clark's house. When she arrived, she was surprised to see, in addition to Ruth Ann and another girl, Pam Nish, three boys as well, including Ruth Ann's brother, Lloyd Clark. The two girls quickly disappeared with two of the boys, leaving her in the living room with Clark, who was three years older than Debbie and in short order managed to put his arm around her shoulder. Desperate to escape but equally concerned about causing offense, Debbie suggested they go out for a walk. Clark agreed, and as soon as they got outside, Debbie bolted toward her house.

She then spent the entire night on the rear steps rather than wake her parents so they could let her in.

One can imagine that if Debbie stayed out all night rather than tell her parents she left a sleepover early because Lloyd Clark had put his arm around her shoulder, then her sister Valarie would surely rather have chewed off her own arm than tell them that their relative Gary Thompson and neighbor Bob Dahle had done such terrible things to her that she was losing her mind.

But John wanted to seek accountability from her assailants. "John called me and said that he and Valarie would like to come out and meet Shirleen and I at our home," Denzel recalled. On the afternoon of Sunday May 12, 1985, John and Valarie drove up to Clarkston. Valarie cried on the way up. She would do what he asked of her, but she insisted on one thing: They would not name the two men who had attacked her. She was afraid of the trouble it would cause her parents in their community.

Once they arrived, John and Valarie were ushered into the den, which had a view of the backyard and its flowers and birds. Denzel remembered that Valarie looked sick. "She was taken aback," he said. "Usually she was very forward." He could tell she'd been crying. John began by saying he wanted to let them know that while Valarie was hospitalized for depression, after the administration of truth serum, she had remembered being raped as a young girl. He asked whether Denzel knew anything about it.

Denzel immediately said, "I know who did it. It was that Gary Thompson and Bob Dahle."

Shocked once again and recalling that Helen Godfrey had said exactly the same thing, John pressed Denzel to explain.

"Because for many years"—Denzel seemed suddenly to realize—"both those men would say things to me about Valarie that were inappropriate for anyone to say about someone else's daughter. They spoke lewdly about her."

Later Denzel recalled, "They used to say, 'That Valarie, she is really *something.*'"

Despite this, Denzel said he never suspected them of any wrongdoing. But come to think of it, he recalled, "they didn't say, 'Denzel you have such beautiful daughters.' They talked about Valarie as if they knew her better than I did."

After getting over the surprise of Denzel's revelation, John encouraged Valarie to tell her story, and she did so, though it was excruciatingly painful for her. She couldn't get through it without long pauses and showers of tears.

John observed that "Denzel was struggling" as he listened to her recollections and evident distress. Dwight Pearce, Denzel's nephew, said, "You know, they were cousins, first cousins, and Denzel loved Thompson like a brother. They hunted deer together. They camped together. He didn't want to believe that in the worst way."

Shirleen sat quietly in her chair. She was "a little hard to read," John recalled. "I don't know if she was angry . . . I'm sure she was shocked and displeased about it, but I don't remember her saying a whole lot other than maybe 'oh my gosh.'" John didn't remember Shirleen consoling her daughter. "I don't remember her hugging Valarie or trying to comfort her or anything like that."

In the end, there was no emotional outpouring, no catharsis. Neither Denzel nor Shirleen rushed to support their daughter, and they didn't ask what they could do for her. They didn't apologize for not noticing her distress. They didn't say they loved her. They didn't rise to gather her in their arms and embrace her. Rather, they sat in their chairs, frozen. Valarie feared they didn't believe her or hadn't quite absorbed the truth and its ramifications.

Years later, when he was interviewed for this book, Denzel said he and Shirleen never discussed the issue further with Valarie.

Around the same time, when Shirleen was asked to describe Gary Thompson, she said he was "a tender man."

With sorrow and self-reproach, Denzel admitted, "I don't know how dumb a parent can be . . . I didn't think such things existed."

—

Valarie was in a fragile and highly enervated state. The unspeakable secret she had tried for so many years to hide from herself and the world was now out, causing her deep shame and anxiety, which sometimes led her to yell at the children. These outbursts brought on regret and more shame, and relief was hard to come by. But there was one thing she realized she could do to feel better: swallow the pills the doctors prescribed for her. With them, she could float away. First were benzodiazepines—tranquilizers like Valium and Xanax. And then the sweet, deep embrace of the opioid Percodan, which she came to like a bit too much.

Why might Valarie have become hooked? Science writer Maia Szalavitz offered a possible answer in a *New York Times* op-ed. She wrote that opioids gave her "relief from my dread and anxiety, and a soothing sense that I was safe, nurtured and unconditionally loved." She explained that the drugs "mimic the neurotransmitters that are responsible for making social connection comforting—tying parent to child, lover to beloved." Szalavitz also noted that "people who experienced sexual trauma and neglect are at high risk for opioid addiction."[4]

On May 13, 1985, John wrote in his journal: "She has admitted she is addicted to a drug called Percodan. We are working to solve this problem. I love her but sometimes lose patience."

Valarie was medicating herself while her doctors were having trouble finding an antidepressant that worked for her, possibly because antidepressants don't work as well for people with a history of childhood abuse.[5]

"Sometimes she goes into the bedroom and I can hear her screaming and banging her hands on the walls," John wrote in his journal. "I suppose there is so much pain she tries to make her physical body hurt so she doesn't hurt so much inside."

A few days earlier, John received a phone call from a policeman saying he had picked up Valarie for running a red light and not stopping immediately when he tried to pull her over. The policeman said he "knew she was high on something" and confided to John that his own wife "had had some mental problems" and that he too was familiar with the drug Percodan.

By the middle of June, Valarie was back in the hospital. "It is very discouraging," John wrote. "Dr. Andrus is very concerned about her progress. Frankly, I'm scared about where she is emotionally. It hurts so much to see her in so much trouble. The past few months have been very difficult. Valarie has attempted suicide a couple of times."

One night, Valarie slipped out of the hospital and police found her wandering around Nolan Johnson's old apartment building. Johnson had been Valarie's college love while John was away on his mission. Amid her regression, she may have felt Nolan would be more understanding of her pain.

As Dr. Andrus tried to treat Valarie, he also offered John some troubling marital advice. John confided to his journal that Dr. Andrus had wondered aloud "if I would be able to sustain any kind of a normal relationship with Valarie in the years ahead." John understood him to mean that divorce was indeed a likely outcome: "He kind of hinted I should get out," he wrote.

John noted that the doctor's words upset him, though he did not remark on the ethical lapse of a psychiatrist telling the husband of his devastated patient that he ought to divorce her. Nor did he remark on the possibility that the doctor was at a loss about how to treat her. In August, John wrote: "She has experienced a lot of pain and suffering for 15 years. I am committed to help for the balance of my life."

In September, John thought he saw improvement. "I hope she can work her way back to good health."

Three weeks later, he canceled a business trip to Japan "because of Valarie's emotional problems." He wrote, "Just don't feel secure leaving the family under the circumstances. I am afraid she is damaging the children with her abusive anger and language." Moreover, he noted, almost as an afterthought, "she has anorexia."

Valarie's friend Sue Saunders said Valarie always "felt terrible" after shouting at the children, but she couldn't help it. Her anxiety in the evenings rose to

levels she couldn't control. "All trauma is preverbal," wrote van der Kolk, quot-
ing William Shakespeare's play *Macbeth* to illuminate the Bard's preternatural
understanding of the primitive nature of panic.[6] Upon finding the king has
been murdered, Macduff cries, "O horror, horror, horror! Tongue nor heart
cannot conceive nor name thee! Confusion now hath made his masterpiece!"[7]

"Even years later many traumatized people have enormous difficulty telling other people what has happened to them," van der Kolk wrote. "Their
bodies reexperience terror, rage, and helplessness, as well as the impulse to
fight or flee, but these feelings are almost impossible to articulate. Trauma
by nature drives us to the edge of comprehension, cutting us off from language based on common experience or an imaginable past."[8]

Valarie felt this terror, an inescapable truth of trauma and its aftermath.
"Psychologists usually try to help people use insight and understanding to
manage their behavior," van der Kolk wrote. "However, neuroscience research
shows that very few psychological problems are the result of defects in understanding; most originate in pressures from deeper regions in the brain that
drive our perception and attention. When the alarm bell of the emotional brain
keeps signaling that you are in danger, no amount of insight will silence it."[9]

John noticed in September 1985 that Valarie had started a new and troubling behavior—staying away in the evenings. "She will tell the kids or me
that she will be home around 4:00 p.m.," he wrote in his journal, "and then
call at 7 p.m. and say she is on her way but not show up until 10:30 p.m. I
sit home and really worry myself sick about it."

Perhaps Valarie was trying to craft a solution for the perilous anxiety
that afflicted her in the evenings and led to blowups with the children—
by staying away. But even as they strained to understand the depth of her
psychological trauma, her male doctor and husband also viewed her as irre-
sponsible and out of control. Dr. Andrus decided that she wouldn't get
better until she could "anchor the memories of her abuse in the past."

Today, therapists use the term *containment* to refer to exercises they use
to help patients safely place traumatic events in the past. These techniques

help the patient feel he or she has some control over the intrusive and traumatic memories or thoughts. For example, patients are encouraged to write a narrative of their frightening memories in a journal and lock the journal in a drawer. Another patient may imagine the memories being recorded on a tape or downloaded to a zip drive to be hidden away. Someone else might write frightening words on a chalkboard and then erase them.

Later in his life, John used these techniques to manage his own anxiety. He would open a shoebox and holler into it his feelings of anger, frustration, and despair. He would then close the box and put it away on a shelf. He kept up the habit for years until the box was battered and worn from use.

Sadly, such techniques were not available to Valarie in 1985. John asked Dr. Andrus if it might help Valarie's recovery if one of her assailants confessed to abusing her. The psychiatrist told John it might, though he felt getting a confession was unlikely. Said John, "I remember Dr. Andrus saying, 'Look, this probably isn't going to work. He's going to deny it. But let's go try,'"

Before making any decisions, on August 25, 1985, John wrote a memo outlining various ways that might get Gary Thompson and Bob Dahle to confess to having raped Valarie. He had discussed the issue with Dr. Andrus, Denzel Clark, and his personal attorney, Brent Hoggan. One was to "approach Gary and try to get a confession and a statement implicating Bob." John suggested adding some muscle including a law enforcement official such as "the State Attorney General or some other state or federal official" who might induce Thompson to confess if he were offered "some kind of immunity for his testimony against Bob." Another option was to approach Thompson and Dahle separately to obtain confessions "on the terms that if they confess, we would not pursue that matter further with state or federal officials." John noted that as an additional impetus, he might threaten to launch a full investigation with the proper law enforcement authorities.

He observed that "most likely, Bob and Gary will deny the entire event. [After all,] Bob knows the court system very well and would probably realize there is virtually no way to prove such an allegation."

As John and the other men mulled over what to do, Valarie's accusations came to the attention of Bob Dahle himself. During the last week of September 1985, he called Denzel Clark on the telephone to say he wasn't happy to hear "that the story was out that he was responsible for rape," said Denzel. "He tried to tell me he didn't do it," Denzel later said. They spoke by telephone a couple of more times, then Dahle told Denzel to meet him in Layton, a town 75 miles from Clarkston.

Why Denzel felt he was required to do Dahle's bidding and drive all that way to see him was unclear. At the time, Dahle was not living in Clarkston, and thus Denzel was technically no longer his bishop. However, custom would have dictated that Dahle show Denzel the respect of traveling to see *him*, and not the other way around. But Denzel, still operating under the weight of the perceived "cloud," was always exceedingly generous with his congregants, and he complied with Dahle's command.

He didn't remember if Dahle arrived at their rendezvous in his official Highway Patrol cruiser or in his personal vehicle, but he recalled that Dahle "jumped in my car, [then] spent an hour telling me how he never done anything. All he wanted to do was talk about how he couldn't have done it."

Denzel said Dahle was nervous and angry, insisting that "everything that's being said is a lie. And I'm not going to take it." Denzel recalled that Dahle appeared angry and threatened to sue John.

On October 1, 1985, a few days after that meeting in Denzel's vehicle, John and Dr. Andrus drove to Clarkston to visit Gary Thompson. In spite of the many strategies John had considered in his memo to create incentives for Thompson and Dahle to confess, or ways to frighten one into implicating the other, in the end, John and Dr. Andrus undertook their mission without carrot or stick, hoping that Gary Thompson might, out of the goodness of his heart, confess to a vile criminal act and an excommunicable sin in the eyes of the church. They did not fully comprehend the cost to Valarie's health and peace of mind if they should fail.

"It was a beautiful day," recalled John. "We were going to surprise Gary

Thompson. We thought that if he came clean it would help Valarie's recovery. I remember it all very clearly. It was, perhaps, naive."

According to an expert in sexual abuse who preferred to remain unnamed for this book, "Whenever you confront an abuser or perpetrator, you have to have very modest goals. Standard expectations are that you have to be prepared (1) for the [victim] to get worse and (2) for the crime to be denied. Very few abusers can confess in the face of a confrontation, whether it's with parents or siblings or strangers."

Sadly, both expectations proved true. John and Dr. Andrus arrived at Gary Thompson's house at 7 a.m. He was already fully dressed when he opened the door and said, "Well, good morning, John. Come on in." John's spirits fell. It seemed clear that Thompson had been tipped off and was expecting them. Perhaps he'd been warned by Dahle.

"We went into his living room and sat down," recalled John. "It was very civilized, and I said, 'Look, we need your help. We believe that you were involved in the sexual molestation of Valarie, and Valarie's life could be at stake here, and we believe that you could help her recover.' I told him about Valarie's problems—extreme depression from being abused as a child."

According to John, Thompson "sat there and just shook his head and denied everything."

Before they left, John asked Thompson if Bob Dahle had anything to do with Valarie's abuse. Thompson denied that as well—a clear lie because he couldn't possibly know what Dahle had or hadn't done.

"Walking out to the car," John later wrote, "Andrus and I looked at each other and we both said that if ever there was a guy lying, it was Gary Thompson. Not just his sweaty behavior—he was fidgety and nervous during our entire visit—but he clearly seemed like a man with something to hide. We both had the same reaction—we both felt much stronger that what Valarie was saying was truthful."

They, too, apparently doubted her. And their clumsy efforts got them no closer to helping Valarie "anchor her memories." Neither did they consider how their physical proximity to one of Valarie's attackers might reignite her fears.

On October 5, John admitted to his journal that "Valarie has taken a turn for the worse since we decided to approach these two men. The pressure . . . has forced her to nearly enter the hospital again."

Around the same time, whether on his own or summoned by Bob Dahle, Lloyd Clark drove down to the offices of the Utah Highway Patrol in Salt Lake City. Years later, he recounted their conversation to a private investigator. "I went in and talked to [Bob] and I said, 'Do you know what's going on?' and he said, 'What?' I said, 'The thing that, uh, that they say that happened with Valarie.'"

Although Dahle had his own office at headquarters, he suggested that he and Clark "go for a ride." He clearly wanted to talk far away from his law enforcement colleagues.

Clark said, "We went for a ride, and he said that he did not do it." Clark told Dahle that since he "hadn't been there," he couldn't say either way what had happened. Dahle then seemed to suggest that, should he be called to appear in court, Clark should go in his stead. Dahle explained that he would be more at risk because "they're gonna bring up a lot of stuff."

Clark said he repeated, "Well, I don't know anything about it, so . . ."

Although both men denied any knowledge of the rape, Dahle urged Clark to "go to court" if worse came to worse because he felt it would be less consequential for Clark to do so.

———

Valarie's condition worsened and John wanted to do something that might bring her relief, so on October 5, 1985, he took her on a short vacation to Jackson Hole, Wyoming.

In March of the next year, he noted that she was "slowly looking better."

In April, he wrote in his journal that she was suffering from a sinus infection that landed her in the hospital. "It seems like it is one thing after another with her."

He didn't know—few outside the medical profession knew back in 1985—that chronic illnesses and immune system disorders are common among those who were sexually abused as children. And there are many maladies survivors suffer from that have no clear medical cause—neck aches, backaches, pelvic pain, and even trouble swallowing.[10]

In June, John sent Valarie on a trip to Norway with a family friend, "thinking it will help her to get away for a while." When she returned, he thought that she seemed "stronger."

In July he wrote: "Valarie has done well this summer. Her depression seems under control although she still struggles with the past. She is taking less medication and has put on a little weight. She has much further to go but I am encouraged."

In November, he noted that Valarie "continues to struggle."

In the two years following Valarie's recollection of the gang rape, the Miller and Clark families descended into a crisis that went far beyond Valarie's physical and psychological breakdown. The very structures of the Miller family life were tested, and the Clark family's faith in the unquestioned goodness of their village and their place in it were set on edge. John had lost the conjugal company of his wife, and the children could no longer count on consistent care from their beautiful and loving, though fragile, mother. Her furies burst through in episodes of self-harm and harsh words. The old family was over and done with, and it wasn't clear what shape the new one would take—echoing the fear about the future that John had noted in his journal from the very start of his marriage.

In January 1987, after years of reorganizing and upgrading E. A. Miller into a profitable business, and after months of difficult acquisition negotiations,

John and Junior completed a $33 million sale of the company to Conagra Brands in a complex deal that guaranteed employment for the E. A. Miller executives. Junior walked away with $28 million in Conagra stock, and John received $5 million in cash and stock.

Six months later, at the age of 35, John was hired as president of Armour Food Company, a unit of Conagra and a diversified family of food products. Armour processed, marketed, and distributed hot dogs, bacon, ham, sausage, and lunch meat. Taking the job required moving to Omaha, so in August, John and Valarie started looking for houses. They soon found a beautiful large two-story brick home in a development on the northwest side of town that had an excellent school system.

Valarie put her all into planning and managing the move, and soon became exhausted. John encouraged her to pace herself and rest when she got tired, but she didn't know how. "I seem to always be telling her to rest. She has no self-esteem. I tell her she can never give the kids the love they need until she loves herself," he wrote.

Nevertheless, with considerable help from friends, she got the family relocated and the children enrolled in school. And she also had a new role as a corporate wife, which required her to host gatherings and accompany John to the occasional social function. Youngest daughter Brooke remembered her mother dressed to the nines, kissing her goodnight before heading out for the evening on John's arm. "I was in awe of my mom," Brooke wrote in a long letter of memories of her mother. "She was kind, smart, fierce, chic, stunningly beautiful and glamorous." Around the same time, in the car one day with their mother, Brooke remembered Ryan announcing out of the blue that "our mom is the prettiest woman in the world!" Brooke remarked, "He was dead serious, you couldn't challenge him, not that we would. She was. She was just so beautiful. She was also very mysterious to me, but was so open at the same time. She was relatable and empathetic and everyone around her adored her. My whole world revolved around her love."

There was, of course, a darker side to Valarie's life in Omaha. In February

1988, John noted that Valarie "has been tired lately and does not look well." In June she came down with a painful case of shingles, which customarily takes weeks to abate. On August 15, he wrote: "I told Valarie that I do not think we should have any more live-in nannies because she treats them more like her own kids than employees and it causes problems. She creates more stress on herself."

On September 4, 1988, without the live-in nanny, John admitted that "the house is overwhelming her."

An incident in November 1988 devastated John. "I came home from work the other night," he wrote in his journal, "and as I walked in the door, I could hear Valarie upstairs screaming and using very bad language toward the children, totally out of control. She was very abusive. I ran upstairs and everybody was crying, and Valarie was completely crazy. I picked her up and drug her into the bedroom and closed the door and told her not to come out until she was in control. It really scared me, and I later thought that I knew something really had to change or all would be lost in regard to my marriage."

John thought most of Valarie's problems derived from her faulty decisions brought on by profound mental anguish. "Much of her illness comes from stress she places on herself," he wrote in his journal. But for people suffering from PTSD, willpower and decision-making have very little to do with how they act and feel. "Trauma is not just an event that took place sometime in the past; it is also the imprint left by that experience on mind, brain, and body," wrote van der Kolk. "This imprint has ongoing consequences for how the human organism manages to survive in the present."[11]

For example, stress hormones in the body usually respond quickly and forcefully in response to an imminent threat, then stop pumping through the bloodstream as soon as the threat has passed, allowing the body to return to normal. However, research shows that people suffering from PTSD are unable to turn off the stress hormones once the threat has passed and continue to feel "agitation and panic." In the long term, this "wreaks havoc with their health."[12]

Valarie was disorganized, sick, overcome with anxiety and fear, and still preoccupied by terrifying flashbacks. The children were suffering along with their mother. John had no idea at this point, three years after Valarie's first recall of the childhood rape, that more memories of violence and abuse were fighting to gain consciousness, tormenting her but unable to break through. But in the fall of 1988, John knew that his wife was profoundly ill, and he had the good judgment to reach out to Sarah Jones, a therapist who had seen Valarie briefly in Omaha, to express his alarm. She suggested that Valarie might benefit from treatment at the renowned Menninger Clinic, then in Topeka, Kansas, known as "the court of last resort" for patients suffering from grievous psychological trauma.

In the LDS way, John and Valarie prayed and fasted together in November to decide whether Valarie should try a six-month inpatient stay at Menninger, but John had already decided that he wanted her to go. He wrote: "I will be lonely without her but this is very important for our family. . . . Her problems have affected all areas of my life and I admit at times they are trying. I wonder how much more I can take."

John had had high hopes—a strange elation in fact—when he discovered that the reason behind Valarie's depression and regression was a childhood rape. He felt that once the source had been discovered, healing would naturally follow, like infection drained from a lanced boil. But the extent and duration of the attacks against Valarie were yet unknown to both him and her doctors, as was the damage done to Valarie's psyche and nervous system from not only the abuse but also the specific shame assigned to female victims of sexual assault in her repressive, closed village. John still had little idea of what had happened to Valarie in her early teenage years. Yet he was acutely aware of how he felt: Over the last few years, he had gone from hopefulness to abject despair.

CHAPTER FIVE

"Dirty, Inside and Out"

JOHN AND THE CHILDREN accompanied Valarie to Topeka, Kansas, on January 11, 1989. She was admitted into the Menninger Clinic and "we all cried and it was very hard," he wrote in his journal.

"I was very impressed that she had a good perception of what her problems are," he continued. "I think overcoming them will be very difficult. I am really discouraged about the whole thing, having a pity party."

In spite of John's apprehensions, Valarie was entering an environment completely different from anything she had ever experienced, the first one that offered her a chance to explore, at her own pace, her experiences, memories, thoughts, and feelings with the help of doctors who were experienced in the treatment of trauma and abuse. The goal was to help her understand herself in a way that was more flexible, open, forgiving, and human than the deeply idiosyncratic Mormonism unique to tiny, isolated Clarkston had allowed.

Her admissions intake report, written by a staff psychiatrist, noted that she expressed "long-standing feelings of being a loner and having difficulty in sharing her problems with others." It quoted her explaining that as a child, "she would ride her horse in order to cope and she liked to be alone." Summing up what had brought her to the hospital, the psychiatrist pointed to the recovered memory of having been raped as a young teenager. "Apparently, she was aware of the rape for several years, but then repressed it. She has never been entirely able to deal with the rape and its aftermath." Additionally, he wrote, she has had "chronically low self-esteem for many years."

He explained that Valarie had checked into the hospital because she could not "tolerate any attempt to explore and understand her underlying feelings of low self-esteem and to explore the trauma and still function well enough to be a wife and mother."

She had endured a very trying three and a half years since she had recalled being raped at knifepoint by Bob Dahle and Gary Thompson—three and a half years without effective therapy, with no relief from her panic and shame except the occasional blackouts offered by pain pills, three and a half years struggling to fulfill her maternal and conjugal duties while driving her self-loathing deeper and deeper, leaving her in a profound depression "marked by numerous suicidal ideas and some attempts through overdose."

The doctor noted she had suffered from "anxiety and agitation" as well as extreme mood swings. She told the Menninger psychiatrist that she could be "functioning right on one day and the next day be extremely depressed, angry, irritable, and agitated." She also said that she experienced "racing thoughts and excessive energy, sometimes staying up for several days at a time and keeping very busy in order to avoid thinking about or dealing with her concerns." She also experienced episodes of "tearfulness, weight loss, and anorexia."

After more than two months of evaluations and tests, a treatment regimen was created for Valarie. She was assigned an in-patient team that included a staff psychologist "experienced and credentialed in the use of hypnosis," according to the intake report. He would continue at Menninger for almost 30 years as a clinician, teacher, and supervisor, and he eventually became the organization's director of clinical psychology and dean of the School of Psychiatry. Because he still practices and sees patients, he requested that the book not use his name. We will call him Dr. Brown. A soft-spoken man with a comforting Southern accent, Dr. Brown listened carefully to Valarie.

He was perhaps the first person in her life who tried to draw out her feelings and thoughts rather than tell her what feelings and thoughts she ought to be having. He observed in his first set of notes for the quarterly reporting period of March 7, 1989, through June 5, 1989, that Valarie's depression and suicidal ideas had appeared after her daughter Annie's bicycle accident, and he surmised that Annie's injuries and prolonged coma stimulated feelings in Valarie associated with her own childhood injury—the rape and, possibly, earlier trauma.

Because it was still difficult for her to revisit the sexual attacks, she had been referred for "psychotherapy which could include hypnosis" as a means of exploring her traumatic experiences. Dr. Brown noted that Valarie "approached the therapy with some trepidation, but with a dutiful sense that this was a necessary part of her treatment." It turned out that Valarie was an excellent hypnotic subject, "achieving fairly deep trance states during which early memories were easily recalled."

In Dr. Brown's office, patients sat in a reclining chair so they were relaxed and comfortable but not feeling as vulnerable as they might be if they were lying flat. He induced hypnosis via one of several standard means—generally a progression of verbal suggestions to concentrate on their breathing, to focus on relaxing their muscles, or to imagine they were in a familiar, restful place. The therapist might also ask the patient to count, suggesting that with each number they allow themselves to go deeper and deeper into a state of hypnosis.

In an interview with the author, Dr. Brown explained that hypnosis induces "a state of focused attention and relaxation so that things that are not ordinarily available in the consciousness can become available." He noted that hypnosis enhances the mind-body connection, which explains why certain disorders such as irritable bowel syndrome and hypertension can be relieved with hypnosis. Trust between doctor and patient is critical because a patient exploring his or her trauma under hypnosis "is not just remembering, they are remembering *with* someone," he emphasized.

If the patient didn't trust the doctor, he knew, the therapeutic process could be impeded.

With Valarie, he wrote, "Our exploration first took us to an event that happened when she was in her early teenage years, when she found herself alone with three grown men, all known to her, in a field near a barn." This event likely took place when she was 13, about to turn 14, in the summer of 1968. She laid out the scenario just as she had done with Dr. Andrus. One of the men was her father's first cousin, Gary Thompson, 33 at the time, who had grown up directly across the street from her family home. The second man was Bob Dahle, 31, who had been Clarkston's town marshal from 1962 to 1964 and had graduated from the Utah Highway Patrol Academy in 1967. He lived two blocks away from the Clarks. The third man was Lloyd Clark, 20, also a neighbor.

Valarie told Dr. Brown that Thompson mentioned that there were some kittens up in the loft of the barn behind his house and suggested she go look for them, and that his daughter, a playmate of hers, would be along soon. Valarie said she climbed up into the loft but found no kittens. After a few minutes, the three men followed her up, and she noticed that they "smelled funny and acted funny"—apparently intoxicated.

Dr. Brown wrote: "Threatening her with a knife, they forced her to remove her clothes, lie down on the straw, and subjected her to oral and genital intercourse."

Valarie told Dr. Brown she had been "quite frightened and disgusted" throughout the experience. At one point, when she protested, "a knife blade was poised at her vagina and she was told it would be shoved all the way up her if she didn't be quiet. Further, she was told that her sister would have the same done to her if she ever told anyone."

Outnumbered and thus unable to fight or flee, she "attempted to dissociate, pretending she was safe at home and not there at all."

She couldn't get the story out completely in one go. As Dr. Brown noted, it took several sessions for her to "slowly relive the memory, and with it came a good deal of fear and emotional tension, but no real outpouring of emotion." Rather, she seemed to "relive it as she had originally experienced it, feeling still the need to suppress her emotions." During the retelling, she was unable to express any anger at the men for this attack, and she was unable to cry over her pain and humiliation. This led, "not surprisingly," he wrote, to painful headaches "almost continually until she was instructed during trance to interrupt the memory and scream at the men to stop what they were doing, expressing to them how frightened and upset she was." The headaches subsided after that session and did not return for several weeks until new painful memories emerged.

During the first three months of her treatment, Valarie saw Dr. Brown twice a week for therapy. Between sessions, she was encouraged to speak to the staff about her feelings and any other thoughts that came to mind, but she found that very difficult. She not only was shy and inhibited but also didn't have the words. After all, at the time of the assault, she was still a child whose parents never so much as mentioned the names of human genitalia to her. How could she even begin to describe what the men had done? Moreover, during an attack so terrifying she believed she might be killed, the men told her at knifepoint not to make a noise. They told her she was not allowed to complain or express her feelings. In a letter to her doctor, she wrote down the words that were too painful to tell: "It's hard for me to explain how I felt when Gary and Bobby would not allow me to show my anger or disgust. It makes me feel nauseated and a little dizzy. It's hard because I can feel myself being there, feeling hot, and sweaty, and dirty, inside and out."

Two men in positions of authority over her—one a fearsome highway patrolman, the other her father's beloved cousin—told her during the most emotionally wrought event of her young life that she wasn't allowed to have feelings or express them. And so she didn't. Not for a very long time.

Dr. Brown tried to develop a cathartic experience for Valarie after she told him of this memory by encouraging her to "dwell on her fear and shame, her strong feeling that she might be killed, and her sense that she would never be the same again." He wrote in his notes that she was finally able to "cry a good bit" but was still "unable to experience anger." He reassured her that she had done nothing to provoke the mistreatment and that she wasn't being punished for being bad. It was the men who were wrong for having done what they did. Dr. Brown wrote:

> For a few sessions we continued to work with the feelings associated with this incident, and also worked hypnotically with images of herself being comfortable with her husband, differentiating clearly between a man who loved her and cared about her from men who would abuse her.
>
> It was easy for the patient to grasp how profoundly this experience had affected her, and how inhibited she has subsequently been in the expression of any emotion, but especially anger. Feelings must be kept to oneself, lest something terrible happen.

Valarie told Dr. Brown she attributed her "lifelong disinterest in sex" to the abuse.

Although Dr. Brown was acutely aware of the shame Valarie felt over these assaults, he could not have known about the teachings she had received in the LDS church about sex and love, as well as the psychological trip wires they set in her young mind. In the 1960s and 1970s, in keeping with that era's conservative rejection of feminism and the sexual revolution, LDS teachings placed particular emphasis on female chastity. "Sexual purity is youth's most precious possession," declared one Young Women's lesson plan for December 1968, reminding Mormon girls that good prospective husbands "want a person . . . who has reserved her personal affection for one she loves in marriage." Teachers warned about the social impact of sex on young women: "Reputations are ruined as the word gets around that 'so-and-so' is 'an easy mark.'"[1]

In vehement opposition to socialism and communism, Mormonism during the Cold War promoted the concept of "free agency"—in its formulation, the divine gift of free will that allows humans to choose good or evil for themselves. This theme, ever-present in the materials from which Valarie was taught, again emphasized chastity as a choice but included no discussion of child sexual abuse or rape. In fact, the teachings suggested that a man's sexual behavior was a woman's responsibility.

The most influential LDS writer on sexual morality was Helen Andelin, author of the 1963 book *Fascinating Womanhood*, a Mormon counterpoint to Betty Friedan's feminist classic, *The Feminine Mystique*, published earlier that same year. Andelin's bestseller made her a celebrity in Mormon circles and beyond, its teachings disseminated in follow-up books, discussion groups, and classes for college students and older adults. For Andelin, chastity was paramount, premarital sex disastrous. In the ideal Mormon marriage, she wrote, "there are no sordid skeletons in the closet. . . . Here starts the nucleus for a family where confidence and love can expand."

Once married, Andelin opined, women could determine when and how often she and her husband had sex. But she advised them to be "generous" toward even the most "oversexed" husbands and to respond with "childlikeness" to male demands, becoming "gentle, tender, frail, and dependent."[2]

To add to the confusion, Andelin suggested that a husband who demanded and received sex "is apt to feel terribly ashamed of himself for his loss of control, selfishness and lack of consideration of his wife's feelings. And, he may hold his wife responsible for yielding and may disrespect her for her lack of respect for her own body. If she had kept control and refused him, she would have preserved his self-respect, which is a far more important feeling to a man than a release of his passions."[3]

Damned if she does, damned if she doesn't. Undersexed or oversexed, a husband was the wife's problem and responsibility. Even if he turned away from her. If a wife learned of a husband's infidelity, Andelin explained, "she must first examine closely her own life to see if she has had a part in or is a possible contributor to his delinquency."[4]

One can only imagine that the many solitary hours Valarie spent riding her horse, Leo, were taken up by trying to square the circle of her experiences with these teachings. How was a gentle, frail child to manage the sexual demands of a grown man? Or two? The answer was unambiguous: submission. And then, how to pivot and respond to a future husband? In this impossible situation, only one thing was clear from the outset: the consequences would be hers to bear.

Andelin, of course, never taught her students about the sexual predation that was rife in Clarkston. One of the Young Women's lessons Valarie most likely heard featured the story of a young girl who found herself "in trouble" and died on the steps of a hospital following a botched abortion. After reading the story, teachers were instructed to ask the young women why the girl "ended up where she did."[5]

Valarie was determined to avoid this fate, and she fought to devise an end to the attacks that would not put her family at risk. The mental damage done to her by these cruel, misogynistic teachings no doubt contributed to Valarie's depression, regression, and psychological paralysis.

Her plight was echoed decades later in the case of Elizabeth Smart, a Mormon girl abducted in 2002 from her bedroom in Salt Lake City by two deranged religious fanatics, Brian David Mitchell and Wanda Barzee. Smart was held hostage for nine months and raped repeatedly. She didn't attempt to run from her captors because the sexual assaults committed against her had, in her mind, rendered her worthless. "Nobody re-chews a piece of gum," she later said. "You throw it away."[6] That crushing object lesson had been presented to her in a Young Women's lesson in her LDS ward.

In subsequent sessions, Valarie told Dr. Brown that the two men who had raped her, Gary Thompson and Bob Dahle, approached her on several occasions later that summer and, through coercion and threats, convinced her to meet them "in remote places" for additional sexual encounters, including a dilapidated old house in Steel Canyon known as Ricks Cabin, not far from the Idaho border. Dr. Brown wrote: "The pattern was pretty much the same on each occasion, with them insisting she undress and then the two men taking turns with her, cursing her and growing increasingly physically abusive with her when any resistance was offered." Dahle, she remembered, was particularly rough with her, and she "became increasingly frightened of him. He often would twist her arm behind her back, pull her head around by her hair." He once raped her with his service revolver. Once, Thompson and Dahle held her head under water to threaten and terrify her. She said Thompson sometimes tried to restrain Dahle when he got overly rough.

Valarie told her father years later that when she was being raped at Ricks Cabin, she fantasized about him coming to rescue her because they had passed through the area together on horseback many times when she was a child. Most of the time, she later told Sue Saunders, when she was being raped and abused, she dissociated, imagining she was in the lap of her Heavenly Father, who would protect her and salve her pain.

She also said Dahle made sure he hit her where the marks could not be seen when she was fully clothed—on her torso or on her head—and he once broke her ribs. As the abuse went on, Valarie never told anyone, terrified the men would make good on their repeated threats, which now included hurting her brother. Even when she wasn't being attacked by them, they invaded all aspects of her life. Valarie told Dr. Brown that Dahle and Thompson told her where to meet them via notes, which they would hand her wherever they could find her—walking to the post office or the store or even on her way to church. Whenever she stepped out of her house, she risked being waylaid by one of the men, who would deliver her instructions about the time and location of her next defilement.

When Valarie began menstruating, the men became angry with her, she told Dr. Brown, and used it as a reason to further brutalize her. But they didn't stop raping her until she lied and told them she was pregnant. This took place at Newton Dam, most likely in November, 1970, when Valarie took Leo out for the five-mile ride to meet Dahle. She hopped off the horse and left him in the woods by the shore before proceeding to walk across the elevated mud embankment that crossed the old section of the reservoir. It was dark and cold. When she met Dahle, who had parked his truck on the berm, she told him she was pregnant, a ruse she had spent months working out. Dahle then surprised her by telling her that he loved her and wanted to marry her, even though he was then married to Ollie Lou and was the father of five children, including a newborn, Diana. Valarie laughed out loud. "Why would I marry you?" she said. "You're a monster."

Enraged, Dahle punched her in the abdomen, "causing her to gasp for breath," and attempted to strangle her. She fell to the ground. He then picked her up, stepped to the reservoir's edge, and threw her in. It was pitch black, the water was freezing, and there was no moon. Valarie told Dr. Brown that she "struggled to remain conscious and above the water." Meanwhile, Dahle pulled the spotlight off the top of his truck to scan the reservoir. Terrified that he would shoot and kill her, she stayed underwater, breaking the surface only for quick breaths. Dahle patrolled the shore for a long time, "apparently waiting to watch her death," according to Dr. Brown's notes. After she heard him finally drive away, she couldn't even see the shore. She whistled for Leo. He whinnied back, as was his habit, and from the sound she figured out which direction to swim. According to Zane, to whom she told the story after she returned from the Menninger Clinic, she suffered terribly in the cold water and was unable at first to drag herself out. Leo nuzzled her body at the shore, breathing on her, and she eventually was able to crawl out of the water and drag herself into the saddle and ride home.

The memory of this attempted murder "was quite alarming for the patient, and she suffered racing thoughts, agitation, and insomnia for some time following its recovery," wrote Dr. Brown. Reliving these experiences made them vividly real, and she had trouble separating this event, though it had taken place almost 20 earlier, from the present. She was left "feeling that this persecuting man might be nearby and that she might be in danger once again."

Her debilitating confusion seemed the unavoidable result of being the victim of savagery in a community that did not believe in evil. Any attempt to sort things out led to logical dead ends. In a Panglossian world in which only good exists, the innocent will suffer—and they will also be blamed for their fate. And Valarie was the only one who knew exactly how it would unfold.

"The patient has struggled throughout with how much to tell her husband and her parents of all these occurrences, since her parents live in the same town and know the men involved," Dr. Brown wrote. Valarie was "very concerned about upsetting them or causing great upset and legal problems in the community."

On the heels of the revelation of the near drowning, "to our mutual surprise," wrote Dr. Brown, Valarie began having fragments of memories from her younger childhood, when she was four or five years old. Gary Thompson was sexually molesting her. She said he would put her on his lap and fondle her through her underpants. This happened at his home, across the street from the Clark house, and in the summer while on family camping trips. During her treatment, Valarie produced a hand-drawn picture of a camping tent with a dark, forbidding opening for the entrance flap.

She also recovered an early memory of Thompson's father, Earl, putting her on his lap and shoving his hand down her underpants. "This is how you do it, son—you don't do it to your own children, but the neighbors' kids,"

Valarie remembered the elder Thompson saying. "That's what females are intended for, men's satisfaction."

Valarie remembered Gary Thompson telling her that if she told anyone what he was doing to her, her family would "throw her away."

Because he lived directly across the street, Thompson could keep track of the comings and goings in the Clark household—when Denzel was away working, when Shirleen was out of the house, when the kids were out playing in the neighborhood. As a close family member, he knew that Shirleen was distracted and depressed by the loss of a baby in 1957, when Valarie was three, stressed and preoccupied by Zane's birth when Valarie was five and a half, and then occupied in the following years with the demands of his treatments and operations.

He knew when to make his moves.

He not only could see when the children were unsupervised at home but also when he vacationed and camped with the Clarks. Looking back, Denzel acknowledged that Gary Thompson had had easy and regular access to Valarie and other children during their frequent family trips to Dry Canyon. He explained that the children usually stayed around the women, near the base camp, while the men hunted with the older children. But some of the men volunteered to stay back to help with the kids while the women cooked. Gary Thompson was one of these men. And, yes, Denzel admitted, he would have had opportunities to be alone in the tents with the children. But he never suspected anything untoward might be happening.

Valarie made some indirect attempts as a young child to alert her mother that something was wrong. When Thompson's increasingly aggressive probing of her body caused her to bleed, she placed her bloody underwear conspicuously in the laundry for her mother to find. She was repeatedly disappointed when her mother failed to notice them.

Valarie made another desperate cry for help to her mother in an undated letter in a childish, loopy script, *i*'s dotted with fat circles—the handwriting of a teenage girl. It seems to refer to a mother-daughter spat no one can recollect. Its dark tone might have alerted a more sensitive mother to a child teetering on the edge.

> *Moma,*
>
> *Tonight I did the worst thing I've ever done in my life, and there is no way I can ever forgive myself, and probably God won't either, so I don't expect you to. I don't know what's wrong with me, I've been slowly changing for a long time. I'm just lost, maybe it's too late to find a way back. You don't have to speak to me, or try to love me, because I see no way anyone could have any love left for me in their heart.*
>
> *When I spoke of hate, it wasn't of you, I'll regret those words the rest of my life. I love you, with all my heart. It's just that I've built up so much hatred of myself—that I take it out on others. I'm so sorry I pray to God every night to take me away before I hurt you anymore, but God won't listen to me anymore, so I guess it's up to me. I wish I could have been the sweet, loving daughter you deserve. But, it's too late to change from a hateful, self-centered hypocrite now. Please just forget me, and my ugly words as if we never existed, and then you'll find happiness, I pray for that with all my heart. I love you always[,]*
>
> *Valarie.*

When Shirleen died in August 2021, this was the only letter from Valarie in her possession.

Valarie told Dr. Brown that her mother's failure to notice that something was not right with her from ages 4 to 10, when she was being molested by Gary Thompson, and then from 13 to 16, when she was repeatedly raped by Bob Dahle and Thompson, led her to believe that her mother was rejecting her and that "she indeed must be just as bad as the men told her she was."

Valarie, he wrote, "has struggled to maintain a good feeling about her mother in the face of memories that her mother was in fact not very attentive or giving, quite content to let the patient spend time with other adult women in the family." Sadly for Valarie, the prognosis for victims of early childhood molestation is worse for girls whose mothers are more remote and less supportive and affectionate. A frequently cited experiment conducted at McGill University on the effects of environment on the neurological development of babies showed that the amount a mother rat licks her pups in the first 12 hours of their lives permanently affects the babies' stress-responsive brain chemicals and modifies the configuration of over one thousand genes. According to the study, "The rat pups that are intensely licked by their mothers are braver and produce lower levels of stress hormones under stress than rats whose mothers are less attentive. They also recover more quickly—an equanimity that lasts throughout their lives."[7] Other studies on child sexual abuse show that victims whose mothers are more nurturing are less likely to repress memories of their abuse.

Had Shirleen been sexually abused herself? Her inability to comfort her daughter when she first told the family of the abuse, to cry with her or embrace her, makes one wonder if she, too, had suffered traumatizing attacks that had left her numb or in denial. I asked Denzel if Shirleen had been abused, and he shook his head. However, he said Shirleen had told him that she was afraid of boys when she was growing up and that they spoke in a very vulgar fashion to girls. "They used terrible, lewd language," he said.

Clarkston didn't change much between Shirleen's childhood and Valarie's. The comments written in Valarie's high school yearbook by her male classmates, though clearly intended to be admiring, were casually crude. And sex education, such as it was, remained the same. Denzel acknowledged that because of religious beliefs and cultural practices, Clarkston kids were not taught about sex by their parents but were left to figure it out on their own—mostly by watching the cows and horses. But the breeding of horses is a violent and unpleasant matter. As historian Ross Peterson confessed in an interview, "I'd rather have been anywhere else when my father took his mare to somebody's stallion."[8]

Moreover, the longer the abuse goes on, the worse the prognosis. Dr. Brown said in an interview that "abuse carries a very long shadow and like other forms of PTSD, especially, the longer it goes untreated the harder it is to ever get well. That's why it's important to treat things right away."[9] Valarie didn't get proper treatment for 30 years.

Dr. Brown surmised that there must have been a few years between the early molestation by Gary and Earl Thompson and the rape in the hayloft, which had allowed Valarie to repress the memories of the earlier abuse. Then, he wrote in his clinical notes, "rape experience and the subsequent sexual coercion were later repressed after she left the home community" and went to college.

Cousin Dwight Pearce's memories of that time support Dr. Brown's theory. Dwight remembered Valarie's behavior changing when she first went to college—around 1972 or 1973. "She got quite emotional at times," he said—not the Valarie he remembered from childhood. For example, if his plans changed and he could no longer drive her somewhere "and then she was going to be alone or be required to drive some place alone," he said, she would often get upset, "unreasonable," or "over the top."

Perhaps she was afraid of finding herself alone in her car in the areas where Dahle patrolled the highways, uniformed and armed.

Valarie's friend Susan Saunders had a disturbing memory of Valarie behaving strangely one day during those early college years. Sue liked to drive fast, and once, Sue at the wheel, they got pulled over. Before the patrolman had a chance to approach the vehicle, Sue recalled, "Valarie got out of her seat next to me, opened the back door, and climbed in the back seat and laid on the floor," trying to conceal herself. It looked as if she was trying to squeeze herself under the rear seat.

Sue was busy gathering up her license and registration for the patrolman and figured Valarie was just joking around. "She had a very fun, teasy kind of personality. I thought she was just pretending to be afraid of the highway patrolman."

The officer spent only a few seconds at the driver's window speaking to Sue. He gave her a warning and sent her on her way. As she drove off, she called out to Valarie, "I only got a warning. No big deal."

But Valarie "seemed shaken after that." She remained cowering on the floor behind the seats, crying and whimpering.

Sue said she never asked Valarie why she was upset, never asked her to explain her fear. "I don't know if it was *that* patrolman," Sue said in 2021, after she had learned of the attacks Valarie had suffered. They had been within Bob Dahle's work area, west of Logan and about 20 miles south of Clarkston, but even if the man was not Dahle, it was clear that Valarie was terrified by the idea of a highway patrolman approaching her.

Valarie's sister-in-law, Allyson Miller, remembered another strange episode on the highway many years later, after Valarie had apparently successfully repressed the memory of her abuse. Valarie and Allyson loved going clothes shopping together. Valarie, then living in Hyrum, would drop Annie and Ryan off in Clarkston at her parents' house for the day, then drive south toward Mendon, where Allyson lived. Allyson would drive north, and they'd meet at a dirt parking area along the Valley View Highway. Allyson would park her car there and climb into Valarie's Jeep Wagoneer, and Valarie would drive down to Salt Lake City to shop. One day, the women were back at the parking spot along the highway, chatting a bit before separating and heading home. When Valarie tried to start her Jeep, she couldn't do it.

Allyson said they saw a Highway Patrol cruiser, and "we kind of waved, and he saw us there and he pulled over and he checked a few things in the car." Allyson noticed that the officer seemed "extremely uncomfortable . . . very curt, almost rude." She said he didn't look at Valarie or speak to her, although Valarie did speak to him, trying to explain what was wrong. In the end, Allyson explained, he didn't help them and "got out of there as quickly as possible."

Valarie and Allyson eventually figured out what the problem was, got the Jeep started, and each proceeded on her way, but not before talking about how rude and unhelpful the officer had been. "That's their job, you know," Allyson said. "That's what they're supposed to do." She remembered that Valarie turned to her and said, "Allyson, I've known that man my entire life. He's from Clarkston. He knows me, you know?"

It was Bob Dahle.

By that time, it appeared, her conscious memory of what he'd done to her had mercifully been sealed up in the furthest recesses of her mind.

CHAPTER SIX

"Her Memory Recall Is Very Painful"

IN THE SPRING OF 1989, Valarie wasn't the only one having trouble dealing with her memories. John wrote on April 2, 1989: "I am in shock over some of the things that are coming out in her hypnosis therapy (rape, torture, beatings, etc). I am feeling a lot of anger toward her abusers. I cried and felt deep sorrow (for her and I). I wonder if she will ever be able to deal with all of this. I try hard not to get discouraged."

On April 18, he reflected on a recent home visit by Valarie. "I overheard her talking to her parents and commented to her that she shouldn't wonder why her parents don't seem too concerned about her welfare, she doesn't share any feelings with them but pretends that everything is going well," he wrote. "In fact, this has been our problem for years. Valarie has never really shared her feelings. This has affected our ability to be intimate. I have decided [just] about anything could come out of this mess my family is in."

It's possible that Valarie struggled to express her feelings to her parents because Gary Thompson told her when she was very young that if she told them what he was doing to her, they would throw her away. Thompson later "got other men to join in," in the words of Dr. Brown—his father, Earl, his buddy Bob Dahle, and according to Zane, other neighborhood men. Then as a teenager, with a knife held to her vagina, Thompson and Dahle told Valarie not to object or complain, or they'd hurt her family as well.

Feelings could lead to danger for herself and her loved ones, so there could be no feelings.

Sometimes Valarie was more comfortable writing her thoughts to herself. She wrote this note five weeks after starting therapy with Dr. Brown, soon after a trip home:

> *I walked six miles yesterday. I finished the walk only to find myself back on the unit, still trying to walk, and think. I had made a promise to Dr. [Brown] about talking often to staff, especially when he was gone. Talking is not my strong point. It took me almost two hours to ask "D" if we could talk. Talking is exactly what I did. I'm grateful "D" pointed out the difference between talking, or explaining, and sharing feelings.*
>
> *Feelings, feelings—I don't know how to talk about feelings about myself. I'm not sure I know what they are. I can share other people's feelings. I can feel them with them. I can cry, and feel frustrated with them. I cannot do it for me. It has been a closed door for a long time. I cannot remember how to open the door. I don't even remember when it closed.*
>
> *I think I remember more things from the past. I have remembered enough. I don't want any more, it's too hard to process, and I'm too frightened already. How can there be more?*

> *FEELINGS*
>
> *1. frightened*
>
> *2. confused*
>
> *3. hurt*
>
> *4. ashamed*

> *I can start with those. It's crazy they almost seem like swear words. I wonder if I'm crazy. I hope there's a cure. I'm going to miss this activity. It will feel strange.*

Only five weeks into her psychotherapy, and she was already preparing herself for its termination. She was used to her life being interrupted by the needs and wants of others. She was accustomed to having her thoughts dismissed.

One day as a teenager, she agreed to go hunting with her father—the first time she had decided to take a shot at an animal—and she had brought down a buck with a single shot. But rather than praise his daughter and celebrate her moment of victory, Denzel froze, suddenly fearing she had mistakenly shot a doe. She assured him that the animal was indeed a buck, but he didn't believe her. They waited there in the woods with their horses for an hour, huddled in silence, Denzel fearful that his license would be taken away from him for killing a doe. They waited long enough to see another hunter approach the prey, dress it, and pack it out. It was a buck.

Valarie never again went hunting.

But she still tried to do what Dr. Brown had asked her to do—explore her thoughts and feelings outside of the therapy room. One day she sat down and penned a note. "It's hard to write," she began. "It's worse not to."

She continued:

> *Something interesting occurred to me yesterday. I was sitting in the family room and I happened to notice my shadow. It seemed to be someone else's, not mine. Funny, it didn't matter, I don't want it. I don't care to look in mirrors or any kind of reflection. They feel like ghosts from the past—3 of them—a tiny little 4 or 5 yr. old, an adolescent and me. We are one, and yet apart. I'm not sure how to put us together. We are, but I don't know who we are.*
>
> *I can't protect the little one, but someone should have, shouldn't they?*
>
> *She couldn't give up the easter bunny or the tooth fairy, unicorns or Santa Claus. "They were magical." She understood those, but she didn't understand the frightening things that were happening, and her little spirit was terribly offended.*

—

On April 29 and 30, 1989, while Valarie was home from Menninger for the weekend, she and John went to Utah together. "She is under tremendous stress and was really nervous to even leave the hospital," he noted in his journal. "Her memory recall is very painful, and she is having a hard time accepting what is coming out. I feel so bad about it all and am terribly angry. Mom is also very upset about it all."

Valarie had told her parents more details about the assaults and for once "expressed some of the pain she is in."

In May, Valarie went home to Omaha for another weekend visit. This was only weeks after she had first recalled the early molestation by Gary and Earl Thompson, and she was very much on edge, preoccupied with the newly available memories. John had little insight into the gravity and complexity of her trauma.

"Valarie had a rough week and was very compulsive while home here on the weekend." John wrote. "I am just sick about the whole situation. Valarie has real blind spots when it comes to handling the children."

But how could Valarie effectively discipline her young children when her mind was tormented by memories of being abused and coerced into silence when she herself had been a toddler? How could she know how she felt about most anything when, to help hold off the dread that seldom left her, she had likely also turned off most of her feelings and sensations?

"I used to be surprised by how often my patients asked me for advice about the most ordinary things, and then how rarely they followed it," wrote Bessel van der Kolk in *The Body Keeps the Score*. "Now I understand that their relationship with their own inner reality was impaired. How could they make decisions, or put any plan into action, if they couldn't define what they wanted or, to be more precise, what the sensations in their bodies, the basis of all emotions, were trying to tell them?"[1]

Valarie's youngest daughter, now Brooke Jacobs, recalled feeling frustration with her mother for buying all kinds of paraphernalia for improving her health and developing menus for more healthful eating but being unable to follow any of them, just like van der Kolk's patients.

"She had a very frail sense of herself," recalled Dr. Brown in an interview. "Poorly organized, poorly integrated."[2]

Six months after Valarie's admission to the Menninger Clinic, Dr. Brown wrote that the focus of the therapy for the next three months would be to help her feel "safe in expressing her feelings, and to be able to ask for help, realizing that the danger to her was in the past rather than the present." But Valarie found it very hard not to be overwhelmed by fears that the two men could still hurt her. "Not only would she be preoccupied with fearfulness and memories of her sexual abuse, but on many occasions actually hallucinated the image of the man (B) who was especially cruel toward her," wrote Dr. Brown. The hallucinations were like snapshots or flashbulb memories of her attackers at various moments and places.

One day Valarie sketched the face of a man—it was a face that a young child would draw—round face, a few squiggles for a patch of hair on top, two circles for eyes, a U for a nose, and a turned down line for a mouth. This face had one outstanding feature: two huge ears. Bob Dahle's most prominent features were his large ears.

"Traumatic events are stored differently than normal memories," Dr. Brown said in an interview, explaining that they trigger activity in a different part of the brain, the amygdala, which is responsible for processing strong emotions and warning of impending danger.[3]

For many people, he said, traumatic memories "don't subside. They're always there, ready to be activated."

However, Dr. Brown noted that for the most part Valarie was "increasingly able to work on the integration of her past experiences with difficulties in her later life, with a greater feeling of personal security." To his mind, having finally gained access to the source of her troubles, she was taking the right steps toward getting better. But it had taken a great many years of driving the unpleasant thoughts out of her mind before she began to try to deal with them, making the endeavor ever so much more difficult. Such delays are common. "The science says it takes decades for victims to come forward," said Marci A. Hamilton, who testifies as a legal expert in child abuse cases and is the chief executive of CHILD USA, a nonprofit focused on child abuse prevention. Indeed, in a study of thousands of young victims abused while in the Boy Scouts, half came forward before they were 50, and half after. It is "rare to have a false accusation in those circumstances," Hamilton added.[4]

As Valarie struggled to deal with her memories, John, too, was on an emotional roller coaster. In May 1989, furious about the violence inflicted on his wife, John reached out to his attorney, Brent Hoggan, who began to do some research about the legal issues in this case. Later, John was introduced to Max Wheeler, a trial lawyer specializing in complex civil litigation and white-collar crime who had served as a prosecutor in the US attorney's office in Utah. In June, on a trip to Salt Lake City for business, John met with Wheeler, who on his behalf, contacted Richard Lambert, an assistant US attorney in Salt Lake City who was open to reviewing the case.

On June 25 John noted in his journal: "Valarie has been really grouchy lately. I suppose it is some of the anger. Sometimes I get really sick of all the abuse she throws at me. I am really worried about how all this is affecting the children. Ryan really cried tonight when I left to take Valarie to the hospital. It makes me angry toward the men."

On July 6, 1989, Valarie gave up one of her therapy sessions so Dr. Brown could use the time to speak with John. "While this arrangement might be unusual and even contraindicated in some individual psychotherapy processes," Dr. Brown wrote in his notes, "the mystery and uneasiness surrounding hypnosis in many people's minds, as well as the explicit sexual focus of the treatment work, made such a meeting seem advisable."

"Indeed," he continued, "the husband did seem quite relieved to meet me in person, be able to ask questions, and vent his frustration as well as his gratitude. He hopes she will not only be free of the depression and more serious episodes of distress that have marked the recent years, but the long-standing sexual inhibition and lack of assertiveness that he discovered at the time of their marriage."

John made it clear he wanted to pursue legal action against Valarie's rapists, and Dr. Brown warned that he should not enlist Valarie's help for now. John wrote in his journal that he "agreed it would be some time before she could personally participate in such an effort."

Valarie was apparently well aware of John's personal expectations for her because Dr. Brown recorded in his notes soon after that Valarie "expresses considerable interest in having access to a wider range of emotions and being able to express them more freely, wants to overcome her sexual inhibitions so as to be more responsive to her husband, and very much wants to be an effective mother for her children."

She was less interested in using the therapy to explore her own hopes and dreams or to begin to build a self that was genuinely hers, Dr. Brown observed. She approached her treatment as a necessary step to be able to meet the needs and desires of her husband and family, reflecting her upbringing and socialization in the LDS faith where a woman's role was to be a facilitator and helper for others.

On July 9, John wrote in his journal: "I long for a companionship with Valarie. It has been seven months. I know it is having a negative effect on the children. I am not happy with my job. It seems [there are] mists of darkness around me."

By this point, John had learned he had few options for holding Valarie's rapists accountable. He knew from his consultations with the lawyers that the statute of limitations for sexual assault on a child in Utah at that time was four years after the commission of the crime, making a criminal prosecution of Dahle and Thompson impossible.

—

On July 24, Dr. Brown upped his psychotherapy sessions with Valarie from two to three times a week. Mostly they just talked, and hypnosis was used only sparingly to, according to Dr. Brown, "flesh out memories that appeared in fragmentary form to her, none remarkably different than what was reported in the previous progress report."

Valarie's development—neurological, emotional, psychological— had been deformed and disrupted by the sadistic abuse visited upon her. Recovery required her not only to remember what had been done to her but also to understand how the abuse had affected her body and soul. The hope was she could develop new and more useful life habits.

Her "ego vulnerability," in the words of Dr. Brown, led him to recommend she remain in the hospital until she could better separate past from present. He told her this in August—seven months after her arrival at the clinic, after only five months of active therapy. She was still at the beginning of treatment, but her husband was impatient. She knew that further hospitalization would disappoint him and the children. Once again, she was torn between meeting the needs of others and doing what was right for herself. There seemed to be no solution, so her body reacted—new MS symptoms emerged. "The distress at remaining separated from her children, heightened by their direct and poignant pleading for her to return home, may have been responsible for an exacerbation of MS symptoms," wrote Dr. Brown.

At first, she tried to ignore the symptoms, but when they affected both her arms and legs, she finally acknowledged her fear of becoming incapacitated and was persuaded to leave the Menninger Clinic on September 9, 1989, to seek treatment at the Rocky Mountain MS Center in Denver. John wrote in his journal: "It is really sad to see someone like her in such a sad situation. Emotionally she is really a mess and is struggling with staying at the hospital in Topeka. She is so angry and directs it towards me quite often."

The steroid therapy for her MS symptoms lasted about a week. But more bad luck followed her back to Menninger when she found herself the unwitting subject of an internal hospital conflict not of her own making but that wound up having a significant effect on her well-being. According to Dr. Brown, she was told that a "review conference" of her treatment team indicated "dissension." Some members of the team felt others were indulging Valarie's tendency not to be "fully involved in the treatment life of the unit." She was criticized for "talking only with her psychotherapist, and 'going through the motions' of other aspects of her treatment without being helped as much as would be ideal." Dr. Brown later said that Valarie was not the only patient subjected to this kind of criticism, and this issue was one that came up frequently in treatment discussions. (Not every patient regularly attended art therapy or the various other activities offered by the clinic.)

But the criticism came at a difficult time for Valarie, after the exacerbation of her MS symptoms and the curtailment of her "long walks in the late afternoons, a coping strategy which had been very important for her," according to Dr. Brown.

Valarie's family was clearly suffering from her absence, and her weekend visits home helped somewhat to ameliorate their distress. So, when the staff doctors decided to punish her for not fully participating in clinic life by taking away these home visits, she found herself once again in an impossible position. Surprisingly, this time, it made her angry, which was a good sign, signaling a newfound confidence and self-assertiveness. "For a time, she thought seriously of leaving," wrote Dr. Brown, "feeling she was somehow recapitulating her past, allowing herself to be controlled by powerful others rather than standing up for herself." And she had a point, he acknowledged: she had correctly interpreted the situation in which she found herself. But after a few conversations, he was able to convince her that staying in the program was arguably her better option.

But the damage had been done. Valarie felt helpless and used. Once again, she had been trod upon by "powerful others" and made to feel she had no options but to submit to their demands. In a weak moment, she swallowed a handful of pills and wound up in a Topeka emergency room.

This suicide attempt, if that is what it was, was not mentioned in Dr. Brown's notes—possibly because he didn't consider it a serious effort, possibly because he didn't agree with the punishment meted out to Valarie by staff doctors. But John took it very seriously. After learning that Valarie had been transferred to the hospital, he called the Menninger Clinic, but he didn't speak with her doctor—he spoke with unnamed staff members who, without explaining the context, told him Valarie had most likely made a suicide attempt. He was beyond himself that after almost a year in treatment, she was still thinking about killing herself.

A door slammed shut inside him. On October 8, he wrote: "I am really discouraged today about the whole situation with Valarie. I am feeling many different feelings including anger, loneliness, and self-pity. . . . I really need a companion who I can rely on and carry some of the pressures of life."

On October 29, he wrote: "I seem to be having a hard time the past few months about my attitude about most things. . . . My reaction is to run and find relief somewhere. I think subconsciously I have been trying to escape from the problems Valarie and I face in our relationship."

John was done with her.

The result of the clinic brouhaha was a negotiation between Dr. Brown and John over Valarie's discharge date. It was decided she would go home in mid-December 1989. This seemed to have less to do with her readiness than with the needs of her family and the end of John's patience. In fact, it would turn out she hadn't yet recalled all the repressed memories of her abuse.

On December 1, two weeks before her departure, John wrote: "She is nervous about coming home and so am I. The past year has been very hard on all of us. I wonder about how she will handle the challenges of the future." As far as he was feeling, he observed, "Faith is easy to say you have, but when the battle continues day after day, it is really easy to get down."

John wanted a normal marriage and a normal life. Valarie knew he had lost confidence in her. it. She wrote one last note while at Menninger.

I know the memories I have been uncovering and the feelings . . . have all been important. It all felt good, even in a melancholy way, the only relief I have felt in years. It has, however, turned into a game I can no longer play. The supportive, caring role is gone, and has turned into a no-win situation with no compromises. I need space and air and room to breathe. I need people to trust, people to trust me. There are a lot of I's floating around I know—but I need to like myself. A whole lot of people doubt what I'm saying, they even wonder if the MS symptoms are real or psychosomatic. I spend hours trying to relax and talk to myself, experiencing a pain that is right up there with labor. It happens through a good share of the day and always most of the night. And I know no one will help.

Dr. Brown said that the treatment group believed that Valarie was referring to her husband when she wrote of the "no-win situation with no compromises."

—

Although John had piloted his own Beechcraft Bonanza out to Topeka with Ryan at the beginning of December to bring Valarie home for the weekend, when it came time to bring her home for good on December 15, 1989, he asked Denzel and Shirleen to go pick her up. He said he wanted her parents to understand what she had gone through and appreciate where she had been. Debbie recalled: "One day, John called Dad and said, 'I need you to go pick up Valarie from Menninger's.' He said, 'You need to be there in two days.' So, Mom and Dad hurried and packed their bags and took off."

It was a 1,000-mile drive. They stopped at a motel in Nebraska the first night, and Denzel recalled that John called them there and told them they needed to be at the hospital early the next morning to get Valarie. They did as they were told and got out of bed and drove straight through.

"I thought it was a little strange that John didn't go get her," said Denzel, but "we wanted to help."

Denzel remembered that when they arrived, Valarie was packed and ready to go, although because of her latest MS exacerbation, she needed help walking. Her parents stood on either side of her to support her as she shuffled from her hospital room to their car. They headed back to Omaha, stopping overnight in a motel. Denzel remembered that although she had been in good spirits when they arrived at Menninger and was very excited about being reunited with the children, the closer they got to Omaha, the more subdued she became. Once in Omaha, Shirleen stayed with Valarie for a week to help her adjust. Denzel drove back to Utah to resume his schedule on the railroad.

Two days after Valarie's arrival at home, John wrote: "I don't remember when I have felt so much pressure coming from so many directions. My life is passing too quickly, and I can't stop it."

Valarie was still experiencing an uptick of anxiety at the end of every day, though now she finally understood why: these were the hours when Thompson and Dahle would arrange to meet with her for sex. Before her departure from Menninger, Dr. Brown taught her how to use self-hypnosis as evening approached to help calm herself by retrieving early positive memories. This helped her for a time. To ease the transition home, Dr. Brown arranged to meet with her on an outpatient basis. Every Wednesday, Valarie would travel from Omaha to Topeka for a late afternoon session, stay overnight in a local motel, and have another hour-long treatment on Thursday before returning home. Sometimes she drove the three hours from Omaha, other times she was flown in on a company airplane. This was an unusual protocol for Dr. Brown, but he clearly felt she was not ready for termination.

During one of those visits, she told Dr. Brown she felt the pressure of another memory trying to emerge. "The patient acknowledged that there was one extremely upsetting event that had happened earlier that she thought using hypnosis to recover more fully and master might be necessary before her late afternoon anxieties could subside," he wrote.

Dr. Brown noted that she "dreaded this effort and was unable to carry through with it on the first attempt." On the second try, however, "slowly and with considerable support and reassurance," Valarie was able to "relive a horrifying experience" of having the family dog, Shadow, a German shepherd and spaniel mix, shot before her eyes as punishment for her having refused to meet with the two men for sex. "Seeing this animal shot, with the highway patrolman using his service revolver and being dressed in his official uniform, further solidified her conviction that these were dangerous men who could not be resisted, but even more importantly, made her feel guilty and responsible, that she had indeed been bad for refusing."

Helen Andelin's teachings had clearly failed her.

Moreover, though Valarie had been forced to leave the hospital, yet she was still uncovering new and highly traumatic memories that required time for processing and understanding.

As her friend Sue Saunders often said, Valarie could never catch a break.

Dr. Brown felt Valarie had made progress at Menninger, but she seemed to fall back into old patterns after she got home. He wrote:

> As the patient made this transition from inpatient care to home, she was quite apprehensive that the family would expect too much of her and that she wouldn't be able to cope with their demands. Her other worry was almost the opposite, that the family would be getting along just fine without her, and she would actually have no place there. At times she would feel that her husband and mother-in-law (who had been living in the home to care for the children) really did not need her and only grudgingly allowed her to resume some of her former responsibilities. At other times, she felt she couldn't possibly keep up with the fast-paced household and assumed that everyone was terribly disappointed with her.

Dr. Brown noted that it "continues to be a struggle for the patient to acknowledge frankly how she is feeling, both physically and emotionally." Moreover, she was still laboring to "overcome the profound sense of inferiority that was linked to guilt and shame surrounding the abuse."

He also noted that Valarie wasn't acknowledging how debilitating her MS symptoms were, particularly the fatigue: "Her experience of psychological fragility was being complicated by a literal sense of physical exhaustion such that she would drag herself from bed in the morning in order to help the children with breakfast and their morning routine, push herself through a day of cleaning and shopping and other errands, greeting the children and occupying herself with them at the end of the day, and trying to be available to her husband in the evenings, always feeling as if she could barely survive from one day to the next."

Dr. Brown tried to help her budget her time and offered her a few books on how MS patients had learned to adapt to the limitations imposed by the illness.

In his notes, he explained why it was so difficult for Valarie to slow down:

> *The patient had spent most of her life concealing her inner turmoil and physical discomforts, fearing that if others knew what she suffered when being sexually abused for so many years, she would be rejected and despised by her family. Further, in order to forestall the rejection and hatred she so badly feared, the patient became a model student and highly successful athlete, finding some reassurance in the praise and recognition she received in these areas. Thus, admitting her physical vulnerabilities, emotional pains, and acknowledging that she is physically incapacitated run directly counter to major defensive and even characterological patterns that are well-formed in her.*

He wrote that he would continue to treat Valarie until she found a suitable therapist closer to home. Their goals would be to continue to help her

expand her ability "to experience and express her emotions, to deal construc-
tively with her marital difficulties, and to overcome the inhibitions and sense
of inferiority linked to guilt and shame surrounding her early childhood sexual abuse." Dr. Brown noted that for a time she "was able to use writing as a
way of maintaining the momentum of expressing her deepest and most secret
thoughts, but now at home she finds it difficult to continue."

Any mother of young children knows how difficult it can be in the tumult
of family life to find time to jot down a few words, let alone the peace of
mind to sort through issues as profoundly affecting as the ones Valarie had.

Valarie continued with her outpatient therapy with Dr. Brown for the
last two weeks of December 1989, then through January and February
1990, but she knew the work was coming to an end. She had no power to
stop it, just as she had had no power as a child to get her mother to see there
was something wrong, just as she had had no way to stop cousin Dwight
from selling Leo, just as she had had no control over the Menninger staff
meeting during which she was misunderstood, misjudged, and punished.
As Dr. Brown recalled in his clinical notes, she said, in something of a fare-
well, that she was "very grateful for the therapist's commitment to her and
willingness to know of all of her pains, both past and present, but fears she
has been sick long enough and that he will soon grow impatient if she does
not behave in a more cheerful and healthy fashion."

CHAPTER SEVEN

"Blood on My Boots"

AT JOHN'S URGING, in the middle of April 1990—only two months after she had recalled the shooting of her dog—Valarie met with Richard Lambert, then an assistant United States Attorney for the District of Utah in Salt Lake City. Furious and heartbroken over the abuse Gary Thompson and Bob Dahle had inflicted on Valarie, John sought accountability, and he had found that Lambert was willing to launch an investigation. Valarie "handled herself really well," John noted in his journal, and Lambert arranged for two FBI agents to look into her complaint. This was, of course, decades before #MeToo and at a time when a woman's or girl's accusation of rape or sexual harassment was not taken seriously unless there was corroboration, which was unlikely to exist considering the private nature of the crime.

Valarie had hesitatingly begun to speak to a few relatives and close friends about the assaults she had suffered as a girl. She shared the story with her sister, with her college friend Sue Saunders, and with her cousin Dwight, whom she invited out for a meal in Brigham City at an old-time restaurant called the Idle Isle.

"It was kind of an old, neat restaurant with a lot of room, and quiet," recalled Dwight. "We had a nice dinner and at the end, she said, 'I have to tell you what happened to me, and it's basically destroyed my life.'" He said that was "the first time she told me the stories of what had happened to her."

"She was a little bit embarrassed to tell me the details, but she told me basically what happened," he added.

"Can you believe that Gary Thompson was involved in this?" he recalled her asking. He replied, "Valarie, I don't want to believe that. He's family. How could he possibly do such a thing?" Thompson was not only Valarie's relative but also Dwight's. Thompson was a first cousin to both Denzel and Dwight's mother.

Dwight recalled Valarie saying, "I'm as sorry as you are. But he was involved. And Lloyd Clark."

Dwight was incensed. Valarie and Dwight had enjoyed a special connection their whole lives. But he'd also grown up across the street from Lloyd Clark and his brother Ralph, and he couldn't believe Clark could have been involved, though he remembered him as "homely, quiet, and backward. Not a polished person by any means . . . kind of strange." According to Dwight, Clark was "never good at anything he did," and Dwight's wife, Bonnie, called Clark "weird" and always asked Dwight why he was friendly with him. Dwight answered that they had grown up together. And, of course, he assumed they had similar moral and ethical beliefs.

After thinking about it during an interview for this book, he said, "You don't really know people, do you?"

After the dinner with Valarie at Idle Isle, Dwight spoke to John and recalled him saying, "If there's anything that can be done, I want it done. I am angry. These guys are gonna pay for this." John asked Dwight to go with him to meet the FBI agents then looking into the case, and Dwight readily agreed.

"There was two of them with John and I, in Logan," recalled Dwight. "It must have been [at] a police station over there."

When the agents learned that Dwight was a childhood friend of Lloyd Clark, they asked him if he would question Clark and prevail upon him to tell what he knew. Dwight recalled that he said, "Yeah, I'll go ask him if he was involved in this, you bet I'm going to ask him. I'm happy to ask him because he always really looked up to me. There's no doubt about it."

Dwight went to Clark's house and said, "Lloyd, I want you to level with me right now. This is what happened to Valarie. You were involved, right?"

He said Clark said, "No, no, no, I wasn't. I deny that. I would never do that."

Dwight recalled replying, "Well it happened. We know that for sure. And we know where it happened a couple of times. What do you know about it?"

Dwight said Clark finally broke down and said the accusations were true. The rape had taken place. He didn't acknowledge that he'd been present but offered this strange explanation: He knew it was true because Burke Godfrey, one of Clarkston's troublemaking drinkers, had told him so.

Dwight thought this rang false. "Why would Burke get involved with this?" he asked Clark.

Clark said that Burke knew about it because Dahle and Thompson told him what they'd done while they were drinking with Burke behind his house one day.

Dwight thought this highly doubtful. Why would Burke tell Clark something like this when Burke was friends with Denzel? And further, it was his strong feeling that Burke Godfrey would never share sensitive information of any kind with Lloyd Clark, who was two decades younger and enjoyed considerably lower social status in town.

Dwight and John reported what had transpired in the meeting to the FBI agents, who then called Lloyd Clark in for questioning. Clark remembered going to meet with the agents in Logan, where he corrected his previous version of the story. The rape had happened, he said, because Burke Godfrey told him so.

The agents then called Burke in for questioning. He was, John wrote, "scared to death" and "denied having any knowledge of anything."

And that seemed to be the end of the FBI investigation. The agents didn't speak with other women in town who may have suffered sexual assaults at the hands of Dahle or Thompson. They never interviewed Debbie or Zane. They didn't speak with Gary Thompson. They didn't ask Valarie to describe any unusual characteristics of the men's bodies that may have identified them and supported her story. They made no effort to search the site where Shadow was shot for bones or bullets or to check Dahle's truck or sheds for evidence. The agents eventually decided it was a "he said, she said" situation, which appeared to stop them in their tracks. As of this writing, the FBI has not produced any records of its involvement in this matter despite several FOIA requests.

Clarkston's unique social dynamic asserted itself during this investigation. Ollie Lou Dahle stood up in church one day to complain about the people she claimed were telling lies about her husband. She also stopped speaking to Shirleen, with whom she sang in the church choir. Shirleen felt she and her entire family had been publicly rebuked.

Debbie played music at church—piano and organ—and her music director was Jill Dahle, Bob Dahle's daughter. "We've known each other our whole lives," Debbie said. "And we still had to get along because we're together all the time, doing different things in the ward."

"I like her so much," Debbie said of Jill. "So what I have to do is just let it be in the past."

The Clarks didn't like the feeling of discord in the town, so they waited patiently until the Dahles "forgave us for saying something that [they felt] was untrue about their dad," as Debbie put it. And life got back to that town's version of normal.

Except that one Sunday at church, Shirleen looked up into the balcony and met Bob Dahle's eyes. He was looking straight at her, and she never forgot what she saw. It was "the awfullest face," she recalled. It was "just like Satan."

But they could think of no way to fight him and right the wrong. Debbie struggled again when Gary Thompson was assigned by the church ward to mentor her family—including her young children—as a home teacher. At the time, home teachers were men assigned to visit families once a month to help them with their temporal and spiritual needs. Debbie didn't feel she could forbid Gary Thompson from entering her home, and she didn't she feel she had the right to request a different home teacher, and yet she was very uncomfortable allowing Thompson access to her children because of what she knew he had done to Valarie. So she decided to "leave it up to God."

Jann Pugmire, who grew up in Clarkston, said Thompson was a home teacher for her family as well: "As I got older, he would say to me, 'I remember when we used to come home teach to your house, and you'd sit on my lap with your dirty diaper and snotty nose.'"

Pugmire, who lived in Clarkston for 28 years, moved away in 2009. "I hate Clarkston," she said. "They're just a bunch of hypocrites." She had to endure a father who drank and beat her and humiliated her mother while everyone pretended not to see. And when she went to her bishop for counseling after she had been raped by her cousin, he told her it was her own fault. "I told him what had happened to me. And, of course, I was crying and I was upset. And he said, 'You know, I pretty much assumed something like this would happen to you because of how you are.'"

She said bad behavior was rampant among the men of Clarkston. She had seen, experienced, and heard about a lot of it—from window peepers to sexual harassers to men who watched pornography with their children to "teach them about life." But most of her neighbors chose not to see what was right in front of them. "I feel like everybody's fake. Everybody's just putting on a show," she said.

Richard Burbidge, a prominent Salt Lake City trial lawyer and acquaintance of John, came to a similar conclusion after reviewing Valarie's case. "There were also those, beyond Valarie's shameless assailants, who should have protected her, who should have drawn out her story and given her comfort and assurance that she had committed no sin," he wrote to this author. "Her family, her church, her community, ignored her suffering and undoubtedly that of many other innocent victims. It was apparently more important to keep up the illusion that something so terrible *did not* occur because it *should not* have occurred."

Valarie's abiding motivation throughout her childhood was to protect herself and her family from violence, sadness, or scandal by remaining silent about her injuries. And although she had experienced some relief telling her story to her psychotherapist, now that it had been made public her worst childhood fears were coming true. First, she wasn't sure that her mother believed her. Second, she watched her family become a target of criticism in the town and her story of pain and shame disavowed.

Rumors abounded. One was this: "Valarie wanted to get attention from her husband, so she made up the story of rape." Bob Dahle and Gary Thompson themselves told everyone they could that Valarie was "crazy" and couldn't be believed.

The old threats of her abusers could not help but ring in her ears—*No one will believe you.*

Despite all this opposition, Denzel wanted to pursue justice for his daughter. He contacted a friend who was a member of the Quorum of the Twelve Apostles of the LDS church, which along with the prophet, were the highest-ranking authorities in all of Mormondom. Denzel shared with him some of Dr. Brown's documentation from the Menninger Clinic. After reading the documents, the apostle was angry and told Denzel that he wanted to have both Dahle and Thompson tried in a church court. Disciplinary courts in the LDS church can be convened for the following offenses, according to an official statement from 1990: "abortion, transsexual operation, attempted murder, rape, forcible sexual abuse, intentionally inflicting serious injuries on others, adultery, fornication, homosexual relations, child abuse (sexual or physical), spouse abuse, deliberate abandonment of family responsibilities, robbery, burglary, theft, sale of illegal drugs, fraud, perjury, or false swearing."[1]

Thus, convening a church court seemed well within Denzel's rights.

After their meeting, Denzel met with his stake president, the local leader who presided over several wards in the small towns near Clarkston. He concurred with the apostle and wanted to move forward with a church court. But then, Denzel said, opposition came from an unexpected place. He said John told him that "he was worried that it was going to get out of hand." John didn't say "you can't do it," recalled Denzel. But John did tell him that if the two men were excommunicated from the church as a consequence of the court, "I think they may sue me."

There was an additional matter the apostle had raised. He told Denzel that if he wanted to continue serving as bishop of the ward, he would have to forgive and love both Dahle and Thompson, and that if he could not do so, he should ask to be released from his calling. This seemed an impossible conundrum. Denzel loved his church and his position serving his people, and he still had projects to complete. But he also wanted to seek justice for his wounded daughter. After reading the scriptures and praying, he eventually came to the point where he forgave the men. He said it took his wife quite a bit longer to do so.

About a year after he first raised the issue with the apostle, he came to the end of his five-year term as bishop of the Clarkston ward. He recalled that his successor, Johnny Clark, a second cousin, after thinking through the dynamics of a church trial—which required the participation not only of the stake president but also 12 high councilmen, six of whom would advocate for the accused, six for the accuser—decided it would lead to mayhem in such a small town where nearly everyone was related. They well understood the dynamic; their grandfathers were brothers.

"You call it off. Don't do it," Denzel remembered Johnny imploring him, "I don't want you to do it. . . . It'll ruin my ward. Everybody will hate everybody."

It was a very anxious time for Denzel, and as per usual, he didn't want to hurt anyone's feelings. But he also wanted to help and protect his daughter, even if it was after the fact. In the end, he succumbed to the pressures swirling around him—John's anxiety about revenge from Dahle, Johnny Clark's determination not to have his ward torn apart, his wife's discomfort with the social approbation, as well as Valarie's poor health—and dropped his request for a church trial. No disciplinary court was ever convened.

Bob Dahle could hardly believe how well things had turned out for him. He approached Denzel in church one Sunday, years later, and took him aside. "I can't understand how you treat me," Denzel recalled him saying. "If I felt that you had done what you think I have done, I wouldn't be treating you that well." Denzel responded that he tried to love everybody.

Denzel and Shirleen decided the only way they could continue to live in town (they ruled out moving) was to reaffirm their friendship with the Dahles. They would treat them with civility and love and would leave it to God to resolve the issue in the hereafter. Eventually, Denzel was once again able to see Clarkston through rose-colored glasses. In 2006, he told the local paper, the *Herald Journal*, that "if there is a tragedy in town, we really come together."

The Dahles just waited out the heat, and in his later years, Dahle made every effort to rehabilitate himself in the eyes of the church—and his wife. He and Ollie Lou were called to serve an adult mission in Charleston, West Virginia, and they also worked together as officiators in the Logan Temple, a sacred position meant only for the worthy. In annual interviews, Bob Dahle had to swear to the bishop that his conscience was clear on all matters to be assigned such tasks. And so he swore, and so it was.

In 2021 in an interview for this book, Denzel said that, as caught up as he had been in the middle of his various responsibilities and the competing interests in town, he had lost sight of the real victim. He realized, seemingly with considerable surprise, that the person who had suffered the most through the town conflicts of 1990 was Valarie.

Shirleen urged her daughter to try to forgive the men who had raped her and to leave it to God to sort out the bigger issues. After Valarie's death in 2017, her daughter Brooke found several folders of Valarie's papers in a storage unit among which were photocopied pages on forgiveness culled from the LDS church's Doctrine and Covenants, a compilation of modern revelations regarded by Mormons as the word of God. On the top of the page were three curt words: "<u>Must</u> forgive <u>all</u>." They were not written in Valarie's hand.

—

There was one more entity from whom John could seek justice for Valarie: the state of Utah. On May 18, 1990, he and his lawyer Max Wheeler met with Mitch Ingersoll, the director of internal affairs at the Utah Department of Public Safety. They laid out their complaint against Bob Dahle, who was then a lieutenant in the Utah Highway Patrol. After they were done, Valarie came in and "very completely went through the story of terror and abuse inflicted by these two men," according to John, who recorded in his journal that "she did a very convincing job and I was proud of her. It was very difficult for her to discuss the details and I was surprised she got through it as well as she did." John felt that Ingersoll believed her and "was quite incensed by what we told him." Ingersoll told them it was the most serious allegation ever made against a major officer of the Utah Highway Patrol, and he assured them it would be a "high-priority" case, which would likely require a three- or four-week investigation.

John warned Ingersoll about deep, long-standing ties between Dahle and the man who would oversee the investigation: DPS Commissioner Doug Bodrero. Dahle and Bodrero had begun their careers at around the same time in the 1960s—Dahle with the Highway Patrol and Bodrero with the Cache County Sheriff's Office. For years, they worked out of the same small building in Logan. They were friends and colleagues, and for a time, Bodrero helped dispatch Dahle on calls. They also occasionally assisted each other in the field. By 1990, they both worked for DPS—Bodrero as commissioner and Dahle in the Highway Patrol. John warned Ingersoll that he feared Bodrero would act to protect his friend and that the investigation might turn into a "whitewash."

After the meeting, John wrote in his journal that "it was quite clear from [the] conversation with Ingersoll that the state would rather quietly handle this matter before it gets to a public trial which would implicate the state and be a very negative public relations debacle with the news media."

John didn't know that a series of scandals had recently rocked the Highway Patrol, making the department even more wary of bad press. Two years earlier, in February 1987, a 31-year-old trooper named Ernest B. Wilcock picked up a 20-year-old woman on a downtown street after she'd been to a party and told her he'd drive her home. Instead, he took her to a construction site and threatened to charge her with public intoxication unless she had sex with him. After a struggle, she managed to jump in his patrol car, lock the doors, and drive away. Wilcock then fired his service firearm 13 times at his intended victim as she drove away in his vehicle. None of his shots hit the target. Wilcock was arrested and charged with aggravated assault and one count of attempted rape. Three additional women subsequently came forward, accusing Wilcock of a total of two counts of rape, two counts of aggravated kidnapping, and one count of aggravated assault. He was allowed to plead guilty to one count of attempted forcible sexual abuse, for which he received a sentence of five years. Four additional victims sued Wilcock in federal district court; three of the four settled, and the state of Utah is believed to have paid each victim $27,000.[2]

That was not all. In the fall of 1989, a trooper was terminated for "off-duty sexual indiscretions" with a teenage girl from Box Elder County, which borders Cache Valley to the west. Another trooper resigned in 1990 and pleaded guilty to charges of "lewdness" after a "two-year off-duty romance" with a 15-year-old. Yet another trooper was suspended for making a statement in front of a convention of corrections officials that "80 percent of the cops I've met are lazy and complacent."[3]

John's fear that the state investigation would turn into a "whitewash" was well-founded. On June 3, 16 days after meeting with John and

Valarie, Ingersoll told John that he had traveled to Kansas to interview Valarie's therapist. Four days later, without revealing anything about his Kansas meeting, Ingersoll notified John that Dahle denied all the allegations against him and had passed a lie detector test with "high marks." John and Valarie were crushed.

Ingersoll then told them that for the investigation to continue, Valarie would have to take a polygraph, too. After consulting with Stan Abrams, a psychologist and polygraph expert, Valarie was advised not to take a polygraph. He explained in a letter that as a sufferer of extreme trauma, she was unlikely to produce a meaningful result. "Because of the patient's rather strong moralistic background," he wrote, the rapes and abuse she suffered were so unacceptable to her that they were repressed. "When repression occurs," he continued, "it is not only the memory that is forced into the unconscious, but all of the feelings associated with these memories at the time they occurred." These "encapsulated" memories include "all the fears and anguish she felt as a child," including "natural feelings of rage, which she still completely denies" that he believes are still felt "inside of her, existing without her awareness." He warned that although she is able to discuss these events in what "appears to be a calm manner," it is inevitable that "anger, fear, and guilt" would be stimulated by any recall of the events, creating "an extremely high likelihood of invalid findings."

The polygraph measures physiological arousal in response to questions and is compared to a control measure. Given Valarie's state of continuing psychological distress, Abrams felt, as a second point, that "there is no control question that could be utilized" effectively to judge her responses, leading to an "extremely high likelihood of invalid findings."[4]

John informed Ingersoll that Valarie would not take a polygraph. Ingersoll then closed the investigation.

Irrespective of the polygraph distraction, Ingersoll's investigation was perfunctory, certainly not the ambitious fact-finding effort he had promised the Millers. Ingersoll did not interview Valarie's father or mother, and he did not speak with her brother or sister, both of whom had information relevant to the case. He did not visit any of the sites in Clarkston or Steel Canyon.

On July 9, 1990, an official DPS document was sent to Bob Dahle stating that the department's investigation of him for sexual assault on a child had been closed.

Valarie's worst nightmare had come true. She had been pressured to come forward with the soul-crushing truth, and she'd been rewarded for her efforts exactly as Dahle and Thompson had predicted: No one believed her.

The FBI, the State of Utah, and the local LDS church leaders had all ignored her plea and protected her attackers.

This is the fate of most sexually abused children. As Dr. Roland Summit wrote in his classic study, "Initiation, intimidation, stigmatization, isolation, helplessness and self-blame depend on a terrifying reality of child sexual abuse. Any attempts by the child to divulge the secret will be countered by an adult conspiracy of silence and disbelief. 'Don't worry about things like that; that could never happen in our family.' 'How could you ever think of such a terrible thing?' 'Don't let me ever hear you say anything like that again!' The average child never asks and never tells."[5]

There was nothing average about Valarie, except her fate. She did everything she could to respond to her impossible situation in a way that would protect her parents and siblings from shame and physical violence while remaining religiously and socially acceptable to her community. She excelled as a youth despite the vicious attacks, directing her energy and anxiety into activities whose successes helped ameliorate her faltering self-esteem. And she was left by herself to figure out how to stop the attacks without putting her loved ones at risk. At this, she eventually succeeded, by falsely claiming she was pregnant. For her efforts, she was rewarded by Dahle's attempt to drown her in Newton Reservoir.

But in the end, Valarie was much like millions of other children abused by adults: She was unable to undo the damage of the injuries she'd suffered or erase the shame they had branded on her soul.

Valarie did, however, contemplate telling her story for the benefit of others. She told Debbie that as she walked home from one of her forced sexual encounters in Clarkston, she noticed drops of fresh blood on her boots. It was flowing from a cut on her head that had been opened by a blow from Dahle, for whom sex and violence were inexorably entwined. Valarie told Debbie, "I want to write a book about what happened to me to help other girls and women who have been abused. I want to call it *Blood on My Boots*."

Debbie remembered Valarie had a pair of red boots when she was a little girl. "We, as a family," Debbie wrote in a journal entry, "cannot imagine how all this went on without our knowing it and we all feel guilty we didn't recognize some sign so we could have stopped this hell for her and put these men where they belong."

In November 1990, an overwhelmed John told Valarie he wanted a divorce. She "refused to hear the message and said she would not leave the marriage," he wrote in his journal. "She is not taking me seriously and I am sick about it."

Divorce meant the destruction of her worldview and all the expectations she had held since she was a child. It would lead to a diminution of her status in society and bring shame upon herself and her family. And she was once again being punished for events that were not her fault. She had done everything John had asked her to do—go to the Menninger Clinic when it terrified her, leave on his time frame before she was ready, tell her parents what "Gary and Bobby" had done to her, and suffer from their bizarrely unemotional reaction, making her fear they didn't believe her. Then she'd gathered together every last bit of strength and composure to speak of her shame to the Utah state authorities at John's insistence, only to learn that

Dahle had reportedly passed a polygraph test. She was then left to suffer taunts from Dahle and Thompson in town that she was "crazy."

And then John had decided to "throw her away."

Richard Burbidge, the Salt Lake City lawyer, observed that "Valarie was raised to live within certain strictures of a 'righteous life,' which included imperative chastity (especially for girls) prior to marriage. Her commitment to that concept of 'purity' entitled her to look forward to a marriage, under the Mormon belief system, 'for time and all eternity' in the Mormon cosmology. She knew it was imperative she present consistent with all expectations of virginity; and she knew after her brutal assaults she could not."

Burbidge felt that:

> *Valarie had the absolute right to make her commitment and to stand at the sacred Mormon marriage ceremony in keeping with her implicit promises to herself and her husband. It was her birthright and she undoubtedly would have met the strictures of her faith but for the brutal rapes at the hands of those who should have protected her.*
>
> *Imagine her heartbreak, as she held herself to a shameful lie, not of her making. Valarie made the decision to hold those secrets and suffer the consequences. She was supposed to live a "righteous life," she knew she would have lived a "righteous life" but for the rapes and degradation. To her, that stain could not be washed away.*
>
> *Valarie was left to bear these burdens of shame and rage on her own, and it ultimately tore her to pieces.*

CHAPTER EIGHT

"All She Had Left Were Her Dreams"

"THIS IS THE HARDEST TIME I have had in my life, and I just want out of the marriage in the worst way," wrote John in his journal on November 15, 1990. "Valarie is not cooperating very well—can't say I blame her. She is certainly frightened and exhausted. She is a good person, and we are really victims."

Since Valarie's return home from the Menninger Clinic, she and John had been in marriage counseling for about six months. Their therapist, Jeanette Davis, "eventually started working with each of us separately, [and] more with me as time went on," he wrote, adding that he now realized he'd been unhappy for many years but had felt obligated to hide his feelings from everyone—including himself. "I am really hurting and sorry for the pain I am bringing to my family, but I need to protect my sense of well-being or I will damage myself and lose my sense of who I am."

"I just can't live that way anymore," he admitted to his journal on November 23. "Valarie and I are not communicating at all and our relationship is very polarized. It is as much my fault as hers. . . . I am distancing myself from Valarie in an attempt not to get caught back in a painful relationship."

He wrote that his bishop had written him a "highly critical letter warning me about getting out of the marriage." He also noted that "Valarie is really trying to prove to me that she is whole. I told her that I did not believe that."

After all she'd been through, hearing this from her husband must have been infuriating. "I will admit she is doing better," he wrote. "But I don't think she rests much and she still is permissive with the children. She is a good mother but not too swift on the parenting side."

Brooke remembers Valarie's permissiveness positively. When she was frightened at night, Brooke recalled, her mother would appear at her bedside and tell her to imagine a protective bubble: "She would ask me what color I wanted the bubble to be, and who was there with me. Nothing could come inside my bubble unless I gave it permission. I was always safe there. It was usually a pink, sparkly bubble and included my mom, probably Jesus, my current pet, and most likely some mythical creature, like a unicorn or a Pegasus. She never made me feel silly about any of the details. She made me feel safe." In spite of her own pain, Valarie attempted to give Brooke the sense of security she had so badly wanted during her own youth.

But John decided he had had enough. He wrote:

> I have lots of feelings right now, and I must admit I am really at the bottom of the barrel. I so much want to run from the pain. I logically can't find a way that feels good in terms of where I should go. It must be a matter of faithlessness on my part. I do love the lord, I love Valarie but not as a wife, it is more as a child. I need companionship and to be one. I do not believe I will ever experience that with her, being impinged by her deep problems of sense of self. Ironically, she does not understand this, but how could she?

Debbie came out to help at the end of November, and she told John that she understood why he needed to get out of the marriage. Debbie explained that she was going to talk to her parents about the impending divorce, as John wrote, "because she felt their encouraging Valarie to have faith and stick in the marriage was damaging and harmful to everyone."

However, Debbie was also very afraid for her sister and shocked by her fragile emotional state. Years later, she said in an interview for this book that she believed her sister never recovered from the shock and shame of John's request for a divorce.

Having decided to end his marriage, John felt it was time to pay more attention to his children. Annie, then 13, was still dealing with the long-term consequences of her brain injury, which included movement and balance problems, hearing loss, memory issues, and seizures. On September 1, 1990, while at their country club's swimming pool, Annie had waded into the water while her siblings were swimming and John was listening to music in a chair on the deck. After looking up and realizing he didn't see Annie, he rushed to the edge of the pool and was horrified to see her lying on the bottom. He jumped in to save her, and as he wrestled her to the surface, he realized she was in the midst of a seizure. Mercifully, she had not inhaled any water, and the seizure subsided on its own.

John was haunted afterward by the sight of her body underwater. "I thought she might be dead," he wrote. He vowed to be a better parent and began taking each child on trips alone with him. "They have really different personalities," he noted in his journal. He took Brooke with him to a business meeting in Dallas, then to Disneyland. "Brooke is a very quiet and shy little girl. I think she is really angry at the world." Brooke was conceived while Annie lay in a coma and was born when Valarie was in the grips of a full-blown breakdown. "I worry about her a lot," he continued. "She doesn't talk much. I would call her an observer . . . with the amount of time she has had her little world disrupted, it is anyone's guess what really goes on in her mind. I can see that I will need to spend much more time with her if I intend to get close at all. She is very reluctant to let anyone in."

In contrast, he wrote that his second daughter, Erin, was "a pistol" because of her energy, athleticism, and daring. She "is rather expressive and will get things off her mind," unlike Brooke and Ryan, whom he thought resembled their mother. They both held "things inside, rather than talking about them."

John took Erin skiing in Park City and saw with delight that she was "becoming a good little skier . . . she is a very bright little lady and a real pleasure to be around. She has a very even temperament and a quick wit. She tends to over-function to deal with her anxiety. On Saturday she wanted to go to a Chinese restaurant for supper. I did not, but finally gave in and I must admit it was good."

In part because of the insights he was gaining through therapy, John was trying to do things differently. He explained in his journal that Ryan called him one morning to say he didn't want to go to Primary, the two-hour period of Sunday instruction for Mormon children. "We talked about it," he wrote, "and I was tempted to just tell him he had to go, but rather than command, I listened, and we talked about it and he finally decided to go on his own. This is a good lesson for me because when kids are not allowed to express their feelings they will be held inside, and they could build into resentment towards us or the church."

John had come to understand that his childhood experiences, particularly observing his mother's periodic melancholia, had caused him to develop a burdensome sensitivity to her moods. John believed that as a child he had taken on a sense of responsibility for the stability of the family. His mother was depressed, his father emotionally unavailable and occupied with the family business. "I felt responsible for taking care of my mother," he wrote.

He also wondered if his powerful attraction to the melancholic Valarie had something to do with familiarity. "I felt at a deep level I was responsible for Mom and this later was part of my attraction to Valarie," he said. "I probably unconsciously responded to the suggestion she was wounded, and was drawn to be her caretaker just as I had been with my mom."

John quit his job at Armour in November 1990, and on November 23 he wrote, "I must admit I am experiencing, for the first time in my life, severe depression." He consulted with psychologists, lawyers, religious authorities, friends, and experts on families in transition. They all told him to proceed slowly for the sake of everyone involved. A family friend who had recently shared a meal with Debbie and Valarie reported back to John that she "wondered if Valarie would survive." She was, he wrote in his journal, "appalled at how sick Valarie was."

John also consulted with Dr. Victor Cline, "a very famous clinical psychologist and also a good member of the church," as John described in his journal. Dr. Cline told John that he was also a victim here. "He told me I was wounded severely and extremely traumatized." He explained that "when Valarie was at Menninger's, what she went through was very traumatizing" to John and that he "probably didn't even realize it."

Dr. Cline told John that "it was not wrong" for John to seek a divorce but cautioned that he needed to "do it in a way that would reduce the impact on the children." John wrote in his journal: "I also agreed to enter a group therapy session once a week in SLC. He said I had battle fatigue. I guess I do." He encouraged John to consider a separation to allow, perhaps, a better perspective on the marriage and his own emotional health. John agreed.

John met with a divorce attorney, who also told him to move slowly for the emotional health of the children.

John noted that his dear Uncle Junior said, "whatever I do now will have an impact on my life in my later years. He said that the older he gets the more sorry he feels for the things he did wrong in earlier life. It is very important for me to do this the right way and with honor."

Nevertheless, John admitted, "I must have patience and that is really hard for me right now. I need to get on with my life."

Every hour was torture, every week a lifetime. He wanted out. And he was going to make it happen. Despite all the recommendations to the contrary, he fast-tracked divorce preparations.

John first met with Dr. Cline on December 15, 1990. According to John's journal, both Valarie and John met with Dr. Cline separately in Salt Lake City a week later. Three days after that, on December 26, *the day after Christmas*, John made an appointment to meet with Valarie at the doctor's home, where Dr. Cline discussed John's plan for the separation, referring to it as a "therapeutic vacation." John and Valarie would take turns living with the kids: John from Thursday to Sunday, Valarie from Monday through Thursday. The family would attend church together on Sundays. John enlisted his mother, Emma, to take care of the children when they stayed with him.

On the drive back to Park City after the December 26 session with Dr. Cline, Valarie "tore into a terrible rage," John wrote. She hit her hand against the dashboard so repeatedly and so hard that John worried she would seriously hurt herself. "I have not seen her so angry in a long time," he wrote. "She told me that she hated me and said about every cuss word in the book. The thing that really hurt my feelings was when she said that she hated me worse than Bob and Gary."

John added, "I told her that there was no one who would put up with what she had thrown at me."

Regarding the separation, John noted that "Valarie really does not want to do this." Nevertheless, on December 30, 1990, John gathered the family together at their ski condo in Deer Valley to tell them that their parents were going to divorce. Ryan was 11 years old. He remembered the reaction of the children: "Shocked, crying, sad. I remember my mom sitting there, she was just super quiet, and mostly it was my dad talking."

———

The earth was giving way beneath Valarie's feet. She was 36 years old. Only one year had passed since she'd left the Menninger Clinic. It had been only 10 months since she'd recovered her final memory, during outpatient treatment with Dr. Brown, of Bob Dahle shooting Shadow as punishment for her refusing to meet him for sex. She'd had barely two years to try to work through the horrors of the abuse that she'd endured from age 4 to 16, not to mention all the self-knowledge she'd missed because 12 years of her life had been locked away and put out of reach. Her feelings had been "buried alive," as Dr. Brown explained it to John.

Her essential understanding of the world up until that point had been a childish patchwork of homilies, religious stories, and storybook expectations, limited by parents who refused to acknowledge the existence of evil and a religion that promised eternal reward for church-sanctioned good behavior. For innocent victims of terrible crimes in the community, no explanation, solace, or apparently, justice, were on offer: self-blame was the well-worn path.

Valarie had moved from a childhood marred by more than a decade of incest and sexual abuse, including beatings and emotional manipulation, to an early marriage and four pregnancies so injurious to her health that her doctor insisted she have no more. After Annie's near-fatal accident and her own subsequent nervous breakdown, she had white-knuckled her way through four years without effective treatment, trying to meet her husband's outsized expectations, until finally, she was able, under the care of an understanding and skilled clinician, to reveal the terrible truth of her youth. Dr. Brown said in an interview for the book, "She did get better when she was with us. I don't know what happened after that."

Less than a year later, John made clear he wanted a divorce.

It was all too much.

On January 6, 1991, after a sleepless night during which Valarie left her bed twice to visit the emergency rooms of two different Omaha hospitals, she called John at 9:45 a.m. and said she was sitting in her car in a park. As he noted in his journal, "she wanted me to know that the children and I were the family and that she was not needed." She told John she loved him and hung up.

He decided not to overreact because he'd heard threats like this before. Instead, he went to his scheduled session with the marriage counselor, Jeanette Davis, and told her about Valarie's disrupted night and the implicit suicide threat in her morning call. The counselor insisted he call 911. John hesitated and instead called a friend of Valarie's—he was surprised when she told him that Valarie had just left a voicemail for her. It said, in John's words, that "she loved her and that she loved me and the kids, she did not want to hurt us and have us looking for her for a long time, that we would find her underneath the water under the Council Bluffs bridge." John wrote that he "about had a heart attack" and cried. He begged Davis to go with him to look for Valarie. Then he asked the friend to call the Omaha police.

When John and Davis got to the bridge, they spotted Valarie's red Mercedes. John felt the engine hood; it was cold. They waited for the police, who came about 20 minutes later, and then began looking for her. Twenty minutes after that, John saw Valarie wandering about 250 yards from where their cars were parked. She was cold and disoriented. "I think she had hypothermia," John said. He took her home and "made her take a bath." He called her therapist and made an appointment for her for that day. After learning about the suicide threat and the fact that Valarie was getting prescriptions for painkillers from several different doctors, the therapist insisted that Valarie check herself into the psychiatric wing at Lutheran Hospital in Omaha. Valarie, John wrote, "did not want to, but really did not offer a lot of resistance."

After discussing the situation with Dr. Cline, John decided to "not be manipulated" by this recent episode; he continued with plans for the separation and divorce.

After they were divorced in 1991, Valarie received half of the community property, which netted her about $3 million, making her a wealthy woman. She rented a house at 2981 American Saddler Drive, near the Park Meadows Country Club in Park City, UT, and soon thereafter purchased a 1.03-acre lot down the street at 2450 Lucky John Drive, in a neighborhood that offered views of the ski slopes and whose street names mirrored those of the ski runs. She settled her children into school and hired John's friend Ron Ferrin to build her a house.

Clarkston, in spite of the old horrors, remained an important respite both for Valarie and her children. In a long letter, Brooke explained how important her grandparents Shirleen and Denzel had been to her and her siblings. After the Millers' move to Park City, Brooke recalled:

> *My mom used to drive us to Clarkston on Christmas Day. They are some of my fondest memories I have. My grandmother cooked a beautiful dinner for everyone and the cousins exchanged gifts. We'd all have slumber parties in her basement, she'd set up all the bedding, she just took care of us.*
>
> *My grandparents gave me the most wonderful, secure, loving environment. My grandmother cooked every meal and regularly made baked goods to always have on hand for us. My grandfather was kind, gentle, entertaining, helpful, and enthusiastic. He was really good with little kids. He could get down and play with them and play pretend.*
>
> *He was silly and cute. And he's really cute with babies. I always felt safe, secure, and loved. I never even heard my grandparents swear, let alone have anything inappropriate go on around them. They took care of me, and that wasn't something I was used to at home. It felt amazing, and I'm so grateful for those beautiful memories. My grandparents never raised their voices. I really couldn't have asked for better grandparents. I truly have nothing but the best memories of being in Clarkston and with my grandparents as a child. And to this day, when I go there, I feel that it's such a calming place to be.*

"I'm a sucker for Utah home cooking because of those good times," she added. "Frog-eye salad, Jell-O salad, soft homemade dinner rolls, turkey, Stove Top stuffing, and funeral potatoes still provide a lot of comfort." She explained that frog-eye salad is made with couscous and tossed with mandarin oranges, canned crushed pineapple, coconut, and mini marshmallows, then mixed up with frozen whipped topping. The small, round couscous swimming in the shiny cream sauce resembles watery frog eyes. Funeral potatoes were a local favorite: an artery-busting dish of cheesy au gratin potatoes made from frozen hash browns, topped with a crunchy layer of ground potato chips sprinkled with Parmesan and drizzled with melted butter.

And vegetables? Brooke said she remembered a green bean casserole, but "I don't remember salads or anything nutritious at all. And it's funny because I think Ryan and I still kind of have the palates of eight-year-olds cause we were raised on that food."

A year or so after leaving Armour, John had an opportunity to acquire a meat-packing plant in Dodge City, Kansas, called HyPlains Dressed Beef Company. He reassembled the old management team he'd put together to modernize E. A. Miller, which had accompanied him to Armour, and got to work. Per their joint custody agreement, he lived in Kansas from Monday to Thursday, while the kids stayed with Valarie. He then returned to Utah on Thursday nights, where his infinitely generous mother, Emma, helped him cook and care for the family until they returned to their mother's at the end of the weekend. Over the next few years, John and his team would revitalize HyPlains and then acquire National Beef. He would remain the CEO and owner of the combined companies for the next 18 years.

In the fall of 1992, when Ryan was 13, Valarie brought him into Jans, an upscale ski store, to buy him a new winter jacket. During an interview for this book in Park City, Ryan pointed out the flagship store on Park Avenue. "That's where my mom met Gary Martin," he said, a local "ski bum" who worked at the store and became her second husband. Ryan said, "I always liked Gary. Gary was just a nice guy. And I think he really loved my little sisters."

Brooke agreed: "He really gave me back a minute of childhood."

Gary remembered very clearly the day he met Valarie and Ryan and outfitted Ryan in North Face clothing. After the mother and son left the store with their purchases, a fellow employee told Gary that while he was taking care of the boy, the mother had gone upstairs to the women's section and asked a lot of questions about him, including whether he was married. A couple weeks later, Valarie showed up at Jans's Deer Valley location at

Snow Park Lodge, where Gary was then working. He noticed she, as he put it, "was really decked out, country chic, you know, cowboy boots on, hair and makeup very nice." She dropped by the store a third time, a few weeks after that, and Gary said his coworkers told him, "Hey, she wants you to ask her out, that's why she keeps popping in." So he asked her if she'd like to go out for dinner, and she eagerly agreed. "Yes, yes, yes, yes," he remembered her saying.

Gary hadn't moved to Park City looking for love. At 36, he was in pursuit of another passion: the great outdoors. "I hit the jackpot and got a little cabin up on Norfolk Avenue in Old Town Park City," he recalled in series of interviews in March 2023. "And that was always my dream, being in a little old miner's cabin, living in a ski town right at the foot of the mountain. I never made a lot of money, but all I was into was backpacking and hiking and mountain biking and skiing."

But Valarie, he observed, "was really courting me."

He asked her out for dinner a few weeks into the future because, he explained, he needed time to save enough money to take her to a proper place, the Riverhorse on Main. On the appointed night, Valarie drove to his place in her red Mercedes sedan and, after a short visit, handed him the car keys, asking if he'd like to drive to the restaurant. Over dinner she explained that she was divorced and that she and her husband were coparenting their four children in Park City. She seemed together and self-possessed. "She had a smile on her face every second. She was sort of lit up, radiant," Gary recalled. "Her hair was perfect and beautiful, real dark, auburn, sort of highlighted. She had really big eyes—that was always something that stood out—and she was very slender and seemed in really good shape. She was beautiful and so sweet and kind and had a good sense of humor. I'd tell jokes, and she'd laugh and she'd over-laugh, like she was really enjoying every second, you know?"

The relationship moved forward slowly. "I'm getting to know this person," Gary recalled. "I'm getting to know the family. The kids are unbelievably awesome, every one of them was a really cool kid." Erin, then 10, was "unbelievable," he said, emphasizing each syllable. "She was the brightest, smartest, most athletic, most gifted little girl I've ever met in my whole life. Never, ever met anyone like her." He noted that she was already an accomplished athlete, then focused on gymnastics. She also played the piano. "All of a sudden, I'm hearing this incredible classical music, like Mozart or Beethoven, coming out of the living room, and I walk around the corner, and Erin's there playing," he recalled. "I'm like, 'Holy cow, Erin, I didn't know you played the piano, and I didn't know you played like that.'"

She was "the queen bee, all the time."

Gary remembered Brooke, then eight, as a very sweet child, also athletically inclined but not as outgoing as Erin. Quiet and introverted, she held back and observed.

"Ryan was the most troubled, as far as his appearance and his demeanor," Gary offered. "He seemed bummed out a lot and wasn't a real happy camper, but a lot of times I'd get talking with him and doing things with him and he would open up." Gary remembered taking Ryan, when he was 13, to Las Vegas to see a Grateful Dead concert. "On the way back, he was just so excited," Gary said. "He was going, 'Man, everybody was smiling. Everybody liked each other. Everybody seemed like a big family. Everybody was having so much fun. Why does everybody like each other?'"

Valarie began dropping by Gary's cabin on the weekends. He had a huge collection of records and a large fireplace but no TV, so "we'd talk, we'd listen to music, we'd snuggle," Gary recalled. Valarie appeared to be hungry for physical attention, and although she was very responsive to his touch, she also seemed oddly incurious about pleasing him physically in return. Gary didn't think much of it, figuring it must have had something to do with her Mormon beliefs. He had been raised a Methodist.

Valarie wrote letters to him after he left the cabin for work in the morning, leaving them beside the bed for him to read. These notes illuminated her halting attempts to discover a world of intimacy that transcended her childhood trauma. In one letter, Valarie awkwardly hinted at her desire for physical affection while confessing trepidation at the prospect: "Gary, feelings of a woman 'passionately' in love, with every part of your body and soul is a gift, and it is new. It has also brought other awakenings and feelings about masculine energy that I must explore."

But the specter of her violation at the hands of Bob Dahle and Gary Thompson was never far off. In a letter to Gary dated January 25, 1994, Valarie wrote:

> I will not be taken advantage of, abused or ignored because I am a woman, and I come across in a very soft and sweet picture. But there is a warrior inside determined to keep myself and every other child or woman within my touch safe. Gary, please trust me. It hurt when you implied I let things slide. You can't know the inside of my mind as God does. Please trust, let me feel free to tell you anything and everything—I know what I am about, and I have battled demons and ghosts, and climbed Mt. Everest with my fingers to get there. Let me explore and conquer all my ghosts. Listen, trust me, believe in me, you are my life.

Gary tried to keep up with his own life, but Valarie was pushing for increased closeness—and time. "I need you in my home, in my bed," she wrote. "I need to wake up and go to sleep listening to you snore, and watching how beautiful you are. I want to sit by you in church, and pray with you every day."

For the year and a half of their courtship, Gary recalled, Valarie "just seemed very confident, very self-assured, and full of energy." He adored her children, taking them to amusement parks, waterslides, and even bungee jumping towers. And they all, he marveled, had a "wonderful time."

Although she was enjoying this new phase in her life, the building of her massive new home was causing Valarie great anxiety. Brooke said that her mother had been unable to restrain Ferrin, whom Brooke said wasn't much interested in listening to her anyway. And he was also distracted with other, competing construction projects. In the end, Valarie got much more house than she wanted or could afford. "She was really frustrated when it became clear he had totally gone above and beyond," said Brooke.

"My darn house has thrown me into such a world of chaos and stress," she wrote to Gary, "I am really struggling to get centered and to slow down." The house had five bedrooms, eight baths, a large backyard, and many patios. An indoor "endless pool" that Valarie thought she'd use to strengthen her back was added. But the pool didn't work and was never used.

On the weekends and when John was minding the kids, Valarie visited Gary's cabin. The notes continued, revealing her struggle to integrate her new romance into a life still dominated by past sexual abuse and a difficult divorce, and to integrate Gary into the Mormon worldview she still held dear. Her terror at the thought of Gary abandoning her was palpable. "Oh, I love you," she wrote, "and something I have been afraid to feel or ever want to acknowledge to anyone—out of fear—I need you. I need you. Please take my hand and never let it go—come home with me." Valarie coped with such fears by reasoning that she and Gary must have become soulmates before birth, in the now-forgotten "pre-existence"—a Mormon doctrine popularized in the 1970s via Sunday lessons, church-produced musicals, and even an album by the Osmonds. "I could not love you this much unless I have already loved you for eternity, could I?"

In the winter of 1994, after they'd dated for a little over a year, Valarie told Gary that they should get married. "She sort of gave me an ultimatum that she was Mormon and she can't keep doing this," Gary recalled. She sent a couple of young missionaries his way, and while Gary listened politely, he firmly rebuffed their efforts to convert him. Valarie probably hoped "they'd come over and I'd go, 'Wow, right, sign me up,'" Gary remembered. But as the missionaries struggled to respond to his questions, he concluded that Mormon theology was "crazy." He remembers that period as "troubling."

But Valarie accepted his decision not to convert and began to plan a June wedding anyway.

"Thank you, thank you, thank you for the magic, the forever, for all the answers I seek just by looking in your eyes," she wrote to Gary on February 27, 1994. "Oh, I love you. I want June to hurry her journey here so we can begin the chapter together. I am a goner! I miss you!"

All in all, the period in which she was dating Gary Martin stood out to all who knew her as a return of the old Valarie—healthy, strong, vivacious, and hopeful about life. Ryan said it was the best he'd ever remembered her. Sue Saunders also noticed how rejuvenated Valarie seemed during this period, pointing out that she had even returned to her old ways as a practical joker. Before her wedding to Gary, Valarie had playfully sewn up the fly in all of his underpants and returned them to his bureau drawer. Sue thought this was a hilarious example of Valarie's fun-loving personality. Gary himself thought it was an example of her "country humor." Nobody seemed to see it as a warning of fears and tempests not yet completely calmed.

There was one very strange thing that Valarie was determined to do before marrying. She scheduled an operation in March to repair her aching back—only three months before the planned nuptials. Gary discussed this several times with her, asking her if she really thought it was a good idea to have a back operation so close to the wedding, especially since she was planning a honeymoon to Tahiti directly afterward. Valarie insisted she'd be fine, and he accompanied her to California, where she underwent surgery to remove bone spurs in her lower back, stabilize her spine with a bone graft, and insert a titanium plate to support two failing vertebrae. She was fitted with a plastic brace and sent home.

Gary remembered that before they drove back to Utah, Valarie collected copious amounts of drugs from the hospital dispensary, including a huge glass jar "like they have at a pharmacy" brimming with hydrocodone, which he knew was a powerful painkiller. She explained that since her doctors were in California and she lived in Utah, she had to get a supply of medicine that would last her months. Although she had struggled with abusing tranquilizers and painkillers during her marriage with John, she evidently didn't abuse the drugs right away, because she succeeded in arranging all the details of the wedding herself—a "beautiful" event according to Gary, which took place on June 3, 1994, in Park City. Gary's parents were there, as was Valarie's family, other relatives, and friends. Valarie wore a pink gown, and the girls were decked out in matching pink bridesmaids dresses, flowers and ribbons in their hair.

The honeymoon flight to Tahiti was long, Valarie made it without fuss, but Gary had to help her through the airports in a wheelchair. He said she ate well on the trip, and in a photo of them at the resort, Valarie appears to be her shockingly beautiful self, the two looking ebullient and suntanned. She enjoyed a couple of canoe rides and a few walks. The consummation of the marriage was hurried and awkward, not least because she was in a back brace and Gary didn't want to hurt her. "It was not an athletic performance," he reported with a rueful laugh.

He did remember an odd image. Unlike their many romantic and physically intimate moments at his place, when her sparkling eyes were intently focused on him, in Tahiti, while lying on the bed in the hotel room in anticipation of sex, she turned her face to the side, away from him.

It would be the first and only time they had intercourse.

—

After the newlyweds returned to Park City, Valarie's gauzy hopes of love, security, and an orderly future were quickly abandoned. Almost as soon as they moved into the Lucky John Drive house, Brooke recalled, "my mom was basically bedridden."

The attentive, athletic woman Gary Martin had fallen in love with disappeared almost overnight, leaving him to become the primary caregiver for her four children, preparing lunches and dinners, driving them to lessons and appointments, all while taking Valarie to doctors and physical therapists.

He was surprised to learn from the children that throughout the time he and Valarie had been dating, Denzel and Shirleen had been coming down from Clarkston every other week to care for them, Monday through Thursday. He had thought Valarie was doing the caregiving herself. It was part of his image of her, which she had assiduously cultivated: she was active, capable, in charge. Instead, he recalled the children telling him, "Hey, you know, Mom's been laid out every week, and her parents have been taking care of us, and then when we go to Dad's, she somehow gets it together to go see you."

It was the first indication that things were not exactly as they'd seemed.

Just as Valarie began sliding away, Ryan was experimenting with prescription medicines and recreational drugs himself. In high school, as a member of the Park City ski team, he'd followed the lead of many of the older athletes who shaved their heads and partied hard, especially when traveling. The team competed all winter and attempted to catch up with their studies by taking summer school.

One day, Ryan found that Gary had a small baggie of weed hidden in his truck. From time to time he pilfered from it. When Ryan got busted by his dad for being stoned, he panicked and told his father he'd gotten the marijuana from Gary. Irked, John had a stern talk with Gary about it. Mortified by the situation, Gary had no idea Ryan had found his little stash, which he'd made a point to keep away from the house and the children.

Ryan felt bad about ratting Gary out and soon came to appreciate his generous nature, which became clear to the rebellious teen after he dropped acid with a few of his friends and arrived at his mother's house tripping. Gary carefully tended to the boys, setting up croquet wickets and leading them through a game. "He literally had to take each of us, put his arms around us, and help us hit the ball," recalled Ryan. "He just made it fun, and he totally knew we were tripping out because I remember him being like, 'What are you guys on?'"

While Gary acted as Ryan's spirit guide, Valarie spent most days in her master suite on the first floor. "She was just gone," said Ryan. "I think the back injury was in a lot of ways just the excuse to be bedridden and to be on drugs, to drown out this pain she felt, you know, and to not have to be responsible." Gary, who had never seen her down and out, was shocked. He assumed she was really suffering from back pain. It took him years to realize it was not pain that was immobilizing her but rather the pain medicine she had been prescribed by her doctors.

When the children came home from school, they walked by her bedroom and frequently found her sprawled on her bed, passed out, often not completely covered up. Whereas Erin would walk over to her, give her a kiss, and pull the covers over her, Ryan was angry to find her this way. At the time of this writing, he said he still couldn't shake those images from his head. "I had a lot of anger about that for a lot of years," he said.

Ryan tried to cope by getting as stoned as possible as often as possible. "That's how I didn't live in reality," he recalled. "I was completely high all the time."

After figuring out how to deceive his father, "I was high all the time around my dad," Ryan added, saying he never let his father catch him a second time. This went on "for two or three years starting when I was 14." Ryan said that he tried to tell his mom what his life was like and what he was into, "kind of like confessing. And she'd just kind of said, 'Oh, it's okay.'"

After a few serious knee injuries and surgeries, he was prescribed painkillers, and like his mother, he became addicted. While dating a Mormon girl in Park City, they together tried to move away from drugs, alcohol, and parties. The relationship didn't last, and Ryan faltered. Despite his struggles, his faith never wavered. "I never doubted the church, for some reason," he said. "I always felt, even from a really young age, that I believed in it. I always felt like I was going to go on a mission. I felt like the teachings were true. I just had my own period of going off the deep end."

Ironically, although his mother's example had led him to seek solace in drugs, her strong religious faith helped lead him away from them. "I was up in my room one day," he explained, "just fighting [with myself] and praying about, How do I overcome these things? How do I change my life? How do I get happy? And I remember my mom knocked on the door." Because of her back pain, intermittent MS symptoms, and drug use, she had seldom climbed the stairs to his bedroom. He was astonished she even had the capacity to do it. "She just put her arms around me and said, 'Ryan, you just have to remember that you're a stripling warrior.'" She was referring to a story from the Book of Mormon about two thousand young warriors known for their bravery. Their ancestors had sworn to put down arms forever, but the youth had volunteered in their parents' stead for a particular battle and fought valiantly. "Had you lived back then"—Valarie said, meaning the ancient time of the Book of Mormon—"then you would have fought with them. You're going to make it. You can fight these battles and get through them."

Ryan said, "It was the one thing that I'll never forget my mom telling me."

He noted that Mormon lore holds that the stripling warriors were relentlessly obedient in battle. And they were this way, he said, because "their mothers taught them to be valiant and to be obedient."

—

While Ryan was fighting with himself to stop taking drugs, he and his siblings faced another family challenge. In 1994, John married Vicki Monroe, a divorced woman with two children—a daughter, Kate, who was Erin's age, and a son, Alex, who was a year older than Ryan. John thought that Vicki, who was confident and well organized, would be able to salve (if not solve) the various hurts of his children and meld them into a happy family, even though the Miller kids were still off to their mother's house for half of each week.

Vicki's kids were well behaved, disciplined, and displayed perfect table manners. The Miller kids tumbled in like a pack of wild animals, and their years of limited supervision and near-constant trauma had created restless souls whose activities included barraging cars and people in downtown

Park City with a fusillade of snowballs from the rooftops and managing to remain one step ahead of the police. At the dinner table, they amused themselves with burping contests.

It would be a rough adjustment. Kate and Erin ceaselessly competed for attention and approval. It was difficult for the Miller children to drop in and out of John and Vicki's home each week, en masse, when different patterns and relationships existed there during their weekly absences. On occasion, Erin and Brooke were left out of Vicki's plans with Alex and Katie, and Ryan remembered some days waiting for the school bus with his sisters and seeing Vicki whiz by in her car, driving her own kids to school without the Millers.

As Ryan struggled to kick his drug habit, a final ski injury knocked him out of competition and, ironically, gave him the opportunity to right his course. Somehow, in spite of the haze, he had kept his mind focused on his goal of serving on a Mormon mission, and he knew that in order to get there, he had to make fundamental changes to his life. He knew he had to separate from his skiing friends and move away from Park City. He found a program at Utah State University in Logan that allowed him to complete high school and begin college simultaneously. Between his family connections in Cache Valley and his father's friends, he was able to cobble together a group of substitute parents who offered him, at various times, places to stay, counsel, mentorship, and care. He found guidance from men who had served missions of their own and warm-hearted mother-types who "adopted" him, monitored him, and advised him while he put himself back together emotionally, spiritually, and religiously. In the end, he embarked on his own mission to Uruguay, where he served two years, from 1998 through 2000. He then returned to Utah State, from which both of his parents had graduated.

As Ryan left Park City for Logan, where Utah State was located, Gary Martin stayed on as Mr. Mom while dealing with his own doubts about his relationship with Valarie and her children. He recalled:

My last whole year with that family, I was it. I did everything. I made every meal. I took every kid to school. I made every lunch, I did the laundry, mowed the lawn, took care of the dogs, took Valarie to all her medical things, you know, took Annie to all her special classes, to where I remember that old movie with Michael Keaton where, you know, he just looked like a rag doll, unshaven and all beat up. I mean, that's the way I was becoming. I was just completely consumed, had no time for myself, but was just doing everything for this family.

At the beginning, he was waiting for the beautiful Valarie, like Sleeping Beauty, to awaken from whatever spell had been cast over her. On a trip to Clarkston, she at last told him about having been raped, and she pointed out the Newton Reservoir where Bob Dahle had tried to drown her. Gary listened, but because the subject was so sad and upsetting, he tried to put it out of his mind. He clearly did not appreciate how deeply the early abuse had affected her. Perhaps she didn't want him to know. He did remember being with her at her parents' house in Clarkston one day when Valarie pointed to an old man sitting in a lawn chair in the yard across the street. In a spooky, quavering voice, she said "That's him . . . that's him." And then she named him: Gary Thompson. He also remembered her creating a scene at dinner once at her parents' home, suddenly crying out in pain and insisting someone take her to the local hospital. Though he was very concerned about his new wife's apparent discomfort, it seemed to him that the family was a bit slow to respond, and he later wondered if her outcry may have had something to do with the opportunity to get more drugs.

By then, Gary had taken over the job of paying her bills, and he was shocked to see how much she was spending. There was also a coterie of hangers-on who seemed to be getting money from Valarie for various dubious services. On occasion she doled out large and puzzling gifts, including $8,000 to a friend's son to study "energy healing" in Hawaii.

"In Park City, everybody took advantage of her, every contractor, every grounds person, every therapist," Gary said.

Valarie also had built up a large consumer debt, which she was paying off slowly, racking up fees and interest charges. She had previously instructed her father, who came over to pay her bills, to write checks for $20, even when those offerings did not reach the minimum payment. One month, Gary said he counted 52 separate bills.

Gary worried that her money had been invested poorly. The market was going up, but her accounts just seemed to be depleting. He called Denzel to alert him to this problem, and a meeting was arranged with Patrick Clark, a relative who was managing her money. During a meeting with Gary and Denzel, Patrick was defensive, claiming the investments were secure and safe. Denzel avoided conflict by detouring the conversation to stories about family. After the investment advisor left, "her dad was standing there," Gary recalled, "with his chest puffed out, saying, 'Yep. I guess we showed him, huh?'"

"No, you never said anything," an astonished Gary seethed. "You never brought up anything. You never seemed concerned. You talked about his dad and his family and Cache Valley, accomplishing nothing."

Bad investments, careless spending, Annie's expensive therapies, Ryan's ski team, gymnastics for the girls—all of these contributed to Valarie's declining fortunes. Worse, after the divorce, she had lost John's health insurance, leaving her saddled with still more debt from out-of-pocket medical bills.

After her marriage to Gary, however, she was covered by his health insurance, and he pleaded with the doctors to help his wife with her pain. In time, he noticed strange looks from medical personnel when they told her they couldn't prescribe any more pain medication. His suspicions were confirmed in Scottsdale, Arizona, where a doctor who had just biopsied Valarie's bladder informed them in no uncertain terms that she did not suffer from "interstitial cystitis," a condition for which she had been prescribed pain medication from another doctor in California.

After caring for Valarie and the kids for two years, Gary finally concluded that she was consulting with endless doctors simply to secure narcotics.

Finally, he told Valarie, "You're addicted to drugs. You won't help yourself. You're damaging your children in ways you can't even imagine. You're damaging me in ways you can't imagine, but mainly it's your kids I'm concerned about, and I'm not going to live here and watch these kids get destroyed by your inability to get off of these drugs and become a person again."

But Valarie couldn't find the strength to do so. "We all just got so exasperated by her behavior with the drug usage," said Brooke. "She would be falling asleep midsentence with her head dropping forward. She was impossible to communicate with and was totally obstinate about everything."

Gary made plans to leave. However, he first wanted to get her into a better financial position. They sold the ill-fated house on Lucky John Drive, paid off her $150,000 in consumer debt, and bought a more modest house not far away on Single Jack Court. He asked her to split with him the $80,000 they had cleared from the sale of the house after paying off her debts. His share of the profits would help him get back on his feet after not working for two years. According to Gary, Valarie agreed to this arrangement.

On June 25, 1996, Valarie filled prescriptions at the Park City Pharmacy for three different prescriptions, written by three different doctors, for Trazodone (an antidepressant and sleeping pill), Estrace, a hormone replacement, and hydrocodone, an opiate. On July 4, she made a list of the drugs she was taking: Zoloft (an antidepressant), BuSpar (an anti-anxiety medication), Klonopin (a benzodiazepine and a sedative), Bactrim (an antibiotic), Robaxin (a muscle relaxant), Neurontin (an anticonvulsant), Cystospaz (for bladder problems), Pyridium (a pain reliever for urinary tract issues), Desyrel (an antidepressant), and Peri-Colace (for constipation).

Under pressure from Gary to get off the drugs, she entered the Betty Ford Center in Rancho Mirage, California, and was quickly thrown out. She then checked into STEPS, a detox facility in Port Hueneme, California, writing checks to cover the daily $695 fee. She stayed for three weeks for a total of $16,680. She received many encouraging letters from her family while she was there—from her parents, her daughter Annie, her sister Debbie, and her niece. Gary Martin sent her humorous greeting cards, and visited her at least once. But as soon as she came out, she returned to taking drugs. As Brooke put it, she couldn't resist the pull of feeling "up in the clouds."

On Gary's final day in Park City in 1997, he arrived home to find Denzel in the house, demanding that he leave. Valarie was sitting in a chair, sobbing. Gary thought that Denzel was trying his hardest to act mean and threatening, but couldn't quite pull it off. But his words were clear, and Valarie did nothing to contradict him. "Get out!" he insisted, which had been Gary's plan, but not in this way. As Gary walked to the car, Erin came hurtling out of the house and threw her arms around him, saying, "I'm gonna miss you so much." Brooke remembered that he said goodbye to her with tears in his eyes. She was 12 years old and had little idea that she soon she would be the one tasked with the daily job of physically caring for her mother.

Valarie never sent Gary the money she had promised him, and he went through a difficult couple of years getting back on his feet. Although according to a prenup he signed, he had $10,000 in savings when he married Valarie, he said he left penniless, and he recalled that he was forced to sell off most of his record collection in the following years to stay solvent. He was hurt that the family had mistrusted him, spreading rumors that he was living high off her accounts, when in fact the one gift Valarie had given him that he accepted, a bicycle, was stolen during his move.

Twenty-five years later, when interviewed for this book, Gary pulled an old briefcase from the back of a closet in his home. In it were some old documents and the notebook in which Valarie had written those love letters that she had left him in his old Park City cabin, when she lounged around there in the mornings after he went to work. Looking through the notebook, he found one last entry that he had never read before. He figured she wrote it and slipped the notebook into his things as he was leaving Utah. On top of the page she scribbled, "Please read this."

She wrote:

Gary, I got caught up in pain and painkillers and didn't have a clue as to how to handle it. I do now and I want many adventures with you. Remember you said we would make love in the back of a pickup when we were 85. Please grow old with me. And all our hikes. I loved walking behind watching the swagger of that great butt, amazed at the beauty of your body. Gary, read this notebook and please read the love letters you wrote to me. It will help you remember and feel how deeply and passionately we loved. My heart is yours and always will be. The love is still there. Please my sweetheart, let's rediscover it together. It's life and home and sweetness we had never felt before. It's alive my Gary.

Even had he seen the letter back then, her apology and explanation would have been too little, too late.

Ryan had long nursed the dream of attending the US Naval Academy, but he realized that his grades weren't good enough and his drug history would be hard to explain away. So Erin picked up the baton in his place, and when she approached college age in 2000, she applied to the service academies herself.

"She was super good at everything," Ryan said. In her freshman year of high school, she parlayed her gymnastics experience to win the state diving championships. But Erin being Erin, she then quit the diving team. She felt she'd "been there, done that," said Ryan. "That's kind of how she was. She was pretty stubborn." And rebellious. She was known in high school as the girl who, moments after setting records in track, would light up a cigarette.

She was fabulous. But her stepbrother, Alex, always worried about her. "There was something fundamental about Erin," he said. "The term would be 'free spirited,' but that doesn't paint a full picture; Erin always had something at risk."

She got into the US Air Force Academy, meeting all the application requirements including collecting a recommendation from a US senator, with one proviso: She had to take some extra math classes to bring her up to speed.

But then Erin reversed course again and decided, no, she wouldn't buckle under and take the course; instead, she enrolled at Simmons University in Boston, Massachusetts, where she joined the diving team.

After her freshman year, in the summer of 2002 while working on her father's Montana ranch, she met Quinn Bingham, a recently returned LDS missionary, who was a churchgoing, straight-arrow young man. Erin worked side by side with Quinn and two of his Cache Valley friends, Tim and Ben Kofoed, six days a week, clearing up the aftermath of a devastating forest fire. On Sundays, the young men invited Erin to go to church with them, which, after a while, she did—in her own fashion, at first wearing very short skirts. But the evenings belonged to Quinn and Erin, and they fell in love. In short order, Erin said goodbye to her pot-smoking boyfriend in Boston, withdrew from Simmons, and transferred to Utah State University. She decided that she would stop smoking, drinking, and using drugs.

"She just decided, 'I'm changing everything for him,'" said Ryan. "He was a great guy, [and] so patient with her." In September they got engaged and planned to marry, as John and Valarie had done, over Christmas break.

Quinn, his friends, and Ryan were all attending USU. Even Annie was close by—she lived in an apartment near campus with two other young women and was enrolled in a childcare training program. Valarie herself began talking about moving back to Logan. Erin moved in with Ryan, who was living not far from campus in the basement of the home of Norm and Winann Thompson, friends of the family. One of the problems Erin faced was that she and Quinn wanted to be married in an LDS temple. To enter a temple required Erin to pass a worthiness interview with her bishop—the same annual interviews that Bob Dahle and Gary Thompson had breezed through for decades, lying through their teeth, of course, about their conduct, allowing them to perform temple ordinances and serve adult missions.

Erin was trying very hard to wean herself from all substances, though her progress had its ups and downs. She was impulsive and liked successes, not failures. She'd be doing very well, explained Ryan, and then "she'd slip." She got in a car wreck, and Ryan thought that drugs were involved. "She was trying so hard to perform this 180-degree turn in one minute," he said, "and she was struggling. She had the same demons that we all had."

Of course, the tragedy at the center of all their lives was never far from any of them. John had promised to include Valarie in every Thanksgiving and Christmas gathering, and he did. John's stepson, Alex, noted that "she was just kind of wheeled in and, you know, would be there for a while and then wheeled out, and you know, you could talk to her and whatnot, but . . . when she was there, she was like very quiet, and it had to be painful for her—bizarre and painful. . . . I don't think she ever accepted her divorce from John."

Her sadness and desperation affected the children in ways both known and unknown, and of course, she had taught them by her example that the way to deal with physical or emotional pain was through pharmaceuticals, which she possessed in copious supply. Brooke observed Erin at times picking out some pills from Valarie's stash, which she kept in a box beside her living room couch. "Erin took stuff from Mom all the time," Brooke recalled. "She wanted to escape." Valarie warned the children away from the most powerful drugs in her arsenal. "Mom did tell us, 'If you take this, it will kill you,'" Brooke said. "'You can't take this dose.'"

A few weeks after her car crash, Erin called Ryan. "She asked me, 'Have you talked to Quinn?'" Ryan said no, but he knew Quinn was toying with the idea of postponing the wedding—to reduce the stress he knew was tormenting on Erin. "The last thing she said to me was 'I love you,'" Ryan said.

The morning of September 26, 2002, Erin drove from Logan to Park City to work on wedding plans. Erin had dinner that night with her father, who dropped her off at Valarie's house afterward. They had plans to meet the next day for lunch and to shop for a wedding dress. Erin went to bed, telling her mother she had a cold. Valarie no longer climbed the stairs to her bedroom but camped out on the living room couch in front of the TV, her box of drugs nearby. John left for work early Friday morning, driving past Valarie's home, and saw Erin's car parked in the drive. He called her cell phone late in the morning to touch base with her, but she didn't pick up. He then called Valarie who told him Erin was still sleeping. He called again around noon, and Valarie told him Erin had not yet come downstairs.

By 2 p.m., with still no word from his daughter, John was alarmed. It was not like Erin to sleep so late or fail to return his calls. He left his office in a state of panic with his personal accountant and assistant in tow. When they reached Valarie's house, he raced up the stairs to the bedrooms, where he saw Erin lying on the floor beside the bed in Valarie's room.

He knew right away that she was dead.

The autopsy report stated she had died of a morphine overdose.

After Erin's death, Ryan had a dream. He and his sister were skiing down a slope, headed toward an icy lake. Every time they approached the ice, Ryan veered away, but his sister did not—she skied over it. Ryan's interpretation of his dream was that Erin didn't mean to kill herself, but "she didn't know she was skiing on thin ice."

Brooke believes Erin knew exactly what she was doing; she feared she wasn't good enough for her fiancé because of her past behavior, and before going to bed, she swallowed a handful of pills that she'd grabbed from her mother's supply—just the pills her mother had repeatedly warned the children against taking.

The family was devastated. John was furious with Valarie, for obvious reasons, and he also blamed himself for not better protecting Erin.

The funeral chapel in Park City was filled with John's and Valarie's extended families and John's employees. All the siblings told stories about

Erin, as did her grandfather Denzel and some family friends. There was music and singing, all religious. Valarie was wheeled in in a wheelchair, and she sat nodding off, zoned out on drugs.

Later, John understood his beloved Erin's death as yet another soul-crushing casualty of the violence committed against Valarie by Bob Dahle and Gary Thompson.

After Erin's death, the surviving children increasingly kept their distance from Valarie. Except for Annie. One weekend, when she was home from Utah State, Annie visited her mother. "I had come home for the weekend to stay with Dad," she recalled. "And I went over to visit Mom at her house. And my mom got all excited that I was there, and I was staying all day and everything. And then I got really tired, and I needed to leave because my mom, as much as I loved being with her, has this 'suck your energy' kind of feeling with her. She just wanted everything from you."

Annie had to be careful to avoid getting too tired or too excited, as these states could bring on seizures, so she called her father and asked him to pick her up. "Then I went to break the news to Mom, and she threw the biggest fit," she said.

Valarie told her the same thing over and over: "I'm so lonely. I just want someone to be with me."

Ryan met a young woman at USU named Leah Roberts, a tall, athletic, mysteriously reserved beauty. As their relationship became serious and he grew busy studying, he had less time for his mother than she would have liked. Later, Ryan regretted that he didn't give his mother more attention. "We'd get in arguments, and she'd just want to be heard," he recalled, "and I'd just be like, 'I don't want to listen, Mom.'"

He came to understand that he and his siblings pushed her away "just to protect ourselves." He recalled that "even we shut her down. Everyone shut her down."

She retreated into her own world, on drugs, staying up all night and ordering things on QVC, many of which she never even opened up. Valarie's sister-in-law, Allyson Miller, said, "If you did too much for her, she kind of wore you ragged." Allyson remembered that sometimes Valarie's psychological pains were manifested in physical symptoms. When Valarie spoke about John, "right before our eyes, her stomach would blow up. Her mental state did that to her physically. I know that sounds crazy, but it was true. It caused her to almost look nine-months pregnant."

Valarie retreated further into a dream life. She told Allyson she wanted to ride horses seriously again and compete in the Olympics, something that her disabilities would not allow. Sometimes she sank into despair and anger, telling Allyson that "John just threw me away." But Allyson knew how difficult it had been to be married to Valarie. "Nobody could have lived with that," she told me. "I could feel for John and I could feel for Valarie, so I tried to stay neutral and just pretty much let her talk."

Allyson knew that Valarie slept during the day and was up at night. Part of this may have been the result of anxiety and PTSD from Dahle's and Thompson's nighttime attacks. But opioid addiction can also alter circadian rhythms. "The craving became so great all I could think of was my next so-called 'legal' hit," Valarie later wrote. "But I believed I could find a solution and control my drugs myself."

At the beginning of her addiction, after the first revelations of the rapes, she had been given pills by her doctors to sedate and quiet her. They began with antianxiety medications: Valium, Xanax, and Klonopin—all benzodiazepines, and the leading prescription drugs of their day. She later developed a habit with the opioid Percodan, a combination of oxycodone and aspirin, a painkiller introduced in 1950 by DuPont. The real trouble came when Purdue Pharma marketed a sustained-release version of oxycodone called OxyContin in 1996, which would destroy many lives, including Valarie's.

Littered with rural, white communities where pharmaceutical companies touted opioids as safe and nonaddictive, Utah was at the center of the emerging opioid epidemic of the mid-1990s. Purdue Pharma "focused the initial marketing of OxyContin on suburban and rural white communities." They wanted to target doctors who were "serving patients that were not thought to be at risk for addiction."

Purdue Pharma and others ran full-on marketing campaigns for the new drugs and paved the way by lobbying lawmakers, sponsoring "continuing medical-education courses," funding "professional and patient organizations," and sending "sales representatives to visit individual doctors." Throughout, they emphasized opioids' "safety, efficacy and low potential for addiction."[1]

As the years went on, Valarie collected more pills, which she hoped would relieve her back and pelvic pain. As her addiction deepened, her pain complaints grew. She was prescribed more drugs. Today, it is better known that opioids are not actually effective for treating chronic pain.

Valarie was treated for a time by Dr. Lynn Webster at the notorious Lifetree Pain Clinic in Salt Lake City, which was under investigation by the DEA from 2010 to 2014 for overprescribing painkillers. According to a feature story in the *Deseret News*, Salt Lake City's church-owned newspaper, "No doctor in Salt Lake City had a bigger influence than Webster. He wrote numerous studies that touted the benefits of opioids, served as president of the American Academy of Pain Medicine, and advanced the notion that addictive behaviors should be seen not as warnings, but as indications of untreated pain." The DEA investigated Dr. Webster for four years, but the United States Attorney for the District of Utah declined to prosecute because of a "lack of evidence." One DEA agent involved in the case said it was "the most frustrating of his career."[2]

More than 20 of Dr. Webster's former patients at Lifetree died of opioid overdoses. Valarie's daughter Brooke once accompanied her mother to an appointment with Dr. Webster. She recalled that the doctor asked her, "Do you have any concerns for your mom?" She replied, "Yeah, she's been on morphine for years. We're all afraid it's gonna kill her." But, she said, "He just reassured me that it was fine." But Valarie knew the truth: "I didn't have control," she wrote later. "The [drugs] controlled me, totally."

In 2004, Ryan began to have an inkling of the extent of his mother's addictions and wanted to get her into rehab. After doing some research, he decided to try to get her treated at the neuropsychiatric unit at the University of Utah, which also had a detox program. His father supported him but took a back-seat role. Because he was in Logan, Ryan explained, "I was kind of the one dealing with it all the time. So basically, I showed up at my mom's place and said, 'Pack a bag. You're leaving.'" Ryan gave her a couple of hours to organize herself. When he returned, he found Debbie with Valarie.

"My aunt Debbie was trying to convince me she didn't need to go, that Valarie was okay," said Ryan. He was bitter that the old forces were trying to operate again, "like everything's okay in Clarkston, in la-la land," as he put it.

Debbie thought, as Gary Martin had eight years earlier, that Valarie was in pain. Addicts can be very clever about concealing their illness, which is at bottom the drugs themselves. Ryan, who knew better because of his own experiences with addiction, told Debbie, "No, she's not okay."

Ryan explained that "it wasn't a fight, but [rather] like 'get out of the way, I'm taking her to rehab.' We hauled her down to the University of Utah." Valarie was appalled. "Oh, she was so upset," recalled Ryan.

They sat down with one admissions staff member, and Valarie maintained that she was okay. She said, "I don't need to go there. This is ridiculous. I'm fine," Ryan recalled in an interview. "She's a great debater," Ryan acknowledged. "She's so persuasive." She insisted to the staffer that there was "nothing wrong with any of the prescriptions" and that her son was "overreacting."

The intake counselor finally pulled Ryan out of the room and told him he wasn't convinced his mother needed detox. Ryan told the man, "You have no idea what's going on here. She is totally manipulating you. I promise you she has a major issue. She needs to be here. We need to get her detoxed."

Ryan spent another hour "convincing this guy that he had it all wrong."

He explained that his mother lived on the couch in her living room, her pajamas streaked with food she spilled on herself after passing out from the opiates. She was unable to perform any duties in her life beyond providing herself with a consistent supply of narcotics; she was rendered unable to manage even the most basic self-care.

Finally, Valarie was accepted into the program, and she agreed to stay.

"But three or four days later," Ryan recalled, "I got a call from the director of the clinic saying, 'Get down here right now. This is the worst patient we've ever had. And we don't want her here. She's threatening people.'" In her panic, it appeared she had resorted to the language of her abusers.

Ryan responded, "No, you're keeping her."

He drove down to Salt Lake City and got his father involved. They discussed her case with the director of the unit. Eventually, the hospital staff discovered Valarie was taking 21 different drugs. "Ninety percent of them, she wasn't supposed to be on," said Ryan. "I had to work really closely with them and go down there a ton."

The detox took a month, and Ryan found her a high-end, longer-term rehab facility, Cirque Lodge in Orem, Utah, which describes itself as "one of the country's most exclusive, trusted, and advanced drug and alcohol treatment centers."

She stayed for about a year. The treatment was based on the Alcoholics Anonymous 12-step program, which holds that alcoholism and drug addiction are diseases and that recovery requires admission of powerlessness over them. Second, the program holds that to aid in recovery, one must believe in a higher power. On an intake questionnaire, Valarie was asked if it would be difficult to "turn her will and life over to the care of God." "No," she wrote, "I have waited for it since I was 4 and 6 and 10 and 21, and 28, and 38, and 41!" These ages presumably mark times when she was severely tested. At four and six, she was molested by Earl and Gary Thompson, then at 10 there was its temporary cessation, possibly preceded by an intensification of abuse. She notably left out the rapes between 13 and 16, and

Dahle's attempt to murder her, but jumps to 21, when she married, with all the responsibilities that entailed including a sexual relationship with her husband for which her preparation had been coercion, rape, and beatings, and soon thereafter, four difficult pregnancies. Then, when she was 28, her daughter Annie nearly died, and she took on the spiritual responsibility for her recovery, which led to her breakdown and an eventual diagnosis of MS. At 38, she was shattered by divorce. At 41, her second marriage ended soon after it had begun. Historian Ross Peterson recalled that "she was brutalized at every turn, and she knew it."[3]

"When I was a little girl, I knew how to leave my body and float in order to escape my pain," she explained on her intake forms. "Using drugs has enabled me to achieve covering pain and float again. I believed drugs were my friends. I now know they are my worst enemy, and their ultimate goal was to kill me. If I let them cunningly draw me back, I will die."

She acknowledged that she couldn't do it by herself: "I believed I could take care of me. I've been trying since age 4! My self-control and self-will has not worked, absolutely. I cannot fix me. I accept that!"

"I think this is my last relapse—terrified I will die. I surrender, not to drugs, but to God," she added.

Her new sobriety led to a surge in hopefulness; after a month in the program, she began to think of her family and future with almost gold-tinged optimism. She anticipated the day when she could "walk in the door of my home and see relief and 'Well done—you did it!' on the faces of my family."

And she thought of even more: She wrote, "I want to enjoy nature, my mountain, my whispering aspens, the smell of pine, the freshness in the air—really notice and become one with it. I do not want to be afraid. Fear and drugs have ruled my life. I will replace it with *love*."

And finally, she wrote, "My relationship with my husband and my children are heaven to me. I want to truly be an integral part of their lives."

For a year, she got lots of individual counseling and support, and she was off "most of the drugs," according to Ryan. As a result, she was "way more clear-minded," and she told her sister that for the first time in many years, her back didn't hurt any more—even though she was off painkillers.

When she got out of Cirque Lodge, Ryan and his father "had to put structure around her." Valarie had run through most of her divorce settlement and had already been compelled to sell her second house. For a while, she had rented an apartment in Logan. This meant she was closer to her parents, sister, and brother but also to the upsetting memories of her youth in Clarkston. Debbie remembered during that time being with Valarie in her parents' kitchen. Valarie looked out the window toward Gary Thompson's house across the street and mused out loud with bitterness and pain about what he might be up to.

Ryan, who was in charge of his mother's care and finances when she got out of Cirque Lodge, had used up the last of her money to pay for her treatment. When she got out, she was more or less indigent. John stepped up to cover her expenses.

"She had a little budget, and we'd let her go out and shop," said Ryan. But they watched her closely. The stakes were too high to make errors. "It was like she was in prison," Ryan said. "I hate to say that, but it was."

But the dreams Valarie had at the start of her detox—to strengthen her body and rededicate herself to the family—were not to be. Her worsening MS prevented her from exercising, and her ability to "stick to it" was not what it had been when she was a girl. Moreover, her furies had, over the decades, worn out her family, and the three surviving children were trying to find their own ways away from the chaos and the grief.

Annie said, "With her, it never really felt like it was a give-and-take kind of relationship, but it was as close as it could be. I knew she loved me. And that's what mattered." Annie was the child who received the most time with Valarie before her breakdown—six years. Ryan only got three, and Erin barely a year. Brooke got none. Annie felt she benefited enormously from the emotional closeness she had with her mother in those early years, though her brain injury had wiped out all of her specific memories. "It's all in there," she explained, meaning the emotional benefit of her mother's early attention. "The retrieval just doesn't happen," she said.

Annie did remember stories people told her about her mother. A friend named Melinda, she said, "remembered my mama being very vivacious and loving and kind, and she also remembered my mom picking me up every day from school in the car, and she wished her mom would do that with her." So she incorporated those memories into her own.

Brooke was the child least able to create distance with her mother. She resembled Valarie physically—beautiful and willowy with dark hair—but made some attempts to look different from her mother. She bleached her hair blonde, for example.

During an interview for this book, her fingernails were carefully manicured, just as Valarie's had been in old family photographs and videos. "We have the same hands," she said. She usually chose light colors of polish, she explained, but that day, in her house in Park City, she had chosen red, her mother's favorite. "I am proud to look like my mom," she later wrote. "I wish I looked more like her. My hair has been most colors of the rainbow, and blonde just happens to be my favorite. If anything, I gravitate towards things she did and emulate her at times."

Brooke held onto many fond memories of Valarie. In Hyrum, she remembered bouncing on the couch as the whole family danced and sang along to Neil Diamond's "America." "It was so nerdy '80s Republican," she joked. In Omaha, Valarie arranged for Brooke and a few friends to sing at an event featuring the pop star Kim Carnes, and Valarie overdressed her relative to the other kids in what seemed to Brooke to be a ball gown.

In a long letter to me, Brooke recalled that "the majority of [her] memories of [Valarie] were actually very sweet and loving, or quirky and funny." Brooke explained:

> *She was very silly at times. She used to stick her head out the front door on Christmas and yell, "Merry Chris-Moose!" My siblings and I*

have no idea why to this day. My mom made Christmas really special overall. I remember in Omaha the decorations galore, the must-have Christmas stuffed bears, silk tartan pajamas, and pink curlers in our hair. She knew how to make it really magic for us. She used to make us wear those pink foam curlers on Saturday nights for those Sunday morning curls. We had to sleep in them. I don't know how you get a four-year-old to sleep in curlers, but she did.

Valarie was also widely known for her imitation of a gorilla. "It was impressive," wrote Brooke. "And it made everyone cry with laughter."

Valarie "prided herself on looking perfect," Brooke wrote. "She had the best hair stylists, makeup, and someone to do her nails. She drove her little red Mercedes, which may have been reserved for herself, like for shopping, as I don't remember riding in it very often."

But there was an odd and terrifying reality about their life in Omaha that collided with their otherwise gilded life there. Although they lived in a grand house with both a basketball court and a hot tub in the basement, "there was an insane amount of crime in Omaha, even in our gated neighborhood," Brooke wrote. Valarie had indoctrinated her kids early in their lives about "how to stay safe." Brooke explained, "She told us these things over and over so that we knew we didn't need to keep secrets from her if something bad happened." But one day, while Ryan and Erin were playing together outside the community gates, "a man in a car pulled up to my brother and sister and told them he had candy for them if they got in the car." Brooke, who was watching safely from inside the gate, watched them as they "ran away screaming." And even though she didn't know why they were running, she followed. That was the end of their playing outside the community gates.

"The sheer amount of crime we experienced must have been triggering for my mom," said Brooke. "Our car was stolen more than once, right out of the garage. A man staked out our house, and eventually got in after watching us for days. He did this a number of times. He was eventually arrested and told the police my mom once came home when he was inside, and he played cat and mouse with her to see how long he could follow her without her knowing." Brooke added, "These things would freak anyone out, but she was fresh out of Menninger's."

"My mom did run us around a bit in Omaha," recalled Brooke. "It wasn't just grandparents or nannies. I remember her picking us up from school and picking us up from gymnastics. My mom said she saw me land a trick when I was four and then do a pretty exuberant victory dance. That was a story she always told me."

And yet Brooke's earliest memory was of being lifted from a floor covered by broken glass and placed on a countertop in the family's kitchen. It wasn't until she was much older that she learned this was an accurate recollection of the day Valarie flew into a rage in Hyrum, broke everything she could lay hands on, and then passed out after Uncle Don and Aunt Mardel appeared at her door.

Brooke was only three and a half years old when her mother went away for a year to the Menninger Clinic—a tough time to lose a mother. When it was time for Valarie to return to the hospital after a weekend visit home, Brooke reacted by kicking and screaming, "and my grandma would have to bear hug me to get me to calm down," she recalled.

Later, when she was a preteen, Brooke would reverse roles and lie in bed with her mother, "talking her out of suicide." Worried about her mother's well-being when she was at school, she left little notes around the house for Valarie to find. They were, as Brooke told me, "little 'I love you' notes, letting her to know that we did love her and that she didn't need to die." She added:

> I also began sleeping on the couch downstairs. I slept on that couch for a year. If I slept there, I could hear my mother if she tried to leave in the middle of the night and hurt herself. The front door, garage door, and patio doors were all within ear shot of that couch.

I was 10, and I thought I had to do everything in my power to keep her alive.

When I started sleeping in my room again a year later, I would sleepwalk back down to the couch. I woke up several times laying or even sitting up on the couch. I apparently even had conversations with my stepdad, but he knew I was sleepwalking and not to wake me. Despite everything, I was fiercely bonded with my mom as a child. I remember thinking I would absolutely lay down and die if anything ever happened to her. She had her rages, but it was like Jekyll and Hyde. She was tender, super loving, and sweet at times, which is what resonated with me as a child.

Valarie told Brooke "she wished [Brooke] was her mom," from whom she had not received such tender, focused care. "I was her emotional keeper for so long," Brooke said.

This, of course, was a terrible job for her to have, but the wider family and community were at a loss. "My mom's friends, people at church, and family members would say, 'You know, your mom's gonna die, right?'" recalled Brooke. The children, showing their toughness and bravado, would always answer that they knew. Brooke added, "So I always anticipated that my mom was gonna die young. I think they were trying to soften the blow, but it was so terrifying."

Stepbrother Alex said Ryan and Erin "had a very similar way of dealing with their mom, which was to push back." Brooke, however, "took it on." In the mid-2000s, when Brooke was in her early 20s, Valarie lived in a small apartment on Vine Street in downtown Salt Lake City. It was, Brooke recalled, "dark, dingy . . . about the most depressing place she could possibly have been." Broke though she was, Brooke bought Valarie meals from the nearby mall food court, attempting to "bring her some cheer."

Eventually, of course, Brooke needed to separate, too, for her own survival. "At some point I had to almost cut ties with my mom. Not completely, but . . . yeah, I failed her too." She added, "We all got pretty bitter . . . and then we all realized that it wasn't [her fault], she couldn't help it. She was so mentally ill."

After the beneficial therapy Valarie had received under the care of Dr. Brown at the Menninger Clinic, Brooke didn't "think she ever got the kind of help she needed." Brooke wondered if there was really anything that could have helped her long term. Every time she got a new doctor, she had to retell the story of her abuse and degradation, which sent her into another downward spiral. She hated doing it, and with all the family demands placed on her, therapy was easy to give up. And there was always something that allowed her bad memories to pass into oblivion: drugs.

For a short while, Gary Martin had been Brooke's savior. "Gary was amazing with me and Erin," she said. "He took care of us like a mom. He did everything."

After he left, there was a short time when Annie picked up the slack. "I was the only child that was really willing to have her in their life," she said. She didn't try to jump into action to try to fix Valarie's problems; she just let her talk. One day when Valarie complained she was lonely, Annie suggested Valarie could move in with her and her husband, Joe. When horrified family members overheard this conversation and told her not to suggest such a thing, Annie shushed them. She knew Valarie wouldn't act on the suggestion.

"All she had left were her dreams," said Annie. "And I just let her dream."

———

Even after Valarie's long rehab, Ryan remembered that, every once in a while, they'd catch her buying sleeping pills and they'd take them away from her. Once her MS had become chronic and she needed two people to help her transfer in and out of her wheelchair, John and Ryan moved her to a public nursing home. Valarie, then about 50, complained about the food and the care and was moved a couple of times to different places, but none were to her liking. She had little real choice because she had no money.

Sue Saunders brought vitamins and protein shakes to Valarie at one facility. "I think Valarie felt desperate to get out of that bed and to change her life," said Sue, who rejected the term *manipulative* that so many people in Cache Valley used to describe Valarie. "*Manipulation* is such a negative word," said Sue. "I never felt manipulated by her."

She said any sane person would do whatever she could do to try to get out of a situation like that. "You're lying there and you can't do anything," said Sue. "You have no control over anything. It makes you feel like pounding down the wall, right? I think any one of us would feel like trying to get people to help do things a little differently."

Sue said that Valarie remained "determined to get better, [and] to beat this MS." But she knew very well that Valarie's life-long fate had been that "everything worked against her, one thing after another."

"If you had met her, you would have felt this lovely warmth and caring," she added. "She didn't focus on herself. She was my example of how a person should be if they want to truly be Christlike. I kept telling her, 'I want to be like you when I grow up.'"

Valarie still maintained the dream of writing a book about what had happened to her to help other women and girls who were victims of abuse. But writing was hard, and concentrating was hard, and Valarie no longer had much confidence in herself. Sue remembered her throwing a laptop in frustration against the wall of her nursing home room.

Denzel and Shirleen didn't make it down to Salt Lake much to visit. Debbie tried as much as she could. There were questions about her care. Valarie fought with the nurses. Once they left her overnight in her wheelchair.

Valarie battled urinary tract infections her whole life. Being restricted to a wheelchair didn't help matters. In the summer of 2016, when she was 61, Valarie lay near death in the nursing home from sepsis caused by a urinary tract infection, a clear indication of neglectful care. John remembered visiting her with Ryan. Overwhelmed with sadness, he asked if he could have a few moments alone with her. He sat beside her, holding her hand and talking to her about his feelings and regrets, and then he leaned over, pulled her into his arms, and embraced her.

She miraculously rallied. She cherished the flower arrangement John sent for her birthday that year on October 15, and told Sue that she knew they would always be together.

"I never stopped loving her," John said. "But I gave up on her," he added sadly.

But still, even though she was unhappy with her living arrangements, and surrounded by old people with whom she had little in common, John and Ryan didn't move Valarie out of the third-rate nursing home. Brooke remembered there was a moment when John's trusted assistant, Teri, was looking for a condo where Valarie could be cared for by a private nurse. But the plan mysteriously fizzled. One year after the bout with sepsis that almost killed her, Valarie contracted another urinary tract infection. She did not recover.

As she lay gravely ill, the children beside her, Ryan remembered the shattering memory of his mother apologizing to her children, saying over and over, "I love you. I love you. I'm sorry. I'm sorry."

On July 7, 2017, at age 62, the infection raging out of control, Valarie passed away.

The hospital staff placed her effects in a single plastic bag. It contained Valarie's Mormon religious undergarments, a teddy bear, and a red Minnie Mouse nightgown—artifacts of a faith somehow maintained and of childhood innocence destroyed. "That Minnie Mouse nightie breaks my heart and haunts me," Brooke said.

Over her bed had hung a photo of a happier time: a light-dappled black-and-white photo of 16-year-old Valarie with a deep tan and wide smile, dressed in a white-lace shirt and hip-hugger jeans, standing beside her beloved horse, Leo.

PART II

CHAPTER NINE

"Mayberry, with a Really Deep Evil Streak"

IN THE SUMMER OF 2020, Ryan Miller, then 40, gave his father a copy of *Mindhunter: Inside the FBI's Elite Serial Crime Unit*, a book about an FBI project in the 1980s to interview imprisoned serial killers in hopes of better understanding their psyches, then using the resulting knowledge to solve other cases. The book had given Ryan an idea—maybe it was time to launch a thorough investigation into what had happened to his mother and to find out all they could about the men she remembered assaulting and threatening her, the men who had, in her words, "destroyed" her life. Ryan, an intelligent and thoughtful man, was married with three children, yet his childhood and subsequent life had been colored in every conceivable way by his mother's suffering—as well as her absences, preoccupations, distractions, and fears.

When Ryan made this suggestion to his father, Valarie had been dead for three years, but her trauma had been passed on to her four children as a permanent legacy. Erin was dead. Annie, with the support of family and aides, lived happily in Salt Lake City with her husband Joe Ferrin, who had special needs himself and was the son of John's friend (the contractor Valarie struggled with to build her first home in Park City). Brooke, the youngest, was married to Thad Jacobs, a naturopathic doctor, and they lived in Park City with Brooke's daughter Ayden Miller and Thad's youngest child. His two older children were in college. Like Ryan, Brooke continued to puzzle through the mystery and madness of their mother and its multiform effects on her psyche.

John was, by this time, out of the beef-processing business after a long and successful career and had moved his fortune into a wide array of investments. He also served as Mitt Romney's campaign finance cochairman when the former Massachusetts governor sought the 2008 and 2012 Republican nominations for president of the United States. John traveled extensively with Romney during both presidential campaigns. In 2021, he was wealthy enough that he no longer needed to worry about being sued by Bob Dahle. In fact, after reading *Mindhunter*, John now relished that prospect because it offered an opportunity to launch an even wider investigation. One of John's lawyers, the courtroom virtuoso Richard D. Burbidge, told him: "I *want* Dahle to sue you. Then I can put him on the stand."

John agreed with Ryan that it was time to conduct a thorough examination of the people Valarie had named as her assailants, as well as the character of the town that allowed the assaults to go unnoticed and uncondemned. Further, he felt that the damage done to Valarie had been so grave, and the effects on his family so wide-ranging, that a written account of the events should be published as a book. His goals were manifold: to unveil the truth, restore Valarie's good name, seek justice and accountability, and explain her tragic story so family members could better understand the generational trauma affecting them all. I was hired to write that book.

When I first met Ryan, he made a heartbreaking declaration that was yet another good reason to do this investigation: "I expect to meet my mother again"—referring to the Mormon doctrine that families will be reunited in an afterlife—"and when I see her, I hope I'll be able to hold my head up."

———

When Matt Lambert, John's chief financial officer and the head of his home office, learned of John's and Ryan's interest in investigating the 50-year-old crime, he mentioned that his father was a retired federal prosecutor who specialized in cold cases. It took a little while for John to realize that Matt's father was the same Richard Lambert who had been briefly involved in the case 30 years earlier. Among his other successful prosecutions since then, Lambert assisted in the conviction of Brian David Mitchell and Wanda Barzee for the kidnapping and rape of Elizabeth Smart.

John and Ryan sat down in the fall of 2020 with Lambert and Brent Ward, a former United States Attorney for the District of Utah. After the two men retired from the US Attorney's Office, they began a law practice focused on cold cases. John explained that his family wanted to seek justice for Valarie to whatever extent was possible, and he let them know that although the events had taken place so very long ago, he had kept a detailed journal of his life in those years. It included a running account of his life with Valarie and their growing family, Valarie's health and behavior, and the recollection of her childhood abuse. John had also carefully documented his attempts to get the state to investigate Valarie's charges against Bob Dahle in the years between 1985 and 1990. Lambert accepted the job and proposed that his longtime investigator, retired FBI special agent Mike Anderson, be provided with the relevant diary entries and be dispatched to Clarkston to see what he could uncover.

Although Valarie's memories of her abuse had been clearly laid out in Dr. Brown's clinical notes, and while he believed her and established how her symptoms, terrors, and recollections all fit together like puzzle pieces, he was unable to stand up in court and swear to the veracity of her story, as he made clear in our first interview for this book. Collecting evidence had not been the goal of his treatment. It was helping Valarie first remember the experiences she had blotted out and then figure out how to live with them.

But if John wanted to pursue justice through the legal system, he needed facts. So he sent Anderson up to Cache Valley for two weeks to see if he could uncover anything that would substantiate her claims.

Nine months later, when I met Anderson in Salt Lake City, he said, "I guess John liked what we found."

———

A six-foot, five-inch, 325-pound enforcer straight out of central casting, Mike Anderson was clean cut and grave. A sad droop around his eyes suggested the toll of a career spent observing humanity at its worst. He served as a special agent in the FBI for 28 years, and for the last 10 years of his service, he worked as an examiner for the Polygraph Unit, eventually managing polygraphy matters for the bureau in Utah, Idaho, and Montana. He retired from the FBI in 2017, then started working as a private investigator.

He picked me up in Salt Lake City in a vehicle that was as conspicuous and imposing as the man driving it: a black double-cab Dodge Ram 2500 with running boards and roof lights. A vehicle, as he put it, that could be seen from space. Since his first trips to Clarkston for this investigation, he'd traveled thousands of miles and interviewed scores of people. I needed to learn what he'd found out and wanted to see firsthand the locations where the story had played out.

I climbed into the cab, and we headed to Clarkston.

Eighty-two miles up Interstate 15, Anderson turned off the highway and onto a paved country road that led east to the Short Divide, a steep, winding road that skirts up and over the southern flank of Gunsight Peak. When he reached the crest of the saddle, he pulled over. We climbed out and took in a panoramic view of Cache Valley—a picturesque expanse of green fields and patchwork agricultural plots bounded by mountains. To the east, across the valley loomed the Wasatch Mountains. On the western side of the valley below, a small settlement clung to the lower foothills.

"That's Clarkston," he said. I saw a small collection of houses, barns, grain silos, and sheds spread over a few square blocks. "It's a *tiny town*," he said. "Think Mayberry, with a really deep evil streak."

Its character was able to flourish in part because of its extreme isolation.

The shortcut we'd taken was closed much of the year for safety, Anderson told me, and Gunsight Peak thereby effectively prevented approach from the west and the state's main north-south artery, I-15. Mike pointed to a strip of green in the medium distance. "Do you see that line of cottonwoods and willows growing along the stream? They call that the Bottom, or the Bottoms. That's important. That's a place Valarie could have been taken and assaulted."

Anderson pointed to another stand of trees a bit to the east. "That's where the Newton Reservoir is, but you can't see the water from here. That's a ride of about 20 minutes from Clarkston on a horse."

We climbed back into the truck and rolled toward Clarkston, past barns, houses, farm equipment, and corrals of livestock. It was very quiet, and nobody was outside. On the southern edge of town, Anderson stopped in the middle of the road and said, "Zane's first wife was taken out there and assaulted as a young woman." He was referring to Kristine Goodey Clark, who when she was 14, woke up in a ditch here at 3 a.m., her clothes "disheveled," according to what she later told Zane, apparently "having been removed and replaced by someone who didn't know what they were doing," explained Anderson. When she woke up, "she had no idea how she had arrived in that ditch—only that she had been out earlier in the evening with Van Dell Henderson and one of his brothers, and she believed that she had been slipped some kind of a mickey that had knocked her out." Kristine later told her sister, Annette Goodey Summers, that the rapist was a different Clarkston man who was a member of Bob Dahle's entourage.

Kristine and Zane were married in 1980. They had five children. On April 7, 1995, when she was 33, Kristine placed a shotgun to her chest and pulled the trigger. Her son Taylor, who was on his way to a friend's house, heard the blast and ran back home. He had to break down the door to his mother's room; she was dead by the time he got to her. The tragedy still causes pain for Zane and his children.

Anderson continued onto 300 South, then took a 90-degree left on Main Street to drive past the houses that had been occupied by the main characters of Valarie's story. Clarkston had five streets running north and south and five east and west, basically a grid of 16 square blocks with some outlying areas of agricultural land dotted with a few houses and outbuildings. We passed a cheerful gingerbread house with narrow purple shutters decorated by a line of diamond cutouts and a red aluminum roof. During Valarie's childhood, this was the home of Kenny Balls, his wife Sarah Ann Clark, and their five children. Kenny Balls still lived there, but now with his second wife, Shirleen's sister, Venna. Right next door was the pleasant, well-kept home of Denzel and Shirleen Clark, a roomy, brown ranch house shaded by enormous box elder trees in the front yard, where Valarie, Debbie, and Zane grew up. Just to the north was a white clapboard house with a blue door where Grandma and Grandpa Thompson, Shirleen's folks, lived. Directly across the street to the west was a two-story pioneer house painted white and tan, with a peaked aluminum roof and cramped front porch with narrow white columns. This was the home of Jack Thompson, the bonesetter, then of his son, Earl, husband of Denzel's Aunt Annie. Earl and Annie's son, Gary Thompson, died in 2019, and his widow, Nancy, still lives there. Behind this house was the barn in which Valarie said Thompson and Bob Dahle raped her for the first time.

Anderson drove north a block, and we passed a red-brick church. "I'll bet you this town is ninety-eight percent Mormon," said Anderson, who grew up in another small Mormon town in Utah. When Valarie was a child here, there was an elementary school next to the church that served about 50 students. (Valarie's was an unusually large class of 16—eight girls and eight boys. Her sister, Debbie, in contrast, had only three girls in her class.) The school was pulled down after it was damaged by an earthquake, and the Clarkston children were bussed to Lewiston, near the Idaho border. The site was now filled with ball fields and a playground.

"Right here is Burke Godfrey's place," said Anderson, pointing across the street from the church. Annette Clark, Zane's second wife, told Anderson they once lived next door to Burke and Alene Godfrey. According to

Annette, since Burke Godfrey "would drive around town in his car and attempt to run over children" when drunk, she "gave her children very specific instructions to get out of the street anytime they saw Godfrey coming down the road in a vehicle." When he died in 2012, Godfrey's obituary euphemistically celebrated his habit of "playing practical jokes on anyone he encountered."[1]

The large lot behind the house had a handful of grain silos and some sheds. "Burke owned 8,000 acres of land going all the way up into Idaho," said Anderson. At various times, he said, Godfrey employed a few of the town's men—including Bob Dahle, Gary Thompson, Lloyd Clark, and another local man named Ross Buttars—to help him gather his grain. When they were done with the work, they'd sit in a shed behind his house and drink. "I got a lot of stories I got to tell you about this town," Anderson said. "You can't buy a beer at full-strength [here]. All that's available is 3.2 beer. You're not supposed to even drink coffee in Mormon culture. But everybody knew these guys would drink together." In fact, both Godfrey and his son LaMont were considered by the townsfolk to be alcoholics. But they wouldn't say it to a stranger. "He liked to drink a little bit," was the expression one heard. Many of the men headed north to Idaho to drink, where the beer had a higher alcohol content, liquor was served in the bars, and they liked to imagine no one would see them.

Jann Pugmire said there were numerous places where people gathered in Clarkston to drink. Zane told Anderson he once saw Burke Godfrey drinking with Bob Dahle in Dahle's truck, then again in a metal shed behind Dahle's old home. He said they also drank in the gravel pit.

Anderson continued driving north along Main Street. On the next block, at the corner of Center and Main, was the firehouse. Valarie's cousin Dwight Pearce lived on the west corner; Lloyd and Ralph Clark grew up in their mother's tiny, gray-and-white painted brick house across the street. After another three blocks north, we passed the area that once held the corral where Valarie's horse, Leo, was kept, behind an old white house previously owned by Valarie's paternal grandparents—Denzel's folks—which looked like it had fallen on hard times. Debbie Clark Cooper lived in a sunny new house that she and her husband Dan Cooper built, facing south, across the street from her grandparents' old place.

Anderson turned around and drove back along Main, again past the firehouse, the ball fields, and the church. At the Clarks' home, he turned west and pulled up behind the Thompson house that was across the street. Anderson got out of the truck, and I followed him. I kicked at some stones and pieces of cinder blocks in the dirt by the road. He pointed to the yard. "Denzel told me this is where the barn was." The sun was high, and it was hot, much like it would have been that late summer day in 1968 when Valarie was first raped here. Anderson pointed a block to the west, where Bob Dahle lived. The barn couldn't have been more convenient to these men—directly behind Thompson's house, a three-minute walk from Dahle's house, with Lloyd Clark two blocks north.

I looked over toward Denzel and Shirleen's house across the street. "These guys decide they're going to rape a little girl right across the street from her own house?" I asked. "Who does that?"

"Who does that?" he repeated, straightening his huge frame. "People in Clarkston."

I couldn't help imagining 13-year-old Valarie stumbling out of that barn and across the street after the attack. Her most important job, she knew instinctively, was to hide any trace of what had happened—from her parents and everybody else. I could see her pulling on her clothes, straightening everything as well as she could, maybe checking for hay in her hair, then hurrying across the street and through the side door of her home, slipping into the bathroom and locking the door before bursting into tears. Or maybe she had run over to her horse, Leo, to grieve in his reassuring presence.

"They took something from her," said Anderson. "Something precious."

Lynette Spackman, who lived for 40 years as a roommate in Logan with

Valarie's friend, neighbor, and cousin Shauna Balls, told me in an interview, "Sad as it is to say, back then, people didn't believe too much in rape. I mean, they did, but you know—the girl brought it on herself."

That was the unmistakable message one got growing up in Clarkston, from the whispered gossip in church, from the Young Women's classes, which girls between 12 and 18 years old attended once a week, from breathing the very air.

My thoughts then turned to the other unthinkable fact in this story: Gary Thompson's abuse of four-year-old Valarie in this very house across the street from her own and on family camping trips to Dry Canyon. I knew that Valarie had been a very small child—Debbie said their aunt Lorraine called her "Tiny," and at 13, she wrote a story about her life in which she said, "I remember being smaller than all the other children my age." This may have made her a target of the pedophile Thompsons.

I said to Anderson, "When another person—an adult, a relative—puts his fingers inside a little girl's body from a young age, how can she possibly develop a true self? She can't even know what is 'me' and 'not-me'?"

"Almost impossible," he replied. "She had no ownership of herself, of her own life."

In "My Story," Valarie had gone on to write that "Since the seventh grade I have grown by leaps and bounds. At the present time I am about 5' 5" and I weigh about 115." Perhaps this growth spurt had also caught the prurient attention of certain men in town such as Dahle and Thompson. Its timing accords with Anderson and Lambert's belief that the attack on Valarie in the barn had taken place when she was 13 going on 14, in the summer before eighth grade—1968.

"Also," I asked Anderson, "what about those blows from Dahle to Valarie's head? Who knows what that did to her health?" Valarie had reported that Dahle liked to beat her after sex but always hit her in places, like her head or torso, where the bruises and marks couldn't be seen.

"The human body is an intensely fragile thing," said Anderson.

Indeed, I later found research that suggested head injury might play a role in the development of MS. "Those who had suffered a single concussion between the ages of 10 and 20 had a 22% higher rate of MS than those who had never had a concussion," declared one study. "The rate of MS more than doubled for those who had experienced more than one concussion."[2]

We got back in the truck, and Anderson continued one block west to the house where Bob Dahle had grown up and then, during Valarie's childhood, where he'd lived with his wife Ollie Lou and their children. The house was a large, gray structure on a corner lot, with a peaked roof and an attached garage. A large wishing well stood out front. Dahle was known for his custom-made wishing wells. Dahle and Ollie Lou's last child, Diana, was born exactly one year after Valarie's rape in the barn—10 years after her nearest sibling. Perhaps this was a wish come true. Or maybe the rape had set Dahle's sexual desire on fire. Or perhaps Ollie Lou, sensing her husband's preoccupation, did what she could to regain his conjugal attentions. In any case, a child was born.

Anderson continued west to the hilly gravel pit, crisscrossed with tracks cut by motorcycles and ATVs. One can see where gravel has been dug up, the surface smoothed over, and grass planted to keep the dust down. "You get a girl down there, or even up here, by herself," he said, "and they might hear her screaming." He pointed to the lower reaches of the pit. "But from down there, no."

Anderson continued on a dirt track to an area of undulating grassland that neighbors call the washboards. "I'm bringing you to this little canyon because Valarie's brother, Zane, brought me here," he said. "As a young man, Zane zipped all around this area on a bicycle and, later, a motorcycle. So, he's zipping around one day, and he comes up over the mountains that way and drops down at this little wash I'm about to show you. And he sees a trailer sitting there."

This trailer, Anderson explained, had been set up by Van Dell Henderson.

The Hendersons were cousins of the Clarks. Zane was about 16 or 17 when he first saw the trailer, and there were several men there, including Gary Thompson and Van Dell Henderson. "And this ground was owned at the time by Burke Godfrey," Anderson said. "See how we're getting all these little tentacles connecting here?"

He parked the truck, and we got out. As soon as my feet hit the grass, I noticed how quiet it was out there. Dead quiet. "I have a loud voice," said Anderson, yelling at the top of his lungs. There was no echo, no bounce.

"Nobody could hear a girl screaming here," I said. He nodded.

He said Zane told him that he saw a local girl named Diane at the trailer one day with some men and wondered if she'd been victimized. Anderson tried to find her, but the trail went cold. Zane said he went into the trailer once when no one was there, and judging by the contents, assumed it was used for eating lunch, drinking, and playing cards. There was also a collection of pornographic magazines.

"In Mormondom," said Anderson, "pornography is sorely frowned upon."

This appeared to be a badly kept commandment, as pornography was omnipresent in Clarkston. Everyone seemed to have a story about it. A month after my trip with Anderson, I drove through town with Ryan Miller, and he told me that when he was a child, he'd been shown a stash of porn under a board in a thicket near the washboards by a neighborhood boy, who also played him pornographic movies at home. Zane's best friend, Mike Dahle, showed him a magazine he'd found in his father Bob Dahle's truck that was so filthy he still remembered every page he saw.

———

Commandment-breaking in Clarkston was not limited to drinking alcohol, coffee, and looking at pornography. Jann Pugmire was raped by her relative, "L," when she was 13 and he was 15. The circumstances reveal a pattern familiar to many a local young girl. Jann said:

We were making out. At first, I was a willing participant, but when he undid my pants and pulled them down, I got scared. I told him I didn't want to. We were in an old, abandoned house. It had an old wire box spring that we were on. He just kept trying to kiss me, and I was trying to get it all to stop. Then it was like I was watching it all happening. He held me down and raped me. I remember how much it hurt, his weight on my body, his heavy breathing, his sweat and the smell after he was done. He didn't hit me. He didn't have anything to threaten me with. He just did it. It didn't take him long. But when it was over, I just pulled up my pants and followed him to his truck. He took me to my house and that was that.

She lived a couple blocks away.

After the rape, she continued to hang around with L. She said she didn't know any better. "I thought he liked me," he said. When she told the bishop what had happened to her, he told her it was her own fault. Decades later, after marriage and children, she's still angry about it. "I hate how girls get a reputation, while the boys get envied and praised when they have sex." Once, she was so upset seeing L at a family event that her husband was compelled to calm her down before she made a scene.

Mike Anderson continued along the dusty track leading north from the grassy canyon up toward Idaho. "I don't know how much you know about Mormonism," he said, "but it totally revolves around family." Mormons believe families are rejoined in an eternal afterlife, and the lessons get "pretty ingrained. Valarie was taught that family is everything. Family will protect you. And you've got to protect your family," he said.

"Let me put it to you this way," he continued. "There are the Thompsons, the Goodeys, the Godfreys, the Clarks—the big four names out here—and they all know each other. Not only are they family, there's a thing called a church ward, the people you go to church with, and the people you socialize with. These are the people you have potluck dinners with. These are the families that your kids play with."

Anderson seemed to be telling me that the town was full of relatives whose obligation was to protect and defend each other. That meant people would be disinclined to see bad behavior—even if it was staring them straight in the face—if it involved a relative. There was self-interest involved, of course: The bad behavior of a relative, were it known, might reflect badly on one's own reputation. And acknowledging the bad behavior of neighbors appeared to violate the unspoken bonds of cooperation in the village.

Silence and secrecy were the currency in Clarkston. But who protected the weak? Who defended the victims?

"Valarie remembered Earl Thompson telling Gary, when he himself was molesting Valarie, 'That's how you do it son, you don't do it to your own children, but the neighbors' kids," I told Anderson. "Also, Valarie remembered Earl saying something to the effect that women's purpose is to provide sexual satisfaction to men. Is that what Mormons believe?"

"That's complete bullshit," he said angrily. "That is Mormonism twisted on its head into an ugly, obscene thing."

"That's not something that's taught?"

"Good God, no."

And what about the idea that "once defiled, you'll always be defiled"? Lessons to girls that if they had sex before marriage, they'd never find a husband? I asked.

"I'm not aware of anybody that told her she was defiled," he said. "But I have no doubt that she felt that way. So much of this, it's just twisted and wrong. Those are not principles taught or espoused by the church that she grew up in."

Angie Curtis, the local hairdresser who grew up in Clarkston, begged to differ. She later told me, "For the girls, it's sickening. You're taught that if you choose to do those things [have sex], you're a licked cupcake, and who's going to want a licked cupcake?" Like Elizabeth Smart, she recalled a lesson for her ward's young women: "The teacher chewed a piece of gum and then put it on her hand and asked any of us if we wanted it. And we're like, 'No, we don't want your chewed piece of gum!' And she's like, 'Well, that's how people are gonna perceive you if you are unchaste.'"

Although both Mormon girls and boys were expected to arrive at the wedding altar as virgins, responsibility for abstinence fell on the girls. "If you're a girl," said Angie, "you're told, 'If you dress immodestly, you're [encouraging] the boys.' They make it sound as if the boys have no self-control. It's all on the girls." Angie said she couldn't bring herself to wear sleeveless shirts for three years after she left the church because "if you show your shoulders, that's pornography."

—

Mike Anderson continued our drive northwest to Idaho, up a sandy road toward Steel Canyon. Clouds of dust swirled behind the truck as we passed Angus cattle munching grass as high as their bellies. We were minutes from the Utah border with Idaho when he stopped the truck on a hill. West of the dirt track, the ground dropped down a steep hillside to a grassy vale. We climbed down the bank and heard a loud trickle of water. "There's a pipe out there that the water comes out of," he said. "That's a pretty nice little flow of water. The cows are sitting there because there's water." He pointed to a sun-splashed flat area. "This is where Ricks Cabin stood."

We climbed down the slope past a couple of discarded bench seats from a truck, rotted down to the metal springs. There was also an old stove and a mattress spring. We saw a few boards, an old recliner, and some rusted Schlitz cans. "When you're out of Schiltz, you're out of beer," he said.

Anderson explained that Denzel, with whom he drove up here the previous fall, told him the cabin used to be owned by the Ricks family. So Anderson tracked down Darrell Ricks, then in his 80s, who owned an appliance store in Benson, Utah. Ricks confirmed that his family once owned a "very livable cabin" near Steel Canyon that had "no air conditioning or that kind of stuff but was a comfortable place for them to come into the mountains" to hunt deer. Ricks remembered the cabin had a kitchen and a couple of bedrooms. He figured the structure was likely built in the early 1900s and said it was never locked. He told Anderson the family sold the land to Young Livestock in the 1990s, and his wife told Anderson she is "certain" the cabin was still there in 1975, and even remembered it standing several years ago. She thought it "curious" that there were no remnants of the cabin or signs of a fire that might explain its disappearance.

Anderson drove a couple minutes farther up the dirt track until we were over the Idaho border. He parked at the bottom of a grassy knoll, to the northeast, and told me that another cabin once stood in that spot, a primitive shelter for hunters if they got caught in a snowstorm. He said he walked the length and width of the area and could find no sign of the structure, though Denzel had told him it existed. "This could be a key right here," he said. "If we had proof that Valarie was taken over the state line, it's possible we could find a means to bring federal charges of rape."

But so far, no one had said anything to him about Valarie being taken to that cabin. Before he turned the truck around to head back to town, I took a mental picture of the place. If Dahle took her to the cabin in Steel Canyon, why not head north a couple minutes to this sun-drenched rise? Being able to charge the one surviving suspect with a crime was a tantalizing goal.

There was one more place Anderson wanted to show me before leaving the area: the Clarkston cemetery. Out of the canyon and back toward Clarkston, the expansive and well-tended graveyard featured an outdoor amphitheater built by the town under Denzel's authority as mayor to accommodate the Martin Harris pageants that Denzel founded in 1983. A sign at the entrance of the cemetery explained that Harris, who was buried there, testified that "a heavenly messenger showed them the Plates of gold and the engravings thereon from which Joseph Smith translated the book." Harris later mortgaged part of his farm for $3,000 and used the money to pay for the printing of the first edition of the Book of Mormon.

He led me past headstones, whose names and dates tracked the history of the town, and stopped in front of one. On the top, taking up one-third of the surface, was "Dahle" in shadowed capital letters. Directly below that was an engraved picture of the Logan Temple, with Bob and Ollie Lou Dahle's marriage date engraved in the ribbon curled below it. On the left was "Ollie Lou Anderson" and her date of birth. On the right was "Robert Norman Dahle" and his date of birth. The headstone also included, on Bob's side, three engraved images: a beehive (the Utah state symbol), the words "Utah Highway Patrol," and a man fishing. On Ollie Lou's side, there was a flower, a hummingbird, a cookie, and a cookie jar. There were no dates of death.

I had never heard of anyone setting up their own headstones while still alive. "Do you think they're afraid the kids won't do it for them?" I asked Anderson. He shrugged.

"There's a part of the story you're not aware of," he then offered. "Dahle had a daughter that died." He walked me a few steps over to a nearby grave. The name Dahle was again engraved in large block letters on the top of the stone. Below that was a black outline, like a tree branch, of Gunsight Mountain. Nestled beneath that was an oval color photo of a young girl and the name Diana in script, and below that, "Nana."

"Beautiful girl," said Anderson, looking at the photo.

Carvings of cats and dogs decorated the corners of the stone, as well as the dates of her birth, August 15, 1969, and death, July 1, 2007.

I checked on my phone and found her obituary in the local paper. It read in part: "She had a great love for animals, especially cats and dogs. She was always nursing injured or abandoned ones back to health. She was a kind, loving, compassionate person who was a friend to the friendless and a guiding light to those who live in darkness."[3]

"I don't know what killed her," said Anderson. "Jann Pugmire said that she got the holy shit kicked out of her by him."

"By her dad?"

He nodded. "I'd like to know the story behind *her*. What it was that killed *her*."

CHAPTER TEN

"The Big-Eared Bastard"

TWENTY MILES NORTHEAST of Steel Canyon, Bob Dahle's father, Reed, was shot dead in a bar in Weston, Idaho, in 1954 by the owner. Reed was only 39, and his death shocked the family and forced Dahle, then 18, to work while finishing high school to help support his mother and two sisters.

On the day he died, Reed delivered milk to nearby Wellsville, Utah, for his employer, the Morning Milk Company, then drove with his Clarkston friend Arnold Rasmussen the 25 miles west to Tremonton, where they bought and drank some whiskey. They then drove to Idaho and found their way to Weston Billiards, where they met up with Farrell Lloyd "Fud" Goodey and Delon Leland Archibald. The men sang and drank beer and played snooker. The owner, William Baker, testified that, late that night, he walked to the back of the bar, where the pool tables were, and asked the men to finish up because it was nearing closing time. There was no argument, but Goodey testified that Rasmussen swung a pool cue at Dahle, accidentally hitting Baker in the face and drawing blood.

Baker's wife, Veda, testified at her husband's subsequent murder trial that Goodey and Archibald left immediately, but Rasmussen and Dahle took their time departing, even though they had been responsible for Baker's injury. As Veda tended to her husband, she saw Dahle re-enter the bar a few minutes later. She asked him to leave, emphasizing that her husband was hurt. William Baker testified that "Dahle was mad about something—I could tell by his voice and his actions." His fists were raised, and he repeatedly said he "wanted to call the cops and get this thing settled" as he slowly inched his way down the bar toward Baker, who twice asked Dahle to leave. "I was scared and frightened and thought Dahle had come back for trouble," he said. As Dahle continued to edge toward him, Baker picked up a .32 Colt pistol from behind the cash register and pointed it at Dahle. Veda Baker heard her husband tell Dahle one more time to leave, and when Dahle did not stop, Baker shot him in the chest, killing him instantly.

Baker was charged with second-degree murder. On January 23, 1954, the jury announced its decision: "voluntary manslaughter in the heat of passion." The Franklin County courtroom in Preston, Idaho, was "jammed to capacity with spectators" according to the *Herald Journal*.[1] Four days later, Baker was sentenced to nine months in jail.

After Reed Dahle was shot dead at Weston Billiards, family members claimed that he had gone back into the bar "to apologize." Nobody at the trial suggested that was true, and both Baker and his wife testified that Reed was aggressive and angry.

Reed Dahle was an alcoholic, said Helen Godfrey, now Helen Godfrey Cooper, and had a violent temper. Denzel confirmed this: "I've been told by the individuals who knew him at the time that he got extremely angry when he drank too much." Denzel remembered that as a 12-year-old, he bumped into a stranger in town one day and asked the man where he was going. Strangers were a rarity in tiny Clarkston and immediately noticeable. The man said, "I'm going to Reed Dahle's, and I'm going to beat the hell out of him. I was drunk last night, and he beat me up. Now I'm sober, and I'm going to repay the debt."

Shirleen remembered Reed Dahle's wife, June, appearing several times at church with black eyes. "His wife was just a thin, mild lady," said Denzel. "I don't know how you'd get mad at her about anything."

Robert Norman Dahle, Reed and June's first child, was born on March 11, 1937, six and a half months after his parents' wedding. It's not hard to imagine that an angry man and a drunk who beat his wife might also beat his son who had been conceived outside of wedlock.

Bob Dahle was often described as "mean," "ornery," and "creepy." About six feet tall, with ears that pointed out from his head at a 45-degree angle, he was snaggletoothed and slightly walleyed, so that when you were talking to him, he couldn't keep both eyes on you. His nickname was "the big-eared bastard," according to Don Anderson, a trucker and farmer in Clarkston. His colleagues in the Highway Patrol knew he was sensitive about his protruding ears, and they knew him to be a moody man. "What they'd say about Bob is that it's his time of the month," said Don.

Bob Dahle grew up in Clarkston, attended elementary school there, and graduated from North Cache High School, the predecessor to Sky View High School. He met Ollie Lou Anderson at a basketball game at Utah State University and married her in 1955. He was 18, and she had just turned 19, and they moved into Dahle's childhood home at 181 South 100 West, one block from his friend Gary Thompson. Mike Anderson found a photo in the *Herald Journal* archives that attested to the camaraderie between the two men. In the photo, they stood behind a pickup on either side of a dead elk they had brought down together in 1965, its head resting on the tailgate, each man gripping one horn. Dahle looked surprised and irked, the fleshy-faced Thompson, self-satisfied.

Dahle held a variety of unskilled jobs that reflected the changing fortunes of Cache Valley. His first job was at the Garland sugar factory, where he processed beets. Later, he worked as a fireman for the Union Pacific Railroad, then repaired engines at the railroad roundhouse in Ogden. He also worked at Thiokol Chemical Company as an engineering aide. A steady employer of Clarkston residents, Thiokol became infamous when the catastrophic failure of the O-rings on its solid rocket boosters were held responsible for the 1986 explosion of the space shuttle *Challenger*.

Perhaps because of his domineering personality, Dahle was selected to serve as Clarkston's town marshal from 1962 to 1964. Having enjoyed the job, he decided to continue a career in law enforcement and graduated from the Utah Highway Patrol Academy on April 28, 1967, when he was 30. At about the same time, Gary Thompson quit the job he'd held for eight years at Thiokol, where he'd worked in the same department as Denzel, testing the fuel used as a propellant for Minuteman missiles. "He had an excellent job at the lab I worked [in] at Thiokol . . . . I don't know why he ever quit," said Denzel, adding that Thompson didn't have enough farmland to support his family.

Zane also dated the first rape to the summer of 1968, when Valarie was 13 years old. Dahle and Thompson were both then in Clarkston, and at least one of them, Thompson, was unemployed and had time on his hands. Dahle was at the start of an 18-year stint as a Highway Patrol officer in Cache County, where he enjoyed status, power, and freedom; there were only six troopers at the time to cover the entire valley.

One day the following summer, Zane headed up to Steel Canyon, about five miles from Clarkston, where he and his buddies liked to ride their bikes up and down along the creek and jump over it. That day, he told me in June 2023, he saw his sister riding horses with a group of Clarkston men, including the Highway Patrol officer Bob Dahle and his friend Gary Thompson. He was eight years old, and his sister was 14.

"I called her down off the mountain. I waved my hand, and I said, 'Valarie, come here. I need to speak to you.' And she rode down, and I said, 'Valarie, what are you doing with all these old guys?' I says, 'You don't wanna ride around with them. You want to be with young kids your age.'" But she waved him off saying, "They can teach me about horses and show me more things."

Zane told me that after she rode off, he followed her farther up the canyon, over the boundary into Idaho, to the area where Mike Anderson and I had stood on a sunny hill, looking for signs of the old cabin.

"And they rode over to a cabin that is not there anymore," said Zane. "It was dilapidated. It was starting to fall down, and, uh, they all went in that cabin with her."

I asked how he knew that, and he said, "I could see with my eyes."

"There'd only be one or two of them in there with her," he said, "and then they'd come out and somebody else would go in." He was too young to understand the meaning of this activity. She returned home that night and said nothing, but he remembered seeing bruises on her torso after that. When he asked her what they were from, she answered vaguely. He also was suspicious when she explained that she had broken a rib because Leo pressed her against a fence. But the way she answered didn't seem to invite further inquiry, so he let it go.

Valarie wasn't the only member of the Clark family that Bob Dahle selected for abuse. For four years, Dahle served as Zane Clark's Scoutmaster. Because of the repeated operations to break and reset the bones of his feet and ankles, Zane had trouble physically keeping up with his peers. For reasons Zane could never understand, Dahle "constantly belittled him and frequently referred to him as 'gimp.'" Once, the Boy Scouts hiked up Gunsight Peak, elevation 8,244 feet, and Denzel, knowing how difficult and painful it would be for his son, carried Zane's backpack partway up for him—though Zane begged his father not to. Dahle was contemptuous of this act of kindness and further mocked Zane over it. Zane told Mike Anderson, "Bob Dahle didn't like me, and he didn't like my family."

One day in 1971, Dahle appeared without notice at the Clark's house with his son Mike and asked Zane, who was then 11, if he wanted to go shoot guns at Molly's Nipple, just north of the canyon through which the Bear River flows from Cache Valley into Box Elder County. Dahle said he was going to bring his .44 Magnum, with which they could stand on the cliffs in the back of Molly's Nipple and shoot down into the river. A .44

Magnum is a huge gun for a little boy, and dangerous. "I remember Valarie being on the front lawn when I left with Bob, and he had that gun," Zane recalled. "I could tell from her eyes something was wrong with her." Such a feeling of menace emanated from Dahle that Zane feared for his life for the entire trip. As they hiked over the cliffs with the gun, Zane struggling to keep up on his broken feet, he thought there was a distinct possibility that Dahle would knock him off balance, causing him to plunge to his death hundreds of feet below. Almost 20 years later, when Valarie finally told Zane about the assaults she'd suffered, Zane saw that old event on the lawn with new eyes. He realized Dahle had staged the entire episode for Valarie's benefit—showing her that he had the power to make good on his threats to hurt Zane if she didn't keep her mouth shut.

Dahle loved to threaten people and play tough cop. Dwight Pearce remembered that when Dahle was the town marshal, he would stop young people in their cars and interrogate them. "He pulled us over for no reason," said Dwight. "He'd just kind of harass us, ask us what we were doing and what we should be doing. 'And what are you guys *really* doing?' he'd ask. I mean, it was kind of weird. It was none of his business."

Dahle pulled over John Miller in the early 1970s. John remembered feeling that Dahle was "creepy." Dahle made the traffic stop for no reason and did not ticket him. John said, "I've always believed he was checking me out since I was dating Valarie at the time."

In addition to his harassment stops, Dahle didn't hesitate to ticket his own friends and acquaintances for various offenses, deserved and undeserved. A Clarkston man named Curtis Godfrey told me Dahle had stopped him for driving without his shirt on. And Dahle pulled Valarie over once when she was driving alone in the orange Ford Pinto her father got for her. She told Zane this was when she was 16 or 17, before she went off to college, and it would have corresponded with the time that Dwight Pearce remembered Valarie becoming very agitated and afraid when plans suddenly changed, requiring her to drive herself around Cache Valley.

"Bob was not a likable person," said Don Anderson. "Even before he'd become a law officer . . . and then when he got to be in the cop shop, he really became an arrogant son of a gun. Yeah, he was something else."

The combination of Dahle's pugnacious anger and a badge produced terrible results. According to Lynn Izatt, who worked as a sheriff's deputy in Cache Valley in the 1970s, Dahle was both "deceptive" and "volatile."[2] "He was supposed to be a big-time Mormon," Lynn said, scoffing. Lynn described himself as "always suspect on that shit." He'd seen Dahle smoking cigarettes at lunch with his fellow troopers, frantically stubbing his out when a ward member walked into the diner; other witnesses remember him drinking to the point of vomiting while on hunting trips. Worse, Dahle and a handful of Utah Highway Patrol officers frequented a grill inside a Logan grocery store, with waitstaff that consisted of college-age women, including, in Lynn's words, "some little gal [Dahle] was a-chunkin'."

According to Lynn, like many of his colleagues, Dahle "had a couple other little chicks on the side," an open secret in Cache Valley's small law enforcement community. What role coercion might have played in these illicit relationships is unknown, but Lynn recalled that Dahle was "very, very hotheaded." Other witnesses recalled him snapping the middle finger of a teenaged boy who dared flip him the bird. "I've seen him so God dang out of control," Lynn said, still marveling at Dahle's "friggin' hot temper" nearly half a century later.

Angie Curtis remembered a much older but still short-fused Dahle harassing her family:

> We were out driving around in the Bottoms, and there were these big elk, and my husband and I pulled off the road to show my son the elk, and a car pulled up behind us and we thought, "Oh, it's their turn; they want to see them." So we drove off. That car followed us to our house and pulled into our driveway, and Bob Dahle gets out of the car and said to my husband, "Get in my car." And my husband says, "I'm not getting in your car." And Dahle said, "Get in my car.

I used to be a highway patrolman." My husband says, "I don't give
a shit who you are, I'm not getting in your car. What do you want,
old man?"

 He said, "I was a highway patrolman, and you don't pull in
people's fields like that." And my husband said, "We had two tires a
foot and a half into the field. Get away from my property."

 So that was an encounter we had with him that just showed how,
even after he was retired after how many years . . . he still had that
cop complex.

Bob Dahle even acted aggressively toward Mike Anderson when the PI was first visiting Clarkston in the fall of 2020. Having heard about a new investigation and seeing an unfamiliar vehicle a few times in town, Dahle followed Anderson out of town in his old green-and-white pickup for about four miles, at one point pulling up close and riding his bumper—long enough, Anderson figured, to get his license number—then dropping back and turning around.

Anderson strongly suspected Dahle had used his old law enforcement connections to run the plates.

Back in the day, Dahle reserved a special kind of aggressive behavior for Denzel. His taunting may have had its roots in jealousy of Denzel's high status. The Clark family curse notwithstanding, Denzel was "on the top of the world," Ross Peterson told me, explaining, "He's as high as you get as a railroader, he's as high as he can be in the town and in the church," serving as bishop and mayor—in contrast to the failures of Dahle's father, who was shot in a bar. Dahle himself ran for mayor in the 1990s and lost and was never called to serve as a bishop.

Dahle also had disdain for Denzel, Peterson surmised, "for the niceness, the kindness, not being a real man" who would "fight to defend things" but who would rather try to "negotiate and arbitrate." Peterson had seen his share of "male harassers" in rural Mormon communities: This kind of man would "want to figure every way he can to make [Denzel's] life miserable."[3]

And so for years, he and his buddy Gary Thompson not only raped Denzel's daughter but also made crude remarks about her to Denzel's face, all of which Denzel ignored or silently excused for the sake of community harmony.

Ominously, given what we now know about abuse in the Boy Scouts of America, Dahle was the first Scout leader ever to produce an Eagle Scout for Clarkston. Curtis Godfrey told me he surmised that Dahle was chosen for the position because of his hard-nosed aggression. "I think they put him in that position for his being law enforcement and the uniform-type thing," said Curtis. And it worked. "He got the first Eagle, and a couple after that."

Dahle may have pushed some boys to become Eagle Scouts, but he was not a leader of men. According to Van Dell Henderson, Dahle was a coward. "Bob was not a fighter," he said. "Bob would make you think he's tougher than all sin, but tell you what, if you pushed back a little or he seen you wasn't going to back down, he'd run."

———

Zane Clark was an observant child. He couldn't keep up on hikes, but he got around town on his bike or motorcycle, and he noticed everything. And in adulthood, he'd already told Mike Anderson about the pornographic magazine his friend Mike Dahle found "under his dad's seat in his truck." But he told this author more: "This was not *Playboy* or *Penthouse*. It was the most obscene thing I have ever seen in my life to this day." It showed "couples in coitus. . . . It showed ejaculate on people, it showed group sex, and it was close-up photography." Mike Dahle told his buddy Zane that his father said he had "confiscated it from someone" as part of his work as a highway patrolman. Zane also remembered once seeing a beer can in the Dahle refrigerator. This was forbidden in Mormon households. When he pointed it out to Mike, his friend told him his father said it was evidence he'd taken from a perp.

But if it was evidence, why keep it cold in the fridge?

Zane knew that the Dahle children were "all terrified of their father." He saw Brad once after he was so badly beaten that he had two black eyes and bruises all over his body. "That poor kid got the hell beat out of him all the time," said Zane. "Bob would take him up to this green Quonset shed behind the house and just wail on the poor guy. I used to feel so bad for him."

Zane continued: "I know that the children were petrified of that man. Their mother would threaten to send them down the basement, and they would scream and cry and try to do anything other than go down that basement to their dad." According to Sarah Clark, the wife of Zane Clark's son, Zach, Mike told relatives that "his father beat the shit out of him." (Sarah's father is the brother of Mike Dahle's wife.) Perhaps he beat his children, as he beat Valarie, to keep them from speaking about what he was doing to them.

In the 1980s, Tonya Goodey was best friends with the youngest Dahle child, Diana. She told Anderson she "spent hours and hours" in the Dahle house, then empty of children aside from Diana, and she was always wary of Bob Dahle. "I was scared of him," she told Anderson. "He'd come home from work and flop his gun down." She described him as "ornery." The girls played upstairs, out of his way. If Diana sensed his mood was too threatening, she'd suggest that Tonya be very quiet—or go home.

She said Ollie Lou also kept an eye on them. "I could see her shielding Diana and I from Bob's [rage] if it was tense," she said. But like many Clarkston women, Tonya automatically blamed herself for a man's violence. "Maybe he was just annoyed that one of Diana's annoying friends was there and they were loud and obnoxious, you know?"

But it wasn't just young friends of Diana's he didn't want in the house. Ollie Lou was part of a ladies' club to which Tonya's mother also belonged. It was called the Variety Club and had 24 members, said Marilyn Godfrey, another Clarkston native Valarie's age who was a member. Dinners were twice a month and included a meal and games, but Tonya said they never met at the Dahle house "because it upset Bob." So Ollie Lou, whom Tonya described as "a very sweet lady, very welcoming, very kind," would bring "all the food" to the home of one of the other ladies for her night hosting, to avoid arousing her husband's ire.

Anderson asked Tonya if Diana had been abused by anyone. She said she didn't have any direct knowledge of that but offered that Diana "was messed up." She "dabbled in the more dangerous" and was "raised in dysfunction." "You could kind of tell that," she explained. "She was lesbian. She feared her dad." She also knew where her father kept a stash of pornography and offered to show it to Tonya.

Zane told me he worried that Diana had no one to protect her from her father and his anger after the older children grew up. Jann Jardine Pugmire had similar concerns. "I know he was very mean to Diana," she said. "She rebelled a lot. Drinking, smoking, running around town. I think she was trying to get away." Of course, since the abiding rule of Clarkston was "Thou shalt not tarnish the family name," Diana surely felt trapped as well as mistreated. Jann coached Diana in softball and befriended the girl because she appeared sad, closed off, and quietly defiant. "I'm sure she was in pain," Jann told me. "Her behaviors definitely showed that to people who knew her well. Alcohol was her way to self-medicate the pain but created more problems for her."

She was hurting, isolated, and lacking an effective ally, Jann felt. Though Diana never admitted that her father beat her, Jann felt they wordlessly communicated with each other about similar experiences. Jann's father would shake her violently when he got drunk. Her mother later told her she would have left her violent, alcoholic husband if there had been a women's shelter or resources *of any kind* in town that helped women escape abusive relationships. There were none—either for abused wives or abused children. "Anyone that goes through mental and physical abuse will be scarred for life," said Jann. "Especially if it's a parent you are supposed to love and trust. It can cause you to make bad decisions as you search for the love and acceptance you are looking for."

Jann, who would have been 22 or 23 then, figured Diana was 12 or 13 when she got to know her. A few years later, Diana appeared one night at the house of Jann's sister, Nancy, who had been her religion teacher. Diana's wrists were bleeding and she said she had accidentally cut herself with a broken bottle. Diana later told Jann and Nancy that the wounds had not been an accident; she had tried to kill herself. "That night we took her to the hospital was the only time I remember her crying," said Jann. "She was scared of what her parents would do."

Jann and Nancy were shocked when they called Bob and Ollie Lou from the hospital. Rather than thanking the young women for their responsible actions, they scolded them for taking Diana to the hospital. They said they should have brought her home to them.

—

In 1985, after Bob Dahle was promoted to sergeant and transferred to the Utah Highway Patrol training section in Salt Lake City, he and Ollie Lou bought a property in Kaysville and built or rebuilt a house there. Mike Dahle, who had been renting a different house in Clarkston, then moved back into the gray family home. Bob and Ollie Lou deeded it to Mike and Kris Dahle, his wife, on March 9, 1989.

Tonya Goodey, now Tonya Goodey Wood, remembered Diana moving to Kaysville when they were both 16; she went down to visit her there and accompanied her to her homecoming dance. Bob Dahle was working as an accident reconstructionist for the Highway Patrol; in fact, he built up that department from scratch. Diana soon found life at home intolerable, and after graduating from high school and enrolling at Weber State University, she moved in with the family of a friend, Kristy Kay Martin, who was four years younger than she was.

Kristy Kay, when contacted by telephone in 2021, was 49 and living in Montana. She told me, "I knew her dad was a monster. He definitely presented an aura about him that wasn't any good. You know when you walk by somebody and the hair on the back of your neck goes up, [and] you haven't said anything to them and your body's telling you something that's not okay and that's not right? I got that from Bob." Kristy Kay was an expert at sizing people up quickly—she had been a cop for 15 years.

She said Diana and her dad "never got along, never." She said there was "a dark side" to Diana that emerged when she drank. And she was a heavy drinker.

And Bob Dahle didn't much like Kristy Kay. She surmised that although she considered herself "a really good kid," she was one of the few children in the neighborhood who was not a practicing Mormon. Apparently, it was important for Dahle—or his wife—to present an image of piety to the neighbors. And he wanted his daughter's friends to be Mormons. Or perhaps that was just the excuse he came up with to try to keep his daughter from getting close to anyone outside of the family.

"When Diana started hanging out with me, he tried to say that I was a drug user," said Kristy Kay, adding that Dahle lied and told Diana that he had found drug paraphernalia near her yard. "He was trying to get me and Diana not to be friends."

Dahle's false accusation against Kristy Kay didn't sway Diana. The two young women moved out of Kristy Kay's parents' house in 1990, when Kristy Kay was 17 and Diana was 21. They later bought a condo together and remained a couple for "four or five years."

After moving in with Diana, Kristy Kay never saw Bob or Ollie Lou Dahle again. She said they no longer visited their daughter. But Diana wanted to go back to Clarkston to fish and sleep under the stars at Newton Dam, a place she remembered with fondness from her childhood, so they visited several times and stayed with brother Mike. Kristy Kay said she remembered older brother Brad as being "rough and gruff," but Mike was "a pretty nice guy." Neighbors described both boys as "twitchy," but Kristy

Kay remembered from staying at his house that Mike "had really violent nightmares" that caused him to "swing out in the night"—sometimes accidentally striking his wife.

What did Kristy Kay see in Diana when she got into her dark moods? "Anger," she said. Also, that Diana was "very, very sad." She never had anything good to say about herself. "It was always really ugly and negative," said Kristy Kay. "I think she hated herself a lot. She had something deep and dark going on." Diana once told her she had built walls inside herself that were "very thick and very high."

Kristy Kay remembered waking up one night and finding that Diana had slashed her shoulder with a knife. "I found her on the floor, with half the bottle of whiskey gone, and she was sewing herself up with a needle and thread."

She remembered Diana saying that her father "wanted to control everything." And soon Kristy Kay saw some of her father's behavior in Diana. If Kristy Kay was late getting home from work, Diana would subject her to close questioning. "I was working at a deaf and blind school, [and] if I wasn't home in seven minutes, I was questioned. Seriously," she said.

Finally, she told Diana, "I can't live my life this way. I'm not under your thumb. And I'm not going to drink my life away."

Kristy Kay is now happily married to a woman with whom she is raising four children.

During their time together, Diana worked with at-risk youth in Layton and Kaysville, "taking them out to work their community hours," said Kristy Kay. She graduated to being a "youth tracker"—similar to an adult probation and parole officer. After they broke up, Diana went to work as a personnel officer in a private prison in New Mexico.

Diana died in 2007 of esophageal varices, a painful condition in which the veins in the lower esophagus swell and bleed, the result of liver damage. She drank herself to death and was forced to return to her parents to be cared for during the final months of her life. Kristy Kay, who had fallen out of touch with Diana over the years, was shocked to learn of her premature death and found it particularly painful to learn that Diana had nowhere better or safer to go to die than at home with her parents.

Kristy Kay said there was one more odd thing about Diana. Although they were young, healthy, and in love, Diana's interest in sex was fraught. "I'm highly intuitive," said Kristy Kay, "and when [your girlfriend] doesn't say anything, but you know something's not okay. . . . It was like that a lot with different aspects, not just in the bedroom."

In that way, Diana was just like Valarie.

CHAPTER ELEVEN

An Environment of Hiding Things from Each Other

A STORY ABOUT LIFE in the early days of Clarkston goes like this: In the winter, everybody in town moved into the church to ride out the cold and heavy snow. Come spring, they left the church, divvied up the children, and went their own ways. The implication was that the villagers were so interrelated, nobody knew who belonged to whom. Siblings and cousins, mothers and aunts, fathers and uncles were almost interchangeable.

People from nearby towns still joke about Clarkston this way.

A typed list of names hangs from a string at the Clarkston City Cemetery, its pages covered in plastic to protect them from the rain and snow. The important families stand out, as they take up much of the cemetery's real estate: Godfrey, Clark, Thompson, Heggie, Goodey, Archibald, Loosle, Buttars, Jardine, Ravsten, and more. Looking at the women's maiden names, one begins to see how the population is bound up in a complex tapestry of interconnected families. Through marriage and remarriage, almost "everyone is related," as Helen Godfrey Cooper put it. Some are related on both sides of the family.

For example, the grandfathers of both Helen Godfrey Cooper and Shirleen Clark were brothers, making Helen and Shirleen's mothers first cousins. Helen's brother, Brent Godfrey, was married to Bob Dahle's daughter Jill. So, Shirleen, Valarie, and Bob Dahle are related, even though a series of alleged violent assaults mars their shared history. And of course, Gary Thompson, another of the men Valarie claimed had assaulted her, was her father's first cousin.

Clarkston's tangled web of family ties originated in the early Mormon practice of polygamy, or plural marriage. Although married to his first wife, Emma, since 1827, Joseph Smith, the founder of the Church of Jesus Christ of Latter-day Saints, began discussing polygamy secretly in the early 1830s. To his mind, plural marriage represented a return to a patriarchal order that had existed under the Old Testament prophets Abraham, Moses, and Solomon—an attractive, if not heretical, proposition for some US men during the 1830s and 1840s, a period that witnessed the birth of the nation's first women's rights movement.

Smith himself took a second wife as early as 1835, later claiming that an angel of God had threatened him with "destruction" if he refused to do so. In time, as the LDS church has only recently acknowledged, he married as many as 40 women, some of whom were wives of his friends and at least one of whom was 14 years old when he was "sealed" to her. Suspicions about the Mormons, including their clandestine marital practices, contributed to their hurried departure or forced expulsion from the states of Ohio and Missouri. In 1843, in the new Mormon settlement of Nauvoo, Illinois, Smith dictated a revelation justifying polygamy as a law of God, explaining that if a righteous man had "ten virgins given unto him by this law, he cannot commit adultery, for they belong to him." Less than a year later, Joseph Smith and his brother Hyrum were murdered by a mob in nearby Carthage.[1]

Under Smith's successor, Brigham Young, both polygamy and controversy accompanied the Mormons to Utah. By 1852, when Young publicly acknowledged the practice of plural marriage for the first time, it had become as fundamental to Mormon society as slavery was to the antebellum South. Young himself married at least 56 women and oversaw a rapid expansion of polygamy among the Mormon masses who were then planting settlements in a great arc stretching from Salt Lake City north into Canada and south into California and northern Mexico. "At its peak in 1857," the church now admits, "perhaps one half of all Utah Latter-day Saints experienced plural marriage as a husband, wife, or child." For most of the period between 1852 and 1890, polygamous families made up 20 to 30 percent of the population in any Mormon community in the American West.[2]

Linked in the minds of white Protestant Americans with supposedly inferior racial and religious groups—Asians, Native Americans, Muslims, and sub-Saharan Africans—polygamy sparked harsh condemnations of the Mormons. In 1856, for example, the platform of the newly formed Republican Party condemned polygamy and slavery as "twin relics of barbarism."[3] Elected president in 1860, Republican Abraham Lincoln sought to eliminate both. In 1862, with the Civil War raging, Lincoln signed the Morrill Anti-Bigamy Act, which outlawed plural marriage and revoked the incorporation of the LDS church granted by Utah's territorial legislature. Still, Mormon men kept taking plural wives, believing they were protected by Utah's remoteness and their First Amendment right to freedom of religion. In a defiant assertion of that right, the LDS church included Joseph Smith's 1843 revelation on polygamy in the 1876 edition of the Doctrine and Covenants, effectively canonizing the practice.

US authorities were unmoved. The Supreme Court upheld the Morrill Act in 1879, distinguishing between the protected right to believe in polygamy and the illegality of practicing it. Addressing Congress in December 1885, President Grover Cleveland railed against plural marriage as a threat to the bedrock of the US republic. "The strength, the perpetuity, and the destiny of the nation rest upon our homes," he thundered, "established by the law of God, guarded by parental care, regulated by parental authority, and sanctified by parental love. These are not the homes of polygamy . . . . There is no feature of this practice or the system which sanctions it which is not opposed to all that is of value in our institutions."[4]

Even as Cleveland spoke, federal marshals in Utah and Idaho were engaged in an aggressive campaign to stamp out polygamy completely. Backed by the Morrill Act and the 1882 Edmunds Act, which declared plural marriage a felony, officials ranged across Mormon country in search of lawbreakers. Backwater though it was, Clarkston was caught up in the dragnet. Many of the town's men turned up in the pages of the *Deseret News* after their arrests for "unlawful cohabitation." In one week in January 1889, for example, Lars Rasmussen, David Buttars, Thomas Griffin, and Thomas Godfrey were all charged and jailed. After unsuccessfully pleading ignorance of the Edmunds Act, Ole Jensen, one of two counselors to Clarkston's bishop, spent the winter of 1888 in jail after paying over $400 in fines and fees.

Jensen's account of those years reveals the real disruptions—religious, familial, and economic—as well as the paranoia triggered by the federal campaign against polygamy. "Some of the officers," he wrote, "came as peddlers, implement dealers," disguising themselves as travelers before pouncing. They "sneaked on the brethren and came by night, and crept through their windows, broke open the doors, and made lights to look for their man." With federal marshals seemingly lurking everywhere, Jensen reported, "nothing of public notice was going on" as Clarkston's social life and economy withered. Some of Jensen's neighbors left the country, while others headed for friendlier states.[5] For his part, Jensen and his plural wives migrated to Wyoming in 1890—very much against the wives' will, according to Jensen's journal. Like the LDS church 's president, John Taylor, who had married eight women, many of Clarkston's polygamist men went "on the dodge," leaving their families behind and retreating to hiding places in the mountains.

Finally, in 1890, as the troubles associated with the federal antipolygamy campaign worsened and with Utah statehood hanging in the balance, the LDS church issued a manifesto disavowing polygamy and advising its members against "contracting any marriage forbidden by the law of the land."[6] Although it did enough to get Utah into the union in 1896, the manifesto did not dissolve existing plural marriages, and it did not stop church leaders from continuing to perform them in secret. In 1904, however, as controversy raged over the election of LDS apostle Reed Smoot to the United States Senate, the church issued a second manifesto rejecting polygamy and vowing to excommunicate any member who lived in a plural marriage or any church official who solemnized one.

In effect, the second manifesto required polygamist men to choose one wife over the others, creating a host of practical, economic, and emotional burdens that weighed heaviest on women and children. Ross Peterson, for example, offers the case of his own great-grandfather, who after fathering nine children with a second wife and taking a widow with two children as his third, left them all to return to his childless first wife after 1904. Some Mormons, of course, simply refused to abandon polygamy; in time, their communities gave rise to religious offshoots, such as the fundamentalist church run by Warren Jeffs, who is now serving a life term in Texas for aggravated sex abuse of a 12-year-old child he claimed to have married. Once-polygamist men who remained in the Mormon fold left behind families mired in legal squabbles over land, property, and even water rights, with less-fortunate branches often descending into poverty. But even in mainstream Mormon communities, "many plural husbands and wives continued to cohabit until their deaths in the 1940s and 1950s."[7]

In towns such as Clarkston, polygamy created the landscape of interrelated families—some favored, others seemingly cursed—that defined social life down to Valarie's day.

Polygamy also led to other social ills. Because it was primarily older, richer men who married multiple wives, many small towns were left with groups of young men who couldn't find mates. As the country became more industrialized, some moved away for jobs, but the least capable remained single. Testifying in a British Columbia, Canada, courtroom in 2011 in a case testing that province's prohibition against polygamy, Professor Joseph Henrich, now professor and chair of the department of Human Evolutionary Biology at Harvard University, explained that polygamy, no matter where it was practiced in the world, inevitably led to a pool of men who could not find wives. This group, already of lower economic and social status, was "left frustrated and adrift," and thus more likely to "to commit crimes, including rape and murder, and abuse drugs and alcohol."[8]

He further explained that in cultures around the world that practice polygamy, competition over mates leads men to seek out younger women, which then leads to teenage brides marrying much older men. Increased competition for wives leads men to exert more control over women, according to Henrich, leading to increases in domestic violence and abuse. Children also suffer in polygamous societies because "men are less likely to invest time and resources in child rearing because they father so many children and are constantly focused on finding new wives."[9]

Perhaps more importantly for Valarie's case, plural marriage and the federal attempt to crush it also helped morph Clarkston's isolation and extreme self-reliance into an enduring culture of deceit and secrecy. That culture can be charted through Latter-day Saints' use of what was then called the Mormon Creed. First deployed by church leaders in 1844, the year of Joseph Smith's assassination, the creed consisted of a call to secrecy in a single phrase: "Mind your own business."[10]

Every 19th-century Mormon knew the creed, which was preached by Brigham Young and, in the 1850s, turned into a popular song whose chorus now seems a bad omen:

> So let us mind the Mormon Creed
> And then we all shall thrive,
> Shall hide a multitude of sins,
> And save our souls alive.[11]

By the 1880s, the Mormon Creed was used as a rallying cry to protect polygamist men in places such as Cache Valley. Dedicated in 1884, the

Logan Temple featured a back-painted glass window whose text loomed over husbands and wives contracting plural marriages: "Mind Your Own Business: Saints Will Observe This, All Others Ought To."[12]

That same year, John Taylor described polygamy as "the secret of the Lord" and advised church members to "keep their own secrets" when it came to family affairs—and to "studiously avoid entering into a knowledge" of sensitive matters among their neighbors.[13] The people of Clarkston listened. Wives and children in polygamist families played a major role in helping husbands and fathers evade capture, donning what one local historian calls "armors of silence" in the face of external pressure.[14]

In Clarkston, the culture of secrecy outlasted the polygamy it had been created to defend. Where once LDS officials had hectored church members into silence over plural marriage, after 1904 they insisted on secrecy when it came to the controversial rituals performed in temples—where even today widowed men may be married to a second (or third, or fourth) "eternal" spouse, thus creating polygamist unions in the afterlife. Where Brigham Young and John Taylor railed against federal interlopers in polygamist Utah, 20th-century leaders such as Cache Valley–born Ezra Taft Benson warned Mormons to shun the "godless conspirators," from government officials to schoolteachers, whom they feared were spreading communism across the land.[15] Remote, conservative, and patriarchal, Clarkstonians assiduously heeded those calls to circle the wagons, especially around their church and the men who ran it, down to Valarie's day.

One artifact of the enduring influence of polygamy and secrecy in Clarkston was posted to the LDS genealogy website FamilySearch in 2017. It is a recording made by Rex Thompson, a distant relative of Gary Thompson, of some family lore regarding Jack the Bonesetter. The story runs that sometime in the 1870s or 1880s, when Clarkston's bishop took a young second wife, "discussion" erupted among the townsfolk. Troubled, Jack decided to make the bishop's plural marriage "a matter of prayer." As he did so, "a beautiful angel appeared," and Jack blurted out his concerns about the bish-op's new wife. The angel pointed a finger at him and responded: "That ain't none of your damn business."

A woman's voice is heard next, snapping off the tape recorder, "And it isn't."[16]

———

Many women and children of Clarkston still wear their "armors of silence." "It's a very closed town," Mike Anderson concluded after long, frustrating days spent trying to talk to its people. The women protect the men much as their great-grandmothers did. Only a few women who had suffered or been victimized were willing to speak their own minds, women like Jann Pugmire, Helen Godfrey Cooper, Marilyn Godfrey, and Angie Curtis. The rest pursed their lips and closed their doors.

Angie Curtis suggested that Shirleen Clark may initially have recoiled from the news of Valarie's abuse at the hands of Bob Dahle and Gary Thompson because "if Shirleen's friends found out that Valarie had been doing that, they would have judged Shirleen." Even if Shirleen didn't feel that way, Curtis's words are as shocking as they are believable, as they speak to the operational logic of a village that protects lawbreaking men and deval-ues its women and girls. How could anyone choose to blame a 13-year-old for her own rape at knifepoint? Everyone in Clarkston knew that Valarie, because of her beauty, brains, and social standing, had the choice of any young man in Cache Valley. Who in their right mind would suggest she "asked" to be raped by an unattractive older married man like Bob Dahle or Gary Thompson?

Historian Ross Peterson told me that for much of its history, the church hierarchy was not set up to punish men who abused girls and women. On the contrary, many church practices were created specifically to protect men from outside law enforcement. At the time of Valarie's assaults, "usually, a bishop wouldn't even ask a man about a suspected molestation," Peterson explained. "It's internally judicial to try to keep it from being externally judicial." Consequently, church leaders were focused on "working more with the sinner than with the person who has been violated."[17]

Don Anderson put it more plainly to Mike Anderson: "If you have a problem, a marital problem or something, you go to the bishop; that's the Mormon way. You don't call the law, you go to the bishop and then he takes it upon himself to straighten it out. If he had any brains, he'd call the cops. But they don't."

Don Anderson was born in 1932. He and his wife were friendly with Helen and Wayne Cooper and Jann and Boyd Pugmire. Mike Anderson affectionately called Don Anderson (no relation) "salty." Referring to incest and sexual attacks on children in Cache Valley, he said: "I'll tell you what—there's a whole lot of this shit that goes on that we don't never hear about."

Men like Dahle and Thompson, "notorious liars," as Peterson called them, were able to avoid punishment for their assaults of women and girls. It was easy to manipulate the system. The only reason a bishop might question a man about abuse, Peterson said, was if a woman or girl in his ward forwarded him a complaint. But these complaints were rare, as most girls knew that they would not be resolved in their favor. Ross Peterson notes that church policies relative to the behavior of individuals has changed since Valarie's youth.

However, the devaluing of girls ran deep, and it, too, was exacerbated by the history of polygamy.

Since one's sister might disappear one day to become part of a distant family, in effect having been offered or contracted to friends or strangers, usually without her prior knowledge, community members developed an attitude of "respect for the mother, but disrespect for daughters," according to Peterson. In some cases, daughters (and sisters) began to be perceived less as family members in whom to invest love and care and more as chattel. This helped create an attitude among some that girls "were there to be used." And this opened the door to behavior like that perpetrated by Thompson and

Dahle. As Peterson said, "if you undervalue girls," then you can "abuse them and it's not going to count."[18]

Adding additional wives into an existing family was not an easy transition. Jealousy, competition, and argument inevitably ensued. Joseph Smith and his closest confidantes had to work hard to convince their wives to agree to additional mates in the house, and Mormon women and girls were eventually offered a sweetener: they were taught that plural marriages offered the chance of reaching the highest levels of heaven. Nevertheless, Joseph Smith's first wife, Emma, remained famously ambivalent about polygamy, and her fights with Joseph on the matter are legion and well documented."[19]

As Professor Henrich's observations predicted, Clarkston included many men who never married and had spotty work histories. They lived on family-owned property (often with widowed mothers) and were fed by relatives or by charity through the church. Many women interviewed for this book remembered the odd single men who hung around the gas station and occasioned fear in them as girls, becoming the subject of derision and colorful nicknames.

Farrel Lloyd "Fud" Goodey fell off a horse when he was young and had a bad crick in his neck, stuttered, and walked awkwardly. He was in that bar in Preston with Reed Dahle before Dahle was shot by the proprietor. Later, at the gas station in Clarkston, he offered candy to young girls, according to Jann Pugmire. Rumors of sexual molestations dogged him for much of his life. He lived with his mother and passed away in 1992 at 66.

When Denzel was a bishop in the mid-1980s, he ministered to two Clarkston men who were convicted of child molestation and incarcerated in the state prison, hoping to encourage them to "straighten their lives out and live decently," he told me. One, Richard Farnsworth, had engaged in sexual relations with his four children—both daughters and sons. He told Denzel he had nothing to repent because what he did was "natural" and that "he had a right to it."

Everyone in Clarkston knew about his beliefs: "He had told those children that it was his responsibility to teach them about sex by having sex with them, including his sons," said Denzel.

And where on earth would he have learned that?

"That's how he was raised," said Denzel.

The other incarcerated offender Denzel tried ministering to was Lee Godfrey, who returned to Clarkston and his wife after serving out his sentence. Boyd Pugmire, who served as mayor of Clarkston from 2006 to 2009, told me: "He's been like a completely changed person from what I've seen. I think that he grew a lot personally from being in prison. It helped him change."

"Lee was an interesting story," said Helen Godfrey Cooper. "I grew up with Lee." She remembered walking through town with her friends and seeing him as a boy "laying on the front lawn, beaten so badly by his dad that he could not get up." Helen said Lee's father, Leon, had been badly beaten by *his* father, Elwin Godfrey. And so it went, down through the generations. Lee Godfrey "turned it into a sexual abuse [issue with his own kids]," Helen said.

She did not condone Lee's behavior with his kids, but, she said, "I do know that my heart went out to Lee."

Even Denzel Clark, a good and decent man, failed to acknowledge evil in the men around him, although it stared him directly in the face. Decades after Valarie's revelations, Denzel said the community should have taken more seriously the prevalence of physical and sexual assault in its midst. "We should have opened our eyes a little bit," said Denzel. "I was one of the leaders, and I should have known."

But there was lots of culture to roll back: "Mind your own damn business!"

Though Clarkston prided itself on being a God-fearing town, it produced a lot of bad behavior. A driver of the elementary school bus once called out to Jann Pugmire's daughter, Amber, as she was walking down the street: "I wish I had a swing like that in my backyard." A married man with five children, he "always bragged about his muscles," remembered Jann. And he liked to tell Jann that she'd gained weight. "A lot of times," she remembered, "it was at church."

Jann said there were village rumors that this man watched porn with his children.

One of those children, now deceased, was "the town window peeper," said Jann. After Jann was married, she heard a noise on her own front porch and found him peeping through the sheer curtains of her living room. "He had the nicest wife. I felt bad for her."

On at least one occasion, the window peeper locked a neighborhood boy in a refrigerated truck with his own young close relative and wouldn't let them out until they performed a sex act for him to observe. The boy was so mortified about having been coerced and abused in this way that he requested that neither his name nor his co-victim's name be mentioned.

Two children of the man who subjected them to porn as youngsters were severely disabled by physical or mental conditions with psychological roots. One was hospitalized for much of her childhood with an auto-immune disease and another became disabled in middle age, suffering from phobias, one of them about dirt. "She didn't like to get dirty," recalled a close friend, who noted that she was also claustrophobic, and eventually had to stop driving and working. "Her anxiety got to the point that she was actually passing out . . . her body would say, 'Okay, can't handle any more,'" said the friend.

Marilyn Godfrey said a neighbor exposed himself to her a dozen times or more when she was in late grade school or early junior high. He was seven years older than she was. When Marilyn reported this behavior to her mother, she told her daughter to "close the curtains." One time, the boy exposed himself to Marilyn when she was standing with his own sister. The sister went home and told her mother what her brother had done, and, according to Marilyn, the woman slapped her daughter across the face and called her a liar.

This boy's bad behavior didn't end with showing his penis to girls. When Marilyn and her girlfriends walked to the swings at the old elementary school, he sometimes followed them and masturbated while watching them. "We'd be up there swinging, you know, just little girls, and [he'd] pull down his pants and have at it," recalled Marilyn.

Marilyn, like the rest of the girls in Clarkston who were molested by men or boys, kept those dirty secrets to herself. She said she was unable to mention it until after she was married. "I didn't tell anybody for a long time," she explained. "I didn't tell my husband 'til after we were married, and you know, he didn't believe me, but that's okay. It really happened."

A cadre of older Clarkston men in town watched for girls who might be sexually active and then planned their moves. After Jann Pugmire's rape at the hands of her relative became public knowledge, Burke Godfrey followed her to her work at Grand Central in Logan one night. She was 16 or 17, and he was the age of her parents. He walked up to her at the service desk and said, "We should go for a ride after." Jann said, "No, I'm not going to." At that time, she worked the 2 p.m. to 11 p.m. shift, and the old Rambler she drove didn't have locks on the doors. She was so rattled by Godfrey's approach that she asked the security guards to walk her to her car. Godfrey followed her home anyway.

She knew it would do no good to tell the bishop about Burke Godfrey stalking her because of his callous response when she earlier sought his counsel after being raped by L.

"They were buddies," she told me. "It would've gotten thrown back in my face."

Zane Clark remembered that as a girl, Jann had an unwarranted reputation of being "loose," the result of rumors generated by Burke Godfrey and other men in town who "closed ranks around" Burke to protect him.

Mike Henderson, who scared Debbie Clark Cooper by peeping into her bathroom when she was a girl, asked Jann to, in her words, "go with him 'driving' around." Van Dell Henderson flirted with her, and all three Henderson brothers "had a way to make you feel uncomfortable," she said, adding that they thought they were "God's gift to women." Van Dell boasted to Mike Anderson he "could get pretty much any girl he wanted." Nice boast in a Mormon town whose religion prohibits sexual relations outside of marriage.

Jann Pugmire also had several run-ins with Gary Thompson. After he observed her with her husband, Boyd, at a bar called Country Friends in Logan, Thompson decided to try his luck with her. He began to frequent the café where she worked. Jann said Thompson and his friends would "all come down and have coffee," a beverage forbidden to temple-worthy Mormons. She said they were "flirty" and that Thompson said "inappropriate things." "A lot of the guys were that way," she recalled. "You kind of brushed it off." But Thompson was not to be ignored. He once goosed her when she reached over the table to pour coffee—grabbing her under the arm near her breast.

Lloyd Clark, who Valarie said was present at her first rape, was arrested for soliciting sex with a child over the internet in June 2007 and served five years in a Colorado prison. Mike Anderson wondered whether watching the violent attack on Valarie had influenced Clark's future sexual proclivities.

Jann said Bob Dahle, too, had a reputation as a man who liked to go to bars and pick up women. Sometime in the 1970s, Valarie's cousin Dwight Pearce saw Dahle and a woman who was not his wife in the Hilton Hotel in Salt Lake City. Dwight and his wife, Bonnie, were spending the weekend there, and after dinner with Van Dell and Julie Henderson, they returned to the Hilton and saw Bob Dahle and Gary Thompson walk into the hotel at 11 p.m. with women "hanging all over them."

Van Dell remembered that night as well:

> *They seen us looking at him. They was like deer in the headlights. Dwight and I are poking each other in the ribs; we knew exactly what they were doing there. When we got to our room, not 10 minutes later— knock, knock, knock—it was Gary and Bob. and they was saying, "Come out here." They said, "Please don't let our wives know we was*

down here. Don't tell anybody, please, please." I said, "We're not gonna go spread shit." Dwight said the same thing while we're laughing on the inside. When we walked back into our rooms, Bonnie and Julie were standing there like two little Cheshire cats.

Bob Dahle was afraid of his wife and didn't mind telling bald-faced lies to get out of trouble with her, Van Dell recalled. "I drank whiskey with him on a snowmobile when I was a lot younger, and Gary and Sterling was there," he said, referring to Sterling Jardine, another neighbor. Dahle then went home and lied to his wife, saying, "They poured whiskey in my mouth and held me down and blew smoke in my face and that's why I smell of smoke," as Van Dell remembered it. "That's the kind of guy he was."

Jann Pugmire's husband, Boyd, who defeated Dahle in a Clarkston mayoral race in 2006, said Dahle tried to pick public fights with him during the race but used his daughter-in-law KaLynne as his proxy—asking her to write letters to the newspaper criticizing Boyd on his behalf. Boyd said the bullying irritated him but he chose not to respond. Don Anderson, a friend, advised Boyd, "If you want to shut him up, just ask him about the redhead at the Bloody Bucket."

The Bloody Bucket was a fabled dive down the hill from a slaughterhouse just west of Preston, Idaho. People were known to ride their horses right up to the bar, and shootings and fights were commonplace. "It was a rowdy place," said L.D. Bowcutt, proprietor of LD's Cafe in nearby Richmond, Utah.[20]

A local woman who didn't want her name used (because Mormons aren't supposed to be in bars) told Charles McCollum at the *Herald Journal* that she remembered a young Willie Nelson coming into the Bloody Bucket. She recalled him as a "scruffy guy with a guitar" who asked if he could play for tips. "He was a good singer," she opined, "but nobody really paid much attention to him and I don't think anybody put any money in his hat." In 1982, Nelson gave an interview to Barbara Walters in which the famed interviewer asked Nelson about the roughest place he ever played. After first mentioning the Fort Worth county dump, he offered, "The Bloody Bucket in West—" before being cut off by Walters's laugh.[21]

Bowcutt, who has vivid memories of the saloon, originally called the Refuge Club, purchased some of its old artifacts at a yard sale and installed them in the pool room of his own café. "That painting right there," he told one reporter, pointing to an oil painting of a naked man skinny-dipping in the Bear River, "hung behind the bar." It was a self-portrait of Shakespeare Newt Hart, the former owner of the bar. "It has some buckshot marks from a 410 pistol someone fired into it."

Newt Hart was the proprietor, but his brother Newell built it out of an old chicken coop, and paneled it with scavenged barn wood. Their 96-year-old brother, Bret, who lived in Salt Lake City, remembered that there was a "four-ton rock right inside the front door and a long rock fireplace on your right as you walk in." Newell "found a huge rock in the Cub River Canyon and wanted to bring it back," Bret recalled. "We used a piano moving truck to move it."[22]

The family was artistically inclined, and the joint was built as a music venue for their Dixieland-style band and included a small stage and a dance floor.

In 1958, Newell decided to attend college at the University of California at Berkeley. While gone, he left the Refuge Club in the hands of various friends, and that's when it got rough. "A farmer friend of mine got into a fight," recalled Bowcutt. The farmer "was about 6'4" and weighed about 250 pounds. His opponent was quite a bit smaller, but he had a knife hidden in his fingers. Every time the smaller guy threw a punch, he cut into the farmer's stomach. When someone told the farmer he was bleeding, he wiped the blood from his stomach, looked at his opponent and knocked him 10 to 15 feet into the wall."

Bowcutt said, "I loaded my friend up into my little sports car and took him to the hospital in Preston. When the doctor was stitching him up, he told him he needed to quit going over there."

Bowcutt added that his friend ignored that advice: "The last time this friend was injured there, the doctor patched him up from a claw hammer to the forehead."[23]

Don Anderson tended bar there soon after its opening, when he was 16 years old. "Holy shit," he said. "You go up there and get the hell kicked out of you." Years later, he was celebrating the birth of a friend's first son. Between them, on the table, was a wine glass with a hard-boiled egg in it. Don and his friend were chatting over beers when "all of a sudden that egg explodes."

Newt had shot it with his .45.

"That was just a common occurrence down there," said Don.

The bar stood on a cliff that hung over the Bear River and was down a sharp slope from the road, so it was concealed and hard to get to. (In the winter, sagebrush was laid down over the snow to help cars get up the hill and back to the highway.) Curious young teens used to drive up to the bar and sit outside in their cars, eager to catch sight of the place but too scared to go in. Nevertheless, there was always a passel of underage girls there.

The place didn't fly completely under the radar, though. There was a single policeman who covered Preston and Weston, according to Don, who remembered he'd come over periodically but usually gave the proprietor a friendly heads-up beforehand. The girls were then told to scram, and they hid in their cars or out in the woods, and the cop came in and looked at a few IDs. He'd asked, "Where's all the young girls?" and the bartender would say, "Oh, they went home a couple hours ago." When the girls couldn't see the cop's taillights anymore, they'd go back in.

Mike Anderson found a woman named Carol Hart Cowgill, who said she was Newt's granddaughter and remembered a perhaps-apocryphal story of a man coming into the bar and grabbing a redhead by the hair and pulling her around, then placing a gun to her chin. As they struggled, his hand slipped, and when he pulled the trigger, the slug hit the ceiling, then fell back down to the floor at the feet of her grandmother, Newt's wife.

The redheaded woman, according to local lore, was more or less "shacking up there." In other words, said Anderson, "she was a working girl."

Anderson wondered if the man who shot the gun into the ceiling was Bob Dahle. "That would explain very nicely why Bob Dahle would want to associate with the redhead at the Bloody Bucket," said Anderson, "and why that information," as Don Anderson told Boyd Pugmire, " would be threatening to him."

—

Don Anderson said Bob Dahle, Gary Thompson, and Burke Godfrey were all regulars at the Bloody Bucket. After quitting his job at Thiokol, Thompson took up itinerant trucking work, one advantage of which was the freedom it offered him to live away from home. "Gary was a little free with himself. Let's put it that way," Anderson said.

Thompson, who died at 84 in 2019, was not an attractive man—wet, fleshy lips, jowly cheeks, thick glasses. Clarkston resident Helen Godfrey Cooper told me he was "one of the homeliest men ever." She thought it was "hilarious" that Thompson was such a bounder. "What the hell? I mean, how did you get anyone to look at you?" she said. "I can't believe your sweet wife stays with you."

Don Anderson had a story about how unsuspecting that sweet wife was. Don had a job hauling flour to a prison in California in the 1970s, and Thompson had a job not too far off his route. Don recalled, "When I was hauling flour out there, [Gary's] wife, Nancy, got ahold of me. And she'd say, 'Would you stop and give Gary these clothes? Or would you take this out to Gary?' Because Gary wouldn't come in, and all the time that he was out there, he was shacked up with some old gal in a motel. [Nancy] didn't know about it. And I didn't say anything about it. Okay. You know, if she found out, [and] asked me about it, I'd probably say, yeah, but if she don't, why stir the kettle? All you do is cause a lot of trouble."

He described Nancy as "the softest-spoken, quietest little old gal you ever seen in your life"—a model Mormon wife.

When Thompson was working for a John Deere dealership in Winnemucca, Nevada, he got involved with a young Native American woman. "And that's the reason that they told him to get out of town," Don told Mike Anderson. "He was screwing around with one of them Indian girls."

He added: "I used to tell him after he quit and come home, that when I'd go out through Winnemucca, that first overpass, there was a little Indian boy out there was always leaning over the railing, hollering, 'Are you my daddy?'" Don thought that was pretty funny. Thompson only a little less so.

At one point, "Gary used to mess around with three or more gals over there. He was messing around with one over in Malad," said Don. He also had a girlfriend in Soda Springs, Idaho, and "he was messing around with one in Preston. We called her Dump-Truck Annie."

Dump-Truck Annie was a "big old gal," not a "neat, good-looking lady," according to Don. She drove down to the Bloody Bucket "in an old ton-and-a-half little gravel truck," hence her nickname. But she had some attributes, and according to Don: "She'd hang them over the pool table and shoot pool. And that's what everybody would go to the bar for."

Thompson worked from time to time on Burke and LaMont Godfrey's farm in Soda Springs. According to Don, Thompson told a woman in Soda Springs that he'd bought half of Godfrey's interest in the farm," a lie to lure the woman into bed.

"Shit," said Don to Mike Anderson. "Gary was *something-else* different."

But that wasn't the end of it. "I know them guys was involved in a gang rape in Preston, and I have no idea who it was, but I know that it happened," said Don. He said the victim was a married woman. "She just got drunk, and they took advantage of her. And every one of them bastards was capable of it."

—

Incest, child abuse, immorality, and ill health plagued Clarkston, but the town was consumed with keeping its secrets from the world—and each other. Bad behavior might sully the image of the perfect Mormon family that was so essential to cultivate and maintain. Clarkston's living room walls were hung with photos of large families, smiling children and grandchildren, and images of the closest temple.

Zane Clark told Mike Anderson that his first wife, Kristine, who was sexually assaulted as a teen, had had trouble when she was even younger. She told him that she had tried to kill herself when she was 12 by swallowing a handful of aspirin. (Her parents brought her to the hospital to get her stomach pumped.) Zane wondered if she had been sexually abused at that time also, but throughout their marriage, Kristine refused to talk about it. When she took her life at age 33, Zane said, she "seemed as though she was having flashback memories of being abused."

When Mike Anderson interviewed Kristine's sister, Annette Goodey Summers, in the summer of 2021, she told him Kristine "absolutely detested and hated Van Dell Henderson, Bob Dahle, and Gary Thompson." Kristine revealed the name of her rapist to her sister, who told Mike. He is a Clarkston man, still alive.

As a young girl, Annette herself was "terribly afraid of Gary Thompson and would have nightmares about him," she said. Retired FBI special agent Mike Anderson thought it was quite remarkable for a neighbor to be so frightening to a young girl that he would appear in her nightmares—if, as Annette insisted, he hadn't actually done or said something frightening to her.

Thompson seemed to have no compunction about spending time alone with any young women he could. "Wendy"—a pseudonym—came to live with Nancy and Gary Thompson as a young teenager in the 1960s.

For years, Denzel Clark observed a strange pattern play out at the house across the street, in full view of their windows. Every Sunday, Gary

Thompson, his wife Nancy, and "Wendy" went to Sunday dinner at Gary's father, Earl's house. (Gary would later inherit this house and live there until he died.) Every week, after dinner, Gary Thompson would go home alone, and Wendy would follow shortly thereafter. Strangely, Nancy stayed on at her in-laws for another hour or so, enough time for her husband and Wendy to be alone together. "It looked suspicious to me at the time," said Denzel of the staggered departures from Earl Thompson's house. "I thought, well, you know, the temptation of a young teenage girl to an older man."

But Nancy seemed not to notice. Denzel said of her, "She's a wonderful lady, and she would do anything not to have trouble."

Though his wife did her best not to see what was going on, others did. Gary Thompson was a "womanizer," said Tonya Goodey Wood, first cousin to Kristine Goodey Clark and Annette Goodey Summers. Don Anderson was blunter: "I knew Gary and I knew what type of an individual he was. If it was female and it walked, it was Gary's aim to take care of it."

Marilyn Godfrey, who was the same age as Valarie, worked with a girl named Lucy at Alvey's candy factory in Richmond. Lucy's boyfriend worked at Newton Market, and he told Lucy that a few local men, including Gary Thompson, used to meet above the store to watch pornography. Clarkston's townsfolk held their tongues because Gary Thompson and his wife had "been called on a mission" as adults despite his indecorous behavior.

Tonya Goodey Wood, who had been friends with Diana Dahle, told Mike Anderson that she had relatives who had been sexually abused by their father. She said the signs were obvious in their later lives, as they suffered from drug abuse and other problems.

Shawntae Reichard, Annette Clark's daughter and Zane Clark's step-daughter, was harassed by a local man named Ed Barson in the 1990s, when she was 15 and had just moved to Clarkston with her mother and sister after her mother married Zane. When Shawntae got in her car to drive to work, Barson, then in his 40s and married with children, followed her almost every other day for years. On one occasion, he got so close to her car while she was driving with her infant son that she was afraid he would hit her, so she pulled off the road, frightened. He followed her and told her he wanted to take her out to dinner. She said no. Nevertheless, his obsession raged, and he followed her to Brigham City, then all the way to Layton. When she told the police, they gave her a mobile phone that was as large as a brick, with an antenna. It was programmed to call the police station. She kept it for two years but never used it. After a while, Zane approached Barson at the local mall and told him to stop. Shawntae believes the police also "told him he needed to stop."

Eventually, he restrained himself from chasing her down in his car but decided to write her love letters instead. He wrote about seven of them, she recalled in a conversation with Mike Anderson, in which he suggested they get a house together and get married.

Zane photocopied the love letters and mailed them anonymously to Barson's wife at her work address, but Shawntae said the harassment ended only after she moved away from Clarkston in 2001 to live with her father.

Shawntae's sister, Stephanie, was assaulted at age 12 by a 22-year-old Clarkston man named Stan Bennet, whose wife had just given birth. He took her for a ride. "Wow, you're so pretty," she recalled him saying, "and you're so fit. You're so much better than my wife." He took her to the gravel pit, kissed her and "fingered" her and tried to get her to go with him into a trailer parked nearby. She said she didn't want to go, and "he didn't force me to do it, to do that," she told Anderson. He asked her to have something to drink with him, she said no, and he brought her home.

The next time she went to the gravel pit to see him, there was a group of young men there. And, she recalled, they said to her, "I hear that you have crooked titties, and you should flash us so we could see." Years later when she recounted the incident to Anderson, she understood they were just provoking her to take off her shirt and show them her breasts, a trick she of course fell for. And as soon as she took off her top, one of the boys started "grabbing on" her. At this point, Bennet appeared and told the others to leave her alone. Playing her savior, "he's like, 'Come in the trailer, and

I'll comfort you,'" she recalled. Stephanie remembered feeling "like I just wanted to cry. And I was so upset, and of course he was there to comfort me and then we ended up leaving."

Bennet bragged to his friends about his new underage girlfriend, but the wrong person overheard him and alerted Stephanie's parents, who called the police. A phone tap was set up, and Bennet was recorded describing what he had done with Stephanie. He was sent to jail. She was too frightened to testify in court, something she had come to regret by the time she talked to Anderson. "Honestly, it ruined my whole life," she said.

At the next Pony Express Day in Clarkston, residents made clear their feelings about the 12-year-old girl who had had the temerity to report her rape at the hands of an adult. They shouted at Stephanie and threw stones at her. "I had a guy friend with me," she explained, "and the kids and adults shouted at him, 'Don't hang out with her. She'll put you in jail. She'll put your family in jail. Don't trust her. She's a little slut.'" She recalled that even the lady at the corner store "called me a slut."

The lady at the corner store, it turned out, told everybody in town that day, including, unknowingly, Stephanie's grandparents.

"And then the whole town stands behind him!" said Annette Clark, Stephanie's mother. The bishop even got in on the action, urging Annette and Zane to write a letter to the judge asking him to let Stan Bennet out of jail.

Annette and Zane were appalled. Annette exclaimed, "He tried to blame my daughter! She was twelve years old!" Zane stood up and told the bishop, "I don't care if she's standing out there with a pair of pasties on and a G-string," Bennet "should not be doing anything to her."

Bennet served nine months in prison.

"That town is scary, the stuff that went on out there," said Zane. "Those little towns breed so much stuff . . ."

"And it gets passed down," said Annette.

But there was a small silver lining. After the rock-throwing episode, Stephanie found a box filled with candy and body wash outside her door.

Attached was a note that read: "Thank you for saying something. He did it to me too. Just keep your head up." It was signed in a girlish script.

Stephanie thought the gift and note might have been left by a girl in town who moved away soon after. The experience "really ruined a lot of things for me," recalled Stephanie, "not just my childhood, obviously, but it was hard to even live there anymore."

She left Clarkston around 2000, and Zane and Annette relocated across the valley to Providence in 2002. Jann and Boyd also said their final good-byes to Clarkston in 2009 after Jann told Boyd she couldn't stay for one more minute.

He knew Jann had been raped as a young woman and that she had been harassed by Burke Godfrey and Lloyd Clark, but he said he didn't under-stand what that really meant and how much it had affected her until he heard the news reports about the Miller investigation. He told me he had come to believe that the town where he had served as mayor and city council member must come clean about its past. "There needs to be accountability," He believed Bob Dahle and Gary Thompson "were capable of just about anything" and Bob Dahle used his position as a cop, more than once, to threaten people. He was just a bully."

"I'm so glad we're not there anymore," he said.

CHAPTER TWELVE

"Never Bring That Up Again!"

VALARIE ONCE TOLD HER SISTER, Debbie, that she wondered if Helen Godfrey Cooper had been abused in Clarkston. Helen ran away from home in high school and was gone for one year. She also presented traits that Valarie knew well—a perfectionism in appearance and care of her home—that Valarie thought might point to her having been traumatized. I drove to Helen's house in Clarkston in June 2022 to find out.

Helen was a beautiful, energetic, and tiny woman whose face was alive with emotion. Unlike most Clarkston women, who speak hesitantly in hushed voices, Helen was eager to speak her mind. We sat in her living room, which looked out to a perfectly tended green lawn.

The first thing she said was, "Every little girl in Clarkston was abused by somebody."

She sat forward in her chair, explaining that she had recently spoken with her sister, who shocked her by revealing—all these years later—that their grandfather had exposed himself to her when she was a little girl. Helen's sister had reported this to their mother when it happened, and true to form in Clarkston, their mother told her "never bring that up again!"

Her grandfather was Ken Thompson, brother of Glen Thompson, who was Shirleen Clark's father. (Ken Thompson offered a eulogy for Bob Dahle's murdered father, Reed, at his funeral.)

Helen said that her mother had had "a complete nervous breakdown" and took antidepressants for most of her life. On the couple of occasions that she stopped—cold turkey—the results were catastrophic.

I asked Helen if it was possible that Ken Thompson exposed himself to her mother when she was a child, or to Shirleen, his niece. This might explain her mother's depression and Shirleen's frozen reaction when Valarie revealed her own abuse.

"That's the $64,000 question," said Helen.

The talk turned to the subject of my visit—whether she knew anything about what happened to Valarie as a teenager.

Helen told me that I needed to understand that her brother, Brent Godfrey, was married to Jill, Bob and Ollie Lou Dahle's second daughter. Because the Dahles were their in-laws, she advised, she wouldn't be able to speak freely about them. Having said that, though, she wanted me to know that she had not been abused by either Dahle or Gary Thompson. "In fact, I would say Gary and Bob were more cold to me than friendly," she said.

I suggested that they were probably looking for girls they could more easily overpower and intimidate. Helen suddenly looked very sad and said, close to tears, "I just feel so overwhelmingly guilty that I didn't notice [what was going on with Valarie]. I just moved from Annie getting hurt to [Valarie] getting sick to her getting divorced. I just feel awful to think I couldn't see any of those signs . . . I'm not sure that Valarie ever had a close friend. Maybe because she never trusted anyone enough."

From the outside, Valarie had everything, Helen noted, but she didn't seem to have confidence or happiness. "Life with John included a lot of money, but that didn't matter to her. Her parents had always given her everything she needed," said Helen. She wasn't a natural mother, Helen thought. But then again, Shirleen wasn't the most effusive person either. "She was a Thompson," observed Helen, as she was herself.

And then there was the terrible time when Annie was fighting for her life after the accident. Helen said Valarie "almost prayed herself to death when Annie was sick."

At one point in the conversation, when speaking about Valarie's abuse, Helen began to cry as if she were reacting to something that had happened to her, personally. When pressed, she paused a beat, then acknowledged that she had been abused as a little girl, too. "I couldn't have been more than eight or nine," she confided. A cousin who had lived out of town convinced her to play "the tickle game"—a favorite of child molesters, I learned from Mike Anderson—which involved him tickling her, then Helen tickling him back. But his tickling had a purpose, and he would eventually tickle her upper thighs, near her private parts. This frightened and bewildered her, she said, and it had a dramatic effect on her feelings about herself.

She ran away from home for a year, and her parents never knew where she was. While attending Dixie Junior College, now called Dixie Technical College, in St. George, Utah, she said she was "promiscuous."

"When I was in college, my friends were drinkers, and we'd drink. And then we'd hook up with guys. "I honestly was never raped," she recalled. "Not really. I never said no, but I really had low self-esteem. I felt like, well, you know, I've already done this, I'm certainly not a virgin anymore." According to Mormon teachings as she understood them, her value had been diminished, so she felt she had nothing to lose. "So why not?" she thought.

After she grew up, if any man even accidentally touched her thighs, she said, she couldn't help but shout, "Fuck you!" She was never able to tell anyone why she reacted so furiously until she married her husband, Wayne Cooper. "A time or two, he'd say to me, 'What in the heck is wrong with you?' Finally, I got the guts to blurt it out."

Helen's abuse at the hands of her cousin—and the decades during which she blamed herself for it—scarred her. She felt she must have done something to encourage him.

She cried again. "But why did he pick me?" she asked. "What did I do to deserve this?"

The eternal curse of the abused—to wonder, "Why me?"

Helen said, "Why do we take it upon ourselves to think, 'Well, I deserve to be hurt. I deserve to be unhappy. I deserve to be miserable'? You know, all those things when someone else is at fault?"

A couple of days after our first conversation, Helen called me from her car on the way home from work to say she was feeling surprising relief from having told the story of her childhood abuse—for having finally told someone. "I don't think you realize how therapeutic this is for me and for people who have been through this," she said. For all her life, she explained, she felt she must be the only one who had endured such behavior—and the resulting feelings of lack of self-worth, guilt, and anger.

"Sometimes you feel like the Lone Ranger, no matter where you're at in life," she explained.

All alone with the guilt.

She struggled with depression, she told me, and believed it had its roots in the "tickle game" and the shame she felt about it. She had been taking antidepressants since her early 30s. Especially in light of her sister's recent revelations about their grandfather, Helen wondered how many other women in town were suffering from assaults they have never acknowledged.

"Maybe my mom, and who knows how many women, ended up dying with all these lies and secrets," she told me. "I believe with all my heart, [talking out loud about this] has been such a good experience for me to open up my eyes, not only about the past, but about the future and what I want for my own children and grandchildren. You know that old quaint saying 'The truth will set you free'?"

There was one last thing she had to get off her chest. Helen didn't remember very much about the investigation into Valarie's assailants in 1990 because in 1987 her first husband, Richard Goodsell, was killed at Thiokol when 100,000 pounds of solid rocket fuel exploded, obliterating a building and killing five workers. Two weeks after her husband's death, Thiokol officials visited Helen and told her they had mistakenly given her pieces of the wrong body. She said she was so devastated that she was not really aware of any investigation of Bob Dahle and Gary Thompson. "I just heard they were accusing Bob and Gary, and I didn't hear much more about it other than they said they didn't do it," she said. She described herself at that time as "engrossed in [her] own wallowing, in [her] own pity."

But there was soon a new scandal to occupy the community that would be settled much more easily. Not long after the explosion at Thiokol, Helen met and fell in love with Wayne Cooper, who served as justice of the peace in Clarkston's Justice Court. And not too long after that, she became pregnant. And even though Helen and Wayne were both middle-aged, were each previously married, and were together raising a combined family of five children that would soon to become six, the situation caught the attention of the community and its leaders. Helen said, "That stake president told Denzel,"—who was then her bishop—"'You need to do something because you need to make her an example.'"

She was excommunicated from the LDS church for, in her words, "doing nothing else but having sexual relations with a guy that I was in love with. Yet, they couldn't rouse interest in a church court against Bob Dahle for raping Valarie Clark. They excommunicated me for getting pregnant with my daughter, but not a year or two later, they [didn't] want to do anything with two guys who supposedly raped a young girl because they didn't want to 'tear that town apart'?"

Denzel later tried to console Helen by saying it would have been harder on her if he hadn't excommunicated her because then the community would have said she'd received favorable treatment from him.

Helen was outraged. "The thing that makes me so sad and makes me feel like crying my eyes out for Valarie," she said, her voice breaking, "is I ended up being on the outside, looking in. And when I looked from the outside, I found out how many people do everything in life for the wrong reason."

As girls, explained Helen, "We were taught if we lived the way we were supposed to, we did what we were supposed to do, everything would be fine. We would never go through bad things. And I'm sure Valarie thought that more so than anybody."

Helen had struggled with the idea of forgiving her childhood abuser and forgiving Thiokol for the explosion that killed her husband and the misidentification of her husband's remains. Consequently, she came to understand very well how the guilty avoid accountability for their crimes. The community's rules of fraternity and self-regulation depended on people telling the truth and fearing God's ultimate judgment. But Helen understood Clarkston's shadow morality: liars could get away with murder or any other crime. "If you never say sorry, you never ask forgiveness, then you never admit that anything happened," said Helen.

Word of Helen's talk with me traveled quickly through town. After all, an unfamiliar vehicle had been seen parked in front of her house, which led to questions and gossip. The day after our conversation, Helen sent me a text: "I've had more than I would like of calls about our visit. I don't want my life turned upside down. I have tried to be honest. But truthfully, it's not going to be worth it at the end of the day. I have the utmost respect for u. My family is too important to me to go through this again. Best of luck. I will love to read the book. I need to be done. It's too painful."

She signed off with a crying emoji.

———

Marilyn Godfrey knew Valarie as a child and teenager, though they were never best friends. They rode on the bus together to junior high and high school, and both tried out for the drill team in high school and went to practice together, though in high school they moved in different circles. Valarie belonged to the group that was "the most popular," Marilyn shyly told me, as I interviewed her in her comfortable, sun-filled living room in Clarkston.

Marilyn, who like many Clarkston women speaks in a soft, breathy voice, said she didn't remember hearing much about the attack on Valarie through town scuttlebutt, and she didn't know anything about investigations by the FBI or the internal affairs unit of the Utah Department of Public Safety. Marilyn said she wasn't surprised to learn from me that Valarie had named Gary Thompson as one of her assailants and said Lloyd Clark had watched the crime. Marilyn thought both men were "creepy." But she was surprised to learn that Highway Patrol officer Bob Dahle would have done anything like that, as he seemed to be such a law-and-order guy. But then again, she had some personal connection with Dahle—her father, Doug Clark, used to run around with him, Sterling Jardine, Max Clark, and Ross Buttars. She also told me that her husband, Curtis, had been friends growing up with Bob Dahle's son Brad and had worked with him at Nucor, a steel company. She seemed to be warning me that she wouldn't be able to speak freely about the family.

But there was one thing Marilyn was certain about after hearing what had happened to Valarie. She fought back tears and, with great emotion, said, "She would've never have asked for it. Never."

I was stunned. Could this question still be bubbling in the minds of Clarkston residents? At a time when the world was consumed by the #MeToo movement, could people—could another woman—believe that a virginal 13-year-old could have *asked* to be raped and beaten by two adult men at knifepoint?

Debbie Clark Cooper, Valarie's sister, told me she was angry about how easy it was for the women of Clarkston to feel that it was their duty to protect the men—regardless of their terrible behavior. "It makes me so mad," she said. "Are they frightened they'll be hurt, or are they just embarrassed cause we're such a small town and they don't want other people to know?" It infuriated and saddened her because the village women, as she put it, "just keep going down the same path instead of changing it. It's just stupid."

As of this writing, Helen Godfrey Cooper and Marilyn Godfrey are neighbors. Helen and Marilyn also share a grandson. When she was 14, Marilyn's daughter Ginger had a baby with her boyfriend, who denied being the father. Ginger had a paternity test done, which proved her boyfriend was indeed the father of the baby. His name was Josh Cooper, Helen's stepson and her husband, Wayne Cooper's, son. Marilyn said she and her husband, Curtis, raised and supported their grandchild until Ginger finished high school and got a job. Josh Cooper, she said, "just never would hold a job." The boy that Marilyn raised was in fact the second child that Ginger bore for Josh. The first, a girl, had been given up for adoption a year before the boy was born.

I asked Marilyn: Is this the story of Clarkston? The girls suffer and the boys just walk away?

She said, "Definitely."

Ginger died under questionable circumstances one winter day while loading up her car before work. It was terribly stormy, and she left the car running with the garage door closed. She was found on the floor beside her car.

"I think it was an accident," said Debbie. "That's what I want to believe."

CHAPTER THIRTEEN

The Most Serious Allegation Ever Made against a Major Officer

ONE OF THE MATTERS MIKE ANDERSON was particularly interested in investigating when John Miller and Richard Lambert sent him to Cache Valley in 2021 was finding out what happened with the 1990 state investigation of Bob Dahle on charges of child sexual abuse. Anderson read what John had recorded in his journals: Lieutenant Mitch Ingersoll, then director of internal affairs for the Utah Department of Public Safety, had been tasked with the investigation, and on May 18, 1990, he had met with Valarie and John. After hearing Valarie's painful story, he told the couple that "a major officer of the Utah Highway Patrol had never been accused of such an act." Ingersoll solemnly assured them it would be a "high-priority" case, which would likely require a three- or four-week investigation.

The next thing the Millers heard from him was that he was headed to Kansas to speak with Valarie's doctor at the Menninger Clinic. Then, on June 8, Ingersoll informed John and Valarie that Dahle had denied all the allegations and had passed a lie detector test with "high marks." He gave no details about his visit to Kansas and relayed no news about what he may have dug up in his investigation of the "high-priority" case. However, he announced that Valarie would have to take a lie detector test for him to continue.

Heeding expert advice, the Millers refused to have Valarie take a polygraph. Ingersoll then ended his investigation, and the charges against Dahle were dropped.

There was something about all this that didn't smell right to Anderson. And as an expert of polygraphy, he knew that no legitimate investigation of a crime ever begins and ends with a lie detector test.

On November 20, 2020, Mike Anderson arrived unannounced at the home of Mitch Ingersoll in St. George, Utah. After identifying himself and announcing that he was representing the Salt Lake City law firm WardLambert, whose principal, Brent Ward, had served for years as a United States attorney for the District of Utah, as well as Richard Lambert, the former chief investigator, criminal division, in the U.S. attorney's office for the district, he stated that the purpose of his visit was to look into an old case involving a highway patrolman named Bob Dahle.

Ingersoll appeared to remember the case clearly—the child abuse allegations, the location of an alleged assault in a barn or shed in Clarkston, and the fact that the victim had been treated at a well-known mental health clinic. But then Ingersoll surprised Anderson by saying that, contrary to what he'd told John Miller 30 years earlier—that he was headed to Kansas to interview Valarie's therapist at the Menninger Clinic—he had spoken to Valarie's therapist by telephone and that the therapist had told him Valarie's claims were "unfounded." Ingersoll said the psychotherapist had called Valarie "a schizo . . . phrenic," pausing in the middle of the word. Ingersoll told Anderson that Valarie's doctor "didn't believe her."

According to John's detailed journal entries from 1990, Ingersoll never reported anything about a conversation with Valarie's therapist, never said anything about his not believing her, or that he called her "schizo . . .

phrenic." He had only told John he was headed to Kansas to speak with her therapist, and the next thing he told him was that Dahle had passed a polygraph with "high marks."

Anderson asked Ingersoll if he had interviewed anyone else in the case, such as Valarie's parents or other family members. "No, I didn't. Like I say, the biggie was talking to the doctor. He didn't even believe her, so . . ."

He repeated the words the *biggie* and *coup de grâce* more than 20 times in his interview with Anderson.

In another astonishing about-face, Ingersoll admitted to Anderson that Dahle might never have taken a lie detector test himself, though he had told the entire town of Clarkston that he had. Ingersoll said, "But yeah, polygraph—there was an issue there. I am thinking that she wouldn't take one, so [Dahle] said, 'Bullshit, if she won't—you have her take a polygraph, then I'll have one.'"

Ingersoll went on to admit to Anderson that he hadn't really conducted much of an investigation at all. He said that since he had no physical evidence and no witnesses, it was basically "one person's word against another."

But there were witnesses, had he looked for them. He never interviewed Valarie's brother, Zane, who had seen bruises on her body, who knew she was sometimes out very late at night on her horse, and who had seen Dahle with Valarie on horseback riding out of town toward Steel Canyon, and who had seen Dahle and other men go into a dilapidated cabin with her over the border into Idaho.

Ingersoll never interviewed Valarie's sister, Debbie, who had seen her sister praying fervently and sobbing night after night in bed. He never made an effort to interview thoroughly Lloyd Clark, who Valarie had repeatedly said was a witness to the rape. Lloyd Clark told Anderson that Ingersoll had spoken with him on the telephone for about five minutes.

He did not interview Gary Thompson.

The following is a list of tasks a diligent investigator could have undertaken in 1990 to investigate the "high priority" case:

▸ He could have interviewed Valarie's pediatrician and tried to match medical records of injuries with those she claimed to have sustained at Dahle's hands.

▸ He could have examined Dahle's truck and his old sheds for evidence.

▸ He could have interviewed Dahle's daughter Diana, who was then still alive.

▸ He could have asked Valarie how the men set up meetings with her.

▸ He could have spoken with her first psychiatrist, Milo Andrus, and looked over his treatment notes for corroborating details.

▸ He could have examined the crime scenes that Valarie described— Newton Dam, Steel Canyon—for physical evidence.

▸ He could have checked Valarie's stories against Dahle's duty logs, personnel files, and radio logs.

▸ He could have asked Valarie about any identifying marks on her attackers' bodies.

▸ He could have asked Valarie where Dahle had shot her dog and tried to find its buried bones.

▸ He could have canvassed the town, asking residents if they'd seen Valarie with Dahle or Thompson.

▸ He could have asked Zane and Denzel Clark what they knew about violence or possible sex abuse in the Dahle family.

Ingersoll did none of these things. Instead, he admitted to Anderson that he was concerned from the outset about the possible damage to his career for investigating an officer—Dahle was then a lieutenant—who might one day outrank him because, as he put it, "you never know when you might be working for that guy."

―――

Mike Anderson tracked down Dr. Brown, Valarie's therapist at the Menninger Clinic, and called him on December 7, 2020. He wanted to know if he remembered speaking with the state investigator, Mitch Ingersoll, 30 years earlier. To Anderson's surprise, Dr. Brown denied having ever been interviewed about Valarie by any law enforcement official from Utah or anywhere else. He also insisted he had never said she was "schizo" because he had never diagnosed her as schizophrenic. Moreover, he had never told anyone that she was not to be believed. In support of his beliefs and these statements, Dr. Brown signed an affidavit on June 17, 2021, stating:

> *I have never opined to anyone that Valarie was a "schizo," ie, suffering from schizophrenia, because that was not my opinion . . . As my documentation in the record reflects and based on my professional training and experience, I concluded, with the proviso that no one's memory is perfect in every detail, that Valarie's account of what befell her was credible and played a significant role in her psychiatric symptoms. At no time during or after my treatment of Valarie Clark Miller, did I communicate to anyone any doubt as to the truthfulness of Valarie's account of abuse.*

John Miller had warned Ingersoll in 1990 that he feared the investigation might be whitewashed because Ingersoll's boss, Doug Bodrero, former sheriff of Cache County and then commissioner of the Utah Department of Public Safety, was a longtime colleague of Bob Dahle. They were also personal friends. Zane recalled that Bodrero "used to come out some summers and they'd go for rides together, him and Bob, up around the loop"—the same loop on which Dahle was rumored to have taken Valarie.

Zane also saw Bodrero and Dahle more than once riding together in cars.

Beginning in 1990, Dahle had worked as a captain in the Utah Highway Patrol under Bodrero's supervision. They retired together in 1997. As commissioner of the Department of Public Safety in 1990, Bodrero held the final authority in any internal affairs investigation of Bob Dahle.

Anderson believed that Bodrero should have recused himself from the investigation as soon as it came across his desk.

However, rather than trying to prevent the whitewash John Miller had warned him might take place, Mitch Ingersoll became a principal participant in it. In their 2020 meeting, Ingersoll told Anderson that he could not recall the name of the commissioner of the Department of Public Safety, his immediate supervisor on the matter. In fact, as soon as Mike Anderson left Ingersoll's house on November 20, 2020, Ingersoll, it later appeared, contacted Doug Bodrero to warn him about a possible reopening of the inquiry.

Anderson had inklings of the contact as soon as he arrived at Doug Bodrero's house on January 8, 2021. First, when Anderson asked for permission to record their conversation, Bodrero didn't even ask what the meeting was about. He already seemed to know. Bodrero's body language was also revealing to Anderson, who noted that he was adopting a defensive posture, "pressing himself into the back of the couch, arms and legs twisted into a pretzel." Then, about 15 minutes into their conversation, Bodrero inadvertently revealed he had been tipped off that Anderson was coming.

To explain why he had arrived unannounced at his door, Anderson told Bodrero he had been hired by a "family out of Logan," and Bodrero interrupted, saying, "Yeah, she's got a lot of family up there." Although Anderson had not yet informed Bodrero of the subject or purpose of his visit, Bodrero already knew. The rest of the conversation further confirmed Anderson's initial suspicions that Bodrero had been warned of his possible arrival by Ingersoll.

At first, Bodrero claimed he didn't know anyone named Bob Dahle, but eventually reversed himself and acknowledged that he did. He tried to further obfuscate by stepping to his bookshelf and flipping through a Utah Highway Patrol yearbook in an awkward attempt to suggest that Dahle had retired in 1991, and therefore could not have been on active duty when the supposed investigation took place. Anderson interrupted his page-turning to inform him that the state internal affairs inquiry had taken place in 1990. Bodrero then claimed that although agency procedure dictated that internal affairs answered to the commissioner, in this particular case, he said, "I don't think it ever got to me."

For the entirety of his conversation with Anderson, Bodrero denied knowledge of the case, which strained credulity since an inquiry as serious as that one had to have been ordered and supervised by the commissioner himself—not to mention that the target of the probe was his lifelong friend and colleague Bob Dahle. Yet Bodrero continued to stonewall and further denied any knowledge of the existence of Valarie Clark or John Miller. He suggested that perhaps Colonel Duane Richens, then superintendent of the Utah Highway Patrol, had overseen the matter.

The day after his visit with Bodrero, Anderson paid a call on Richens who, when asked by Anderson if he could tape the interview, appropriately inquired as to its subject matter. After being informed about the purpose of Anderson's investigation, he agreed to the taping. He remembered Bob Dahle very well but said he was not aware that he'd been accused of the sexual abuse of a child and certainly would have remembered if he had been. As superintendent of UHP, he explained, had one of his officers been accused of a crime as serious as the rape of a child, he would have been informed of the investigation, not only because he may have served as a potential source of information, but also because it would have given him the opportunity to take precautions with Dahle's public role until the investigation had been concluded.

Further, Richens said it would have been very uncommon to use polygraphs in internal affairs investigations—in fact, in his entire career, he could only remember one occasion that a polygraph was used. The proper way to investigate a claim of sexual assault would have been to conduct a complete investigation of the facts.

———

Richard Lambert and Mike Anderson closely analyzed Anderson's interviews with the former DPS men and came to the disturbing conclusion that Mitch Ingersoll, Bob Dahle, and Doug Bodrero had orchestrated a cover-up. They made sure to keep Duane Richens out of the loop so that he remained unaware of the accusations brought by the Millers against one of his officers. Ingersoll repeatedly told Valarie and John the case was the most serious ever directed against a law enforcement officer of the Utah Highway Patrol, yet he never took any serious steps to conduct an investigation. Ingersoll also told the Millers in 1990 he was headed to Kansas to interview her doctor but never did. Instead, according to Mike Anderson's transcription of the 2020 interview, Ingersoll stated that he had spoken "on the phone" to a "mental health facility . . . back East" with an unnamed "psychiatrist" who had called Valarie a "schizo." Ingersoll told Anderson the people at the "famous psych hospital" "didn't believe her," that "in their opinion . . . she wasn't truthful."

Back in 1990, Ingersoll told the Millers that Bob Dahle had passed a polygraph test with high marks. This crushed Valarie and also allowed Dahle to return to the streets and potentially victimize more people. In 2020, Ingersoll told Anderson that Dahle had never taken one. Ingersoll further tried to lay the failure of the investigation on Valarie's refusal to take a polygraph—blaming the victim for his own failure to produce evidence against the man he was in fact protecting. This mistreatment worsened Valarie's psychological state and hastened the end of the Millers' marriage. The Miller children and extended families continue to suffer generational trauma from the original crime and the cynical and mendacious cover-up by state officials to protect one of their own.

CHAPTER FOURTEEN

Denial and Slander

AFTER ANALYZING HIS INTERVIEWS with Mitch Ingersoll, Doug Bodrero, and Duane Richens, Mike Anderson knocked on Bob Dahle's door on April 21, 2021. He gave his name and announced he was a retired FBI agent working as a private investigator. "I was hired by a law firm called WardLambert out of Salt Lake City to take a look at this issue involving Valarie Clark from some 30 years ago," Anderson said.

Dahle's response: "Oh, Jesus."

"Apparently, you're aware of it," said Anderson.

"Oh, yeah."

"I understand there was an investigation done some years ago that resolved this?"

Dahle said, "Well, it was resolved on *my* part. I don't know about the Clarks. What brings you by?"

"Well, obviously, your name surfaced in this."

"Why has this surfaced now?"

"I don't know; they didn't tell me that. They just wanted me to take a look at [the case]."

Dahle invited Anderson inside.

Over the following two hours, Dahle asked 10 times who was behind this renewed interest in the case and said more than 25 times, in various ways, "I better not say anything" or "I'm suspicious."

"Until you tell me, Why now? I'm not . . . ," Dahle stammered at one point. "As far as I'm concerned, it's all over with."

Anderson tried to calm Dahle and focus him on the 1990 investigation conducted by Mitch Ingersoll. He handed Dahle a photocopy of one line in a document that he had received as the result of a GRAMA request, indicating that the accusations against Dahle were "not sustained."[1]

When Anderson asked Dahle what had brought that investigation to a close, Dahle said, "First off, I never had anything to do with this lady. Second, I volunteered for a polygraph test."

"And you took one?"

"Yes."

Dahle asked if any new charges were being brought against him. Anderson made it clear that the statute of limitations had long passed and that the purpose of the investigation seemed to be that someone was "looking for resolution."

Dahle said again that, as far as he was concerned, "It's all over with . . . This lady died. She had I forget what kind of disease, but she died." And, throwing a bit of shade on Valarie, he added, "I know her husband divorced her."

Denial and slander. The Clarkston playbook. Doug Bodrero falsely denied knowing anything about the investigation, just as Gary Thompson, Bob Dahle, and Lloyd Clark denied knowing anything about the rape. Dahle lied that he had taken a polygraph. Mitch Ingersoll lied when he told Mike Anderson that Valarie's doctor called her a "schizo." Even when Valarie was alive, Zane said, "They used to say she was nuts. I have heard that over and over and over and over." Dahle also bad-mouthed other members of the Clark family. When Valarie and John first accused Dahle of sexual abuse in 1990, Mike Dahle told his friend Zane that his father told him that "[Zane] was gonna amount to nothing and that [he'd] probably be a drug addict and go to jail by the time [he] was 30."

Dahle asked Anderson for a business card, and Anderson obliged him. Anderson then managed to work the conversation back to polygraphs. He asked Dahle if he remembered who had administered the lie detector test and Dahle replied, "the Salt Lake County Sheriff's Department."

Dahle volunteered that times had changed with regard to men's behavior toward women and girls. "Sexual assault today," he said, "it's a hot issue. I mean, it's coming out of the woodwork."

Anderson replied: "Well, yeah, 'Me Too' and all that other movement stuff."

"So, I'd better not say anything," said Dahle.

Anderson then got up to leave. "Well Mr. Dahle, thank you. I won't take any more of your time."

When Anderson told Dahle he was off to interview the rest of the people on his list, Dahle perked up. "Well, if you could give me some names, I could maybe tell you where they live, or what's going on," he said.

Anderson asked if he could sit down again. Dahle assented. "One of the things that I've been told is that your name came up in relation to a very specific issue that occurred here in Clarkston in some kind of a barn," said Anderson. "And there were two other names named."

"Well, now you're telling me something I'm not aware of," said Dahle. "I mean, I'm aware that she made some sexual allegations, but not in a barn. So . . ."

Anderson mentioned Steel Canyon.

"Yeah, there's a Steel Canyon up here," Dahle said.

"What that means, I haven't got a clue," said Anderson.

Dahle responded: "Well, I just don't know what to say, so I'm not going to say anything."

"I'm not playing any kind of mind game here," said Anderson. "I'm just trying to gather some very fundamental information. All I've been told is that there were three persons named, you're one of them. There are two others—one of whom I think has also passed."

"Yes, that was Gary Thompson," said Dahle. And as far as the third one—"I don't know where he lives. His mother died."

"And his mother was Barbara?"

"Yes."

"Okay, then we're talking about the same person," said Anderson, and he let Dahle know he was aware of Valarie's accusation against Lloyd Clark.

Dahle then tried to derail the conversation by suggesting the third man had been someone other than Clark. Ollie Lou, who Anderson sensed was hovering in the next room listening to every word, offered helpfully, "Gary took a polygraph, too."

"One more question that I would ask you before I walk out the door," said Anderson. "Did either of these two guys ever come to you or did you ever talk to them about this? Because these are really pointed allegations."

Dahle said, "I talked to Gary, and Lloyd. I, I, I, I don't know. I don't know."

Then Ollie Lou interrupted with a surprising claim. "We didn't live here. We were in Henefer."

An article in the local *Herald Journal* about recent hires in the Highway Patrol stated that the Dahles lived in Henefer from April 1967 to March 30, 1968.

Possibly realizing the peril of this line of questioning, Dahle tried to end it. "I don't know whether Gary Thompson took a polygraph or not," he said. "My wife said yes, so probably it did happen."

"But this Mr. Lloyd Clark, you never heard about him taking one?" said Anderson.

Dahle said no, then tried again to get Anderson off this track by telling a story about an event that took place many years later, probably 1982. He said he came upon Valarie and another woman, whom he could not name, when they were having car trouble in the parking area on Valley View Highway.

"I got it into gear for her," Dahle told him. "She thanked me, and that was the last I saw her until these allegations came."

Anderson said, "You stopped to render aid, and allegations are made?"

Dahle didn't answer.

Anderson of course knew about Allyson Miller's recollection of that day on Valley View Highway. But she had told Anderson a vividly different version: The highway patrolman had acted so unhelpful and uncomfortable before speeding away in his squad car that the women had spoken about it.

Back to their interview, Anderson asked Dahle: "Did you ever pull her over as a child?"

"No, no, no," said Dahle.

It appeared he was lying yet again. Zane said Dahle did stop Valarie once when she was driving the family's Ford Pinto.

Anderson steered the conversation back to the internal affairs investigation. He asked Dahle who would have authorized an investigation into an officer. Dahle answered without pause that it would have had to be the commissioner. Then Anderson asked who the commissioner was at that time.

"Doug Bodrero."

Dahle then offered that at the time he was on the verge of suing John Miller, but then realized that would have forced him to leave his job and decided against it. "Because I didn't want to bring any publicity to the Highway Patrol," he said. "But then the trouble kind of died off until now, so . . ."

Anderson asked about Ingersoll again, and Dahle said he might be able to get some information on him and walked out of the room.

After a few minutes, he invited Anderson to follow him into his study, which was immaculately neat, like the rest of the house and the yard. Anderson glanced over the photos displayed there and commented on an old squad car from the '60s. Dahle said the photo showed a then-brand-new patrol car, a Chrysler, in which he had just run over a skunk. He parked it a ways from the sheriff's office to let it air out, and someone had taken a photo of it and given it to him.

Anderson asked who had taken the photo, and Dahle said, "Doug Bodrero." Anderson noted this close association between the two men but said nothing.

Dahle was holding a thick folder of papers and fiddling with his printer, which he said wasn't working. Anderson tried to move the conversation back to the polygraph. Might he happen to have the report?

"Well, that's what I was looking for," said Dahle, fussing. "I thought I had a copy. When they brought these allegations, I said, 'I will take any test. I'll take any test imaginable. You can give me truth serum or whatever. I'll take a polygraph test. Any test you want to give, I'll take.'" He then made a big show of rustling through his folder, ostensibly to produce the polygraph that he had passed with "high marks." But he couldn't find it. *If I had a polygraph pointing to my innocence for a crime like that*, Anderson thought, *I'd have it bronzed and hung on the wall.*

Anderson asked Dahle if Valarie took a polygraph.

"I have no idea."

Instead of his polygraph, Dahle handed over to Anderson a copy of a letter dated July 9, 1990, printed on stationery of the Utah State Department of Public Safety, with the state logo above the names of Governor Norman H. Bangerter and DPS Commissioner D. Douglas Bodrero. The letter was addressed to Lieutenant Robert M. Dahle, notifying him of the "completion" of the investigation into a complaint against him for "sexual abuse of a minor." The letter announced the claim was "not sustained . . . There is not sufficient evidence to either prove or disprove the allegations, therefore, it is resolved IN FAVOR of the employee."

Anderson got up to leave and thanked Dahle for his time.

Dahle said, "Well, you've ruined my day."

—

Once Mike Anderson examined the letter closely, he realized Dahle had inadvertently showed his hand. The cop who had managed to hide his savage abuse of Valarie Clark for 50 years had just seemingly slipped the noose around his own neck. Rather than the "get out of jail free" card Dahle believed he had been holding for 30 years in his files, the letter actually carried proof of the cover-up that would ruin him. It was tucked into the cc, or carbon copy, list at the bottom, the seemingly benign administrative traffic signs that determine who receives copies.

The letter, signed by Mitch Ingersoll, was cc'd to Commissioner Doug Bodrero and his deputy Brant Johnson. Curiously absent from the cc list was Duane Richens, the head of the Highway Patrol and Bob Dahle's direct boss. To Anderson, this intentional oversight showed that Ingersoll and Bodrero wanted Richens kept out of the loop. Bodrero, Dahle's longtime friend, was the senior man in this fake investigation; Ingersoll had previously told Anderson "all the investigations came through the commissioner's office."

Of course, Bodrero, should have recused himself immediately from overseeing an investigation of his old friend. But he did not. Instead, he protected Dahle, instructed Ingersoll to slow walk the investigation, and then quash Valarie's complaint, all the while making sure Richens knew nothing about it.

Anderson was also quickly able to demolish the claim that Dahle had passed, or even taken, a polygraph. Dahle told him he'd been tested by the polygrapher for the Salt Lake County's Sheriff's Office. Anderson already knew the polygrapher's name from Ingersoll: Steve Bartlett. Anderson discovered that Bartlett had passed away in 2017, but he tracked down his widow, who had saved her husband's meticulous handwritten logs for the Salt Lake County Sheriff's Office and other state law enforcement agencies.

According to those records, Steve Bartlett never conducted a polygraph examination of either Bob Dahle or Gary Thompson.

—

On November 19, 2021—a day less than a year after Mike Anderson's visit to Mitch Ingersoll—Richard Lambert sent an official notice of claim to the State of Utah via Utah Attorney General Sean Reyes.

A notice of claim is filed by a person or persons to inform a governmental entity of their intention to file a suit for monetary civil damages. The statute of limitations on a criminal complaint against Bob Dahle, Mitch Ingersoll, and Doug Bodrero had long passed, but Lambert thought a civil complaint against the state had a chance. His intriguing theory was that since the Millers had been deceived by state employees about the nature and results of the 1990 investigation, and since those lies and misrepresentations had caused the Millers to abandon their quest for justice, they had, in effect, been lied to every day, every year, and every decade since. Therefore, the clock on any statute of limitations should have started not 30 years ago from the conclusion of the flawed 1990 investigation but rather on the day Mike Anderson discovered the cover-up: November 20, 2020, the date of Anderson's interview with Mitch Ingersoll.

Lambert's letter stated that the members of the Miller family, "on their own behalf and on behalf of Valarie Clark Miller, deceased" intended to sue "the State of Utah, including the Department of Public Safety, and its former state employees Robert Dahle, Mitch Ingersoll, Doug Bodrero," and others.

The Miller family would sue the state for "violating Valarie's constitutional right to equal protection under the Federal Constitution and for violating Article I, Section 24 of the Utah Constitution." The complaint alleged that, among other things, "Officer Dahle used his position of authority to sexually abuse Valarie. Moreover, Respondents knew about the sexual abuse, and they had the ability and authority to address the abuse, but they were deliberately indifferent to the abuse. Accordingly, Respondents sexually abused Valarie and/or subjected to her to sexual abuse by acquiescing in it. Respondents also violated Valarie's constitutional rights when they treated her based on gender stereotypes."

This meant that the family intended to prove that the state of Utah had failed to properly supervise the men in charge of the investigation of Bob Dahle. Moreover, the charge of a violation of Valarie's "constitutional right to equal protection" meant the family believed the DPS investigation of Valarie's sexual assault complaint was inadequate because it was motivated by gender bias; that is, investigators failed to take Valarie's allegation seriously because she was a child and a female, thereby violating her rights to equal protection.

The family, the notice continued, also intended to bring various causes of action against the respondents for violating Valarie's constitutional right to bodily integrity "under the Substantive Due Process Clause of the Federal Constitution and for violating Article I, Section 7 of the Utah Constitution." This action would sue for damages for the rapes.

The Millers also intended to bring various additional "state law causes of action, including but not limited to claims for fraud, intentional infliction of emotional distress, negligent infliction of emotional distress, negligence, wrongful death and loss of consortium." As Paul Cassell, a celebrated faculty member at the University of Utah's law school, more elegantly explained it to me in an interview, this was legalese for throwing spaghetti against the wall to see what would stick. "In novel areas of law, lawyers routinely allege a lot of different theories, since it is not clear how the law and facts of the case will develop," he said.

Cassell was an expert on victims' rights whom Richard Lambert approached about joining the team in December 2021, just after the filing of the notice. A Stanford Law School graduate and former president of the *Stanford Law Review*, Cassell had clerked for Supreme Court Chief Justice Warren Burger before going on to serve as associate deputy US attorney general and assistant US attorney for the Eastern District of Virginia. He was later sworn in as a US district court judge for the District of Utah. Cassell resigned from the bench in 2007 to return to teaching, scholarly research, and representing crime victims, which he customarily did pro bono. He was awarded the Ronald Wilson Reagan Public Policy Award by the US Department of Justice's Office for Victims of Crime for his "monumental impact on the victims' rights field" and his "decades-long passion for the just and equal treatment of crime victims." He also cowrote the nation's only law school textbook on crime victims' rights, *Victims in Criminal Procedure*.

Cassell specialized in several areas critical to the case. In October 2018, he had filed a petition in the Utah Supreme Court on behalf of four "Jane Does," sexual assault victims whose cases had never been prosecuted. He argued that the failure to prosecute was the result of gender-motivated discrimination. "Sexual assault cases are not being taken seriously in Utah," Cassell explained. "Women and girls are being undervalued when they report those crimes."

He was working in collaboration with lawyers at the Utah Crime Victims Legal Clinic and others on an untested legal theory regarding a provision in the Utah constitution that might allow the Utah Supreme Court in special cases to appoint a temporary special prosecutor to pursue cases that had not been properly investigated. In 2019, the State of Utah "agreed to create a procedure where first-degree felony crimes could be reinvestigated by the Attorney General's office," said Cassel. "In exchange for getting that law put into effect, we agreed to drop our lawsuit in the Utah Supreme Court."

With Cassell on the case, the attorney general's office was put on notice that it would face an aggressive and effective advocate for justice for victims of sexual abuse. He rounded out a growing team fighting for the Millers. Richard Lambert, who had steered the case to this point, had served as an assistant US attorney for the State of Utah for 33 years and, after his retirement in 2013, had made a specialty of taking on cold cases. His longtime investigator, Mike Anderson, brought along 10 years as a polygraph expert for the FBI and a meticulous interest in the structures of law enforcement agencies and their chains of command. These skills had produced valuable evidence in the questioning of Mitch Ingersoll, Bob Dahle, and Doug Bodrero. In the spring of 2021, former Utah Supreme Court Justice Christine Durham joined the legal team to evaluate the various causes of action the Millers could bring and to judge the difficulty of overcoming the statutes of limitation for each. Richard Burbidge, a well-known litigator known for his courtroom flair and barn-burning closing arguments, was brought in as an advisor for potential lawsuits against the state and the individual perpetrators.

The notice of claim acted as a placeholder. If John Miller was going to sue the state for damages, he'd have to do it within one year. In that time, of course, the two parties could arrive at a settlement. But first, there was one final important lead to follow up on. According to Valarie, there had been a witness to the crime. Was Lloyd Clark ready to talk about what he had seen in the shed in Clarkston in 1968?

CHAPTER FIFTEEN

"My Memory Is on My Mind"

AS AN EXPERT IN HOW CRIMINALS TELL LIES, Mike Anderson was highly attuned to not only what people told him but also how they relayed that information. He noted that throughout Valarie's life, she was "remarkably consistent" and "detailed" in her account of the first rape in 1968. In every telling, she said three men were present in the barn owned by Earl Thompson and located across the street from her house. Bob Dahle, then 31, and Gary Thompson, then 33, took turns raping her, and Lloyd Clark, then 20, serving as a lookout, watched.

In contrast, Lloyd Clark's accounts of what he saw the day Valarie was first raped by Dahle and Thompson changed several times. When Denzel confronted Gary Thompson, Bob Dahle, and Lloyd Clark after Valarie first spoke of the rape after her 1985 hospitalization, Clark insisted he didn't know anything about it—as did Dahle and Thompson. When approached by FBI agents in April 1990, Clark again denied any knowledge of the event. (The FBI had been brought in to investigate by then Assistant US Attorney Richard Lambert.)

Then in 1990, after Dwight Pearce, mortified by the stories Valarie told him about her childhood abuse, questioned Clark harshly about what he knew of the rape, Clark changed his story. He admitted to Dwight that there had been a rape, but he insisted he hadn't been there. Rather, he knew it was true because Burke Godfrey had told him so. He called the FBI agents back and changed his story.

That same year, Clark was questioned again in a five-minute phone call by Mitch Ingersoll during his sham investigation. And Clark's story changed again; this time, he repeated the same denial that Thompson and Dahle had offered. He said he didn't know anything about a rape, and furthermore, he had the audacity to say, he was tired of being asked about it.

This was about the same time that Thompson and Dahle were both loudly claiming to anyone who cared to listen that they had both passed lie detector tests, though there isn't a shred of evidence that either took one.

Gary Thompson's daughter, Angie, told Mike Anderson that her father was "a shit" but that he had passed "three lie detector tests" about the rape—she had no idea when or by whom they had been administered—and she told Anderson that she had held the results in her own hands. "I know Bob and Dad both took multiple lie detector tests, and both of them passed their tests without a problem," she claimed.

Anderson found this highly doubtful. "You only give somebody a second polygraph if you've got inconclusive results," he told me. "And if you give somebody a third polygraph, the polygraph examiner doesn't have a clue what they're doing."

Despite all this polygraph activity, no law enforcement officials had thought of giving a lie detector test to the one alleged witness to the rape.

Not, that is, until Mike Anderson asked Clark in 2021 if he'd sit for a polygraph in the comfort of his own home in Logan. Clark, surprisingly, agreed.

An experienced polygraph examiner, Anderson made sure to create appropriate control questions to accurately assess the range of Clark's physiological responses. Then he asked Clark about that day in the barn. Although polygraph results are not generally admissible in a court of law, when a suspect is confronted with the results of a failed exam, Anderson told me, oftentimes they will then tell the truth or offer more information. In this way polygraphs can serve as effective investigative tools.

When Anderson told Clark the test indicated he was lying, Clark "got upset," in Anderson's words, but he didn't add any additional information or change his story. Anderson later played the tape of the polygraph interview for Richard Lambert and discussed the results with him. Lambert told me that Clark "consistently showed deception" during the interview. "He failed on the very point about whether or not he saw the two men go into the barn with Valarie," Lambert said.

When Lloyd Clark arrived in Logan in 2012 after being paroled from prison for trying to solicit a minor for sex over the internet, he wasn't sure what people thought of him, so he lied to his ex-wife, Kathryn Wixom, and he lied to his family, to his parole officer, and to himself about his crime.

Mike Anderson interviewed Kathryn, at her home in Nibley, Utah, on April 15, 2021. She explained that Clark, from whom she'd been divorced since 1980, had told her he'd been caught in a 2007 sting operation because "he acted interested in this little girl because he wanted to get to know her because he was lonely."

Wixom added, "That's what he swears."

But then she searched online and found a video of his arrest by a dozen armed police officers. "I seen them taking him down," she said. The violence, and its suggestion that Clark was a dangerous criminal, shocked her and their four children.

Though Clark tried to convince his family he hadn't done anything wrong, the police report included pages and pages of explicit online communications Lloyd had with an undercover officer posing as a mother looking for an adult male to have sex with her underage daughter. In those messages, he described a vivid and salacious smorgasbord of sexual wishes, including full penile penetration of the child.

He had apparently kept these details from his ex-wife.

Kathryn was desperate to believe Clark was telling the truth, and even accompanied one of their daughters on the long drive to Colorado to pick him up from prison when he was released in 2012. "He was so apologetic for what he had done," she told Anderson. She believed he had reformed, explaining that he was back in the church, having earned his way out of excommunication. "He's a good person now, I think."

Anderson asked her about their granddaughter, whom Clark had admitted to touching sexually while talking to the Colorado undercover police officer involved in the sting.

"I understand he was grooming her," she answered, "but she won't talk about it. . . . He says that nothing happened, but he was grooming her. I think he was messed up with child porn."

The only thing Clark admitted to with regard to his granddaughter, she said, was that "he sat her on his lap and they watched some porn. When she was 11. But he swears up and down that he didn't touch her inappropriately. He just watched porn, and he was starting to groom her."

Anderson was quiet, seemingly at a loss for words. Then Kathryn said, "I don't understand how far grooming can go."

Anderson explained that what Clark had done was "pretty far down the road."

She couldn't imagine he was doing anything wrong, she told Anderson, because he was "going to the temple."

There was also the question of what he was doing in 2021, the ninth year of his 10-year parole in Logan, Utah, where Clark had been living since his release. According to Anderson, Clark's parole officer was performing perfunctory COVID-19 era drive-by check-ins; the officer would cruise by Clark's apartment, and Clark would give him a wave from his window. But Mike Anderson and his team were busy watching Clark's every move via surveillance. One night, Anderson watched Clark drive to Wilson Elementary School and park in the schoolyard. He followed Clark down to Salt Lake City, observing him driving many extra miles to, Anderson surmised, "dry clean" his tracks before heading to the Hilton Hotel, where he checked in and stayed overnight. Anderson explained to me that criminals share instructions with each other about how to avoid being followed by law enforcement via driving around, including taking frequent turns to assure themselves they are not being followed.

Anderson and an associate staked out the hotel lobby, and they saw no children enter, nor did Clark leave. However, they did see Clark waiting in the lobby as if expecting someone. Although Anderson thought Clark intended to have an encounter with someone at the Hilton, it was also possible he wanted the opportunity to use unlimited internet without being surveilled.

Over the next several months, Anderson watched Clark going about the humdrum routines of his life, meeting his son, eating at local restaurants. Anderson got lucky one day when Clark walked into Café Sabor in Logan. He asked an acquaintance who happened to be there to snap a photo of Clark. Anderson was horrified to see Clark dining with a woman and a young girl. This was a clear violation of Clark's parole terms, which forbade him from being in the presence of a child. Anderson also discerned a wrapped gift in the photo, and its similarity with the circumstances of his prior arrest, before which he had purchased a gift for the child he expected to meet, looked like a very dangerous situation.

Anderson discovered that the woman was a work colleague of Clark's named Amanda Warren. After interviewing her, he learned that she and her daughter had been meeting with Clark for more than three years—since the girl was one-and-a half years old. Anderson acted quickly and gave the photo to the Adult Probation and Parole Division of the Utah Department of Corrections, which led to Clark's arrest. Anderson's goal was twofold: to get a dangerous predator off the street and to maneuver Clark into a position where it would be in his interest to tell the truth about what had happened to Valarie.

The official story, as set down in legal documents, went like this: On July 22, 2021, Detective Kyle VanAmen of the Investigations Division of the Logan City Police was contacted by Nathan Argyle, the investigator for the Cache County Attorney's Office, about a possible child sex abuse case in Logan. VanAmen looked through his list of known sex offenders to see if any matched the profile of this new case, and he came upon Lloyd Clark's name.

In Clark's file was information Anderson had provided to authorities that Clark was meeting regularly in Logan with a woman and her now five-year-old child. There were also documents from the police in Cañon City, Colorado, in which Clark spoke about touching his granddaughter. Argyle then took the initiative to identify the granddaughter, K. H., and he discovered that she had never been interviewed about her grandfather's abuse and that Clark had never been investigated for his statements about touching her inappropriately.

VanAmen created a case file and interviewed K. H., then 26. Based on the account she gave on July 30, 2021, VanAmen prepared an affidavit for Lloyd Clark's arrest on five counts of aggravated sex abuse of a child, each one a first-degree felony.

On August 17, 2021, a warrant for Clark's arrest was signed by Judge Angela F. Fonnesbeck of Utah's First District Court. He was arrested shortly thereafter.

Clark's children were shocked and ashamed. Two refused to have anything further to do with him, and two others struggled over maintaining contact. It was most difficult for his son, Ryan, because for years since his release from prison, Clark had been helping him out with his business, stocking grocery shelves with Little Debbie snack cakes.

Kathryn told Anderson that when the kids were young, "their dad wasn't in their life a lot." In fact, he decided to completely ignore his fourth child, a girl, because "he had only wanted three." They had all suffered from his early abandonment, but, Kathryn said, once Ryan became a teenager, Clark "really wanted to do things with his son."

When the news broke of his rearrest, Ryan couldn't handle the shame, particularly the news that Clark had sexually abused his own granddaughter—Ryan's niece. To make matters worse, many of his clients had met his father and knew they were working together. Kathryn explained that Clark's three daughters "can hide, because they've got different names. But Ryan is a Clark."

Ryan moved away.

Clark lied to his family and to Amanda Warren about his past. Kathryn said Clark told their eldest daughter, Monica, that he'd informed Amanda Warren that he was a registered sex offender. And Kathryn had the impression that he'd had dinner with the woman, who was in her 40s, and her daughter, only a few times.

She was shocked to learn from Anderson that they had met *dozens* of times. In fact, every week or every couple of weeks for the last three and a half years, they'd met for dinner or lunch.

Amanda Warren told Anderson that Clark had said nothing to her about being on the sex offender registry. She told Anderson that she was an orphan and her daughter had no grandparents, so Clark was very dear to them as a grandfather figure. Mother and daughter had even gone to Clark's apartment to help him when he had injured his foot. She added that Clark had asked her to go to Salt Lake City with him, but she had declined. Amanda said Clark was helpful to her in offering boyfriend advice in a grandfatherly way.

She seemed reluctant to believe he was a pedophile or that her daughter was not safe in his presence.

Kathryn was outraged to learn about these meetings and angrily admitted to Anderson that Clark had exhibited inappropriate behavior with girls when they were married and owned a restaurant in Logan called Kelly's Basket. In those years, he had taken it upon himself to drive the teenage female workers home at night after their shifts. "He'd drive 'em home so their parents wouldn't have to come get 'em, but I just felt like that was inappropriate," she said.

"He always wants younger and prettier," she said, her tone seeming to blame herself for his behavior.

—

When Mike Anderson first met Van Dell Henderson, polygraphs were again on his mind. It was August 2021, and Van Dell, a successful cattle broker in the West and beyond to China and Mexico, was then 70. Though he'd grown up in Clarkston, he'd been away for many years when Anderson arrived at his door in Rochester, Washington. He was alert and lively, though in poor health. He was shocked and aggrieved when Anderson told him about what had happened to Valarie, and sure of one thing: Bob Dahle and Gary Thompson would never have volunteered to take a polygraph. "I'll give you a hundred-dollar bill for each one of them reports you find, if you *can* find them, and I tell you what, you might as well pay me now," he told Anderson.

Gary Thompson was "a creep" in his personal life, Van Dell said, but "whip-smart" on mechanical matters and other things he put his mind to. He was certainly "smart enough to know not to take a polygraph test," he said. And Dahle? "Bob Dahle, good God, was law enforcement! Not unless they forced him."

Van Dell was an engaging storyteller with tales aplenty, and he and Anderson covered a lot of ground. But then he remembered an odd call he'd received one night from Lloyd Clark in the late 1980s, when he was still living in Clarkston. It was likely in August 1989, he said, in the evening, when he remembered his then-wife, Julie, picking up their phone and saying, with surprise, "Lloyd Clark?"

Van Dell got on the line, and Clark asked him, "Are you still going back and forth to Salt Lake?"

Van Dell remembered saying, in the rude tone he used on those who occupied a social status well below his own, "Well, yeah, what business is that of yours?"

"Are you going down soon?"

Van Dell answered that he would be heading down the next day, and Clark asked, "Can I get a ride?"

Van Dell said yes, so Clark asked to be picked up at his mother's place.

Their drive down was unremarkable, he recalled, and on the outskirts of the city, Van Dell asked Clark where he wanted to be dropped off. When Clark named the federal building, Van Dell said he was shocked. So he asked, "Lloyd what have you gotten into now?" Clark didn't answer and Van Dell dropped him off.

Van Dell had an early model mobile phone, and he gave Clark the number. He told Clark to call him when he was ready to be picked up.

Just as Van Dell was finishing up his meeting, his mobile phone rang, and Clark said he was ready to go. When Van Dell reached him, he noted that Clark looked "very upset," like he'd been "put through the grinder." Once they got on the freeway, Van Dell asked, again, "What have you gotten yourself into?"

This time, Clark admitted that he'd been to see the FBI. He said, "There's an investigation going on that Valarie Clark was abused."

Van Dell said, "What? You're involved?"

Clark said, "They're questioning me about it. But no, I didn't do anything to her."

"Well, who in the hell else are they talking about?"

"Burke Godfrey, Gary Thompson, and Bob Dahle."

"Jesus Christ!" Van Dell recalled saying. "What have you done?"

Clark insisted he was innocent.

"I didn't do anything, Van," he said. "They're questioning me because my name got involved somehow."

Van Dell was outraged; just the way Clark was speaking about it made Van Dell believe that he was lying and knew more than he was saying. Van Dell told Anderson, "I remember letting a few expletives out. I was upset because I figured it had happened. I assumed it had happened from what he told me."

Van Dell told Anderson that he loved and admired Valarie, and he was furious and heartbroken to learn of her abuse. "I mean, she was not seductive, she did not wear improper clothing, she was a straightlaced gal at that time in her life . . . she'd have been great to have your kid marry," he said. "Decent all the way through. Athletic, good grades, a good Mormon. That's Valarie. Bright, physically beautiful, spiritually beautiful. . . . Take the skin off that girl, she was as good inside as she was out."

And as far as Clark's claim that he knew about the rape because Burke Godfrey had told him so, Van Dell thought that claim absurd on its face: "Burke Godfrey would never talk to Lloyd Clark in confidence." According to Van Dell, Burke was not the kind of man to gossip about such things, and he never would have shared information of any kind with Lloyd Clark. "He would never speak to him unless [Lloyd] was working for him or to say 'good morning' or 'get on that tractor Lloyd, or this tractor, Lloyd.'"

By the time Van Dell had driven back to Clarkston, that day in 1989, he was sure that Clark had been involved in the sexual assault. He told Anderson he barely kept himself from attacking Clark. "I physically wanted to handle that," he recalled. "There was not going to be any goddamn judge and jury. I'd made my mind up." As he explained, driving back "was hell for me. And I think very nervous for Lloyd. There was no nice talk, or conversation going home after I found that out. If I were not cussing, I was gripping the steering wheel as hard as I could grip so I didn't have to pull over and kick the living hell outta him right then and there."

He restrained himself. But after taking Clark back to his mother's house, he was still so wound up that his wife was scared of what he might do, so she called one of her husband's friends who worked in the sheriff's office. Van Dell remembered the man came over and helpfully asked, "Hey, you want to end up in jail yourself with a bunch of crooks?" Van Dell said, "Well you know me, Jerry."

And Jerry said, "Yeah I do. That's why I'm here."

Van Dell told Anderson he remembered one more thing about that incident. Clark kept saying that he didn't really have anything to worry about because "they said, 'Don't worry, she's not gonna say anything. She's too scared to say anything.'"

Anderson interrupted Van Dell to say that from his 25 years in the bureau, he knew that the FBI would never make a statement like that to a suspect. If anyone made that statement to Clark, it had to have been Dahle or Thompson, which meant that the two men had conferred about the situation and were assessing their risk.

By this point in the interview with Anderson, Van Dell was fuming and imagining revenge on Bob Dahle in the traditional ways of the West. "I hope that before I die, I can look Bob Dahle in the eye and tell him, once again, what a fucking prick he is and always will be, and always was, and a goddamn liar," he said. "And that motherfucker can't even leave her alone now that she's dead."

Van Dell imagined the beating he'd give Dahle were he still in his prime—large, strong, and quick to raise his fists: "I'd give a lot to go back even 30 years if I got ahold of that miserable no-account." But then he thought for a moment and realized he'd never have had the satisfaction because, in his estimation, Dahle was a coward and he would have run away from him. And, he added, Gary Thompson would have run as well.

After Lloyd Clark's rearrest in 2021, Mike Anderson told Kathryn Wixom that John Miller and Richard Lambert wanted to reach out to her ex-husband. He told her they had "every reason to believe" Clark had information about the attack on Valarie Clark 53 years earlier and that, if he were able to "provide truthful information" about it, they would be willing to try to influence his upcoming sentencing. However, Clark would have to make his mind up soon. "The clock is ticking," he told her.

Ryan and Monica, Clark's eldest daughter, urged their father to cooperate so he wouldn't die in prison. Clark, then 74, asked Richard Lambert to provide something in writing about what he might expect to receive in return for any information he gave. Lambert prepared a letter, which was forwarded to Clark through his children. It began:

Mr. Clark, I'm writing this letter in response to your request that I put something in writing that explains how we might be able to help you if you can remember and truthfully relate what you witnessed regarding the sexual assault of Valarie Clark Miller in Clarkston, Utah.

Assuming you were able to relate a detailed, truthful account of people and events involved in Valarie's assault, this is what we will do. We will contact the Colorado parole authorities handling your case and inform them of your truthful and helpful cooperation in our very important investigation and urge them to release you on parole. . . . Additionally, we will approach the Cache County Attorney to explain the extent of your cooperation and recommend that you be allowed to plead to a reduced charge that will not carry a mandatory sentence of imprisonment in order to allow the court to fashion a lesser sentence, including the possibility of a probationary one.

Lambert emphasized, "Of necessity, we must be the sole judge of the extent of your helpfulness. We can't promise any particular outcome since that is beyond our control. We will, however, give it our best effort based on your recollection and cooperation."

He also told Clark that he was arranging for him to meet with a forensic psychiatrist named Dr. Michael Welner, who would conduct an interview with him at the Bent County Correctional Facility and try to help walk him through his memories.

Clark agreed to the terms, and Dr. Welner made room in his busy calendar to fly to Colorado. On December 1, 2021, Welner set up a video camera in a visiting room at the prison in Las Animas, Colorado, 85 miles east of Pueblo. Mike Anderson, Richard Lambert, and John Miller, who had all flown to Colorado, reviewed the taped interviews at the end of each day.

In the videos, Clark appeared to be a meek, rotund man with a round, pink face and glasses. He held his body very still, his hands clasped in his lap, though he occasionally gestured with one or both arms in languorous movements.

The mystery of memory was the theme that Clark settled on early in his interview. "I was told that you have a way of going back, deep into my mind, to find out if I know anything," he told Dr. Welner. "And, uh, just wondering if it's going to have any effects on me later on in life. Um, my memory is on my mind."

Dr. Welner tried to reassure him: "I'm not doing anything biological, and I'm not doing anything hypnotic. We're actually just going to have a conversation."

Anderson believed Clark's question was a feint. The idea of seeking help to find something lost in his memory was "a ploy that I've seen before," he said. It was Clark's attempt to protect himself from the truth. "After all, at this point," Anderson concluded, the story that he knew nothing about the rape was "a 50-year-old lie."

Dr. Welner started by asking Clark about his current circumstances at the jail, and Clark said he was quite comfortable, a situation much different from the prison in Fremont County, Colorado, where he had been housed a decade earlier. Back then, "there was a lot of guys getting beat up, getting their lives threatened," he said. "I got mine threatened three times, and because I was a sex offender, those that wasn't wanted to take care of the ones that was. And so it was a very stressful time there." He told Dr. Welner that he'd found people who protected him.

Where he was currently housed, at Bent County Correctional, life was "a lot more relaxed," according to Clark. He was "in a pod where there's just older guys, and there's no threats on my life."

This answer was meaningful for Dr. Welner, who was trying to gauge how motivated Clark might be to make a deal. Dr. Welner pressed on, asking Clark to speak about his early childhood. Clark explained that he was born at Hill Air Force Base near Clearfield, Utah, on August 24, 1948, where his father, Venis, was stationed. Venis hailed from a tiny agricultural town called Tetonia in Idaho, but his family moved to Clarkston, where Venis met and married Barbara Jardine, who already had a son, Ralph, fathered by another man out of wedlock. The two boys looked nothing alike; Ralph was tiny, about 5 feet, 6 inches, wiry and athletic, with dark hair—"small and rawhide mean," according to Mike Anderson, who interviewed him. Lloyd, however, was 5 feet, 11 inches, light-haired and heavyset.

Because Venis was in the air force, the family moved frequently. After Clark's birth, they moved to San Antonio, where the family welcomed a new baby, Ruth Ann, in 1951. A couple of years later, they moved to Sacramento, then to Fairbanks, Alaska, where in 1954 Clark's youngest sister, Jane, was born with Down syndrome. The family then lived in Denver for seven and a half years.

Clark remembered spending pleasant Christmases with his grandparents in Clarkston through the years, but he was never invited to stay for the summer, like his brother was. "I always felt bad about that because I felt that I was good enough to go and stay with relatives, too," he said. But there was a hitch. "If they didn't want you to, you couldn't go."

When asked which of his siblings he was closest to, he answered that he was now close to both surviving siblings. (His youngest sister had passed away at 52 of natural causes.) But earlier in his life, he wasn't close to either one because, he said, "I had a lot of problems mentally. And, I hated myself. I didn't like what I was doing. I just didn't like life in general." He didn't know what was wrong, except, "I was so mixed up." He didn't explain why he hated himself.

In 1961, Venis was transferred to Korea, and Barbara gathered up her brood and moved to Clarkston. Clark entered the seventh grade and found that transitioning from big-city life in Denver to Clarkston, population 500, was difficult. With their dad away, the kids had more responsibility to help their mother. Clark remembered having to break up coal for the stove that they used for cooking and heating the house. Clark said that he had been close to his brother in Denver, "but for some unknown reason, when we moved to Utah, that didn't happen anymore. So I didn't have him. And we argued a lot and fought."

"My brother has always been the one that's got the recognition," he said. Unlike Clark, Ralph made friends and was good at sports. He played football and excelled in track, earning state records for sprinting the 100- and 220-yard dashes.

Clark said he was bullied at school: "I was picked on, and it was very traumatic for me because the people that I thought would accept me, didn't. And so the only ones that was left was those that was doing wrong, and I went with them. I even started drinking a little bit."

He said a neighbor, Kendon Godfrey, bullied him on the school bus. Many years later, after Kendon returned from his Mormon mission, Clark got crosswise with him. "He took my girlfriend away from me," explained Clark. "I mean, I *thought* she was my girlfriend. I don't know whether *she* did or not." That girl was Jaydene Buttars, whom Jann Pugmire told me she thought Clark was stalking but never dating. Jaydene and Kendon later got married, and Clark acknowledged that "they've been together ever since."

High school was frustrating for Clark. "I couldn't get a date," he told Dr. Welner. "I didn't have any real friends. In fact, I haven't had any real friends most of my life. A lot of times I thought I was doing better with the girls and come to find out I wasn't."

Clark wasn't good enough at basketball to get on a team in junior high, but he discovered he "excelled at baseball." He didn't excel enough, however, to make the high school team until his senior year. "Then I quit and went out partying," he said. One time, Bob Dahle caught Clark riding his horse drunk in Clarkston. "He got mad at me, and told me to go home," recalled Clark. "He said that he could get me for drunken driving by me even being on a horse. So I went home and took the saddle off. Took care of that."

Clark wasn't always so docile. Curtis Godfrey remembered that he had a "very, very bad temper." Curtis told me in an interview that he had observed Clark's handiwork after he beat up a Clarkston man: "I seen [the victim] the next day, and he looked like [Lloyd] took a baseball bat to him."

Dr. Welner asked Clark what he liked to do as a young man.

"I liked to race my car," he replied. "I always drove fast and exceeded the limits of trying to see how fast I could go around the corner." On at least one occasion, he played this dangerous game while driving his sister Ruth Ann and her friend Debbie Clark home from school when they were 15. As Debbie recalled it, as they "were going around that corner into Clarkston, I was terrified he was going so fast. I thought, *We're gonna die.*" But he made it around the curve without flipping the car. Debbie also remembered Clark driving so fast by her husband, a triathlete who competed in the Ironman competition, that he almost knocked him off his bicycle. Debbie said she thought "maybe he didn't like bicycles."

Clark seemed to have courted death a few times himself while driving. "I tried to run off the road at one hundred miles an hour doing this," he told Dr. Welner, wiggling his hands left and right, as if handling a steering wheel.

One time, he sped toward an oncoming train at a railroad crossing near Newton, turning away only at the last minute and flipping his car into a ditch. Again, it was Debbie Clark Cooper who, coincidentally, saw this accident. "I thought, *Oh my gosh, this car is gonna hit this train*, but all of a sudden, it turns to the left and rolls," she said. She pulled up and saw, "the car's lying on its side, and the door opens, and Lloyd Clark comes out. It was him, and he hadn't been injured at all."

Clark said he'd just been "waiting for an angel to come and take me away."

He graduated from high school in 1967 and studied for two years at Utah State University before dropping out. He got a job at the Utah-Idaho Sugar Company plant in Garland, which was owned by the LDS church. He had an industrial accident there—deep cuts on his chest and behind one ear. The injuries would later keep him from being sent to Vietnam, but Clark, in typical fashion, turned what others might have hailed as a stroke of good fortune into another occasion for self-pity. He told Dr. Welner, "I went down [to the draft board] with fourteen other guys, and they all went, and I was watching them getting sworn in, and they wouldn't take me."

He got a job as a shipping clerk at Schreiber Foods in Logan, Utah, and met Kathryn Hansen, a girl who worked in the office. They dated for about two years. "All that time, two years, she did nothing but break my heart," he told Dr. Welner. After bringing her home from a date, he parked down the street and watched her leave the house again, only to return soon after with another man. On another occasion, he called and asked to see her, and she said she already had a date. He questioned her, saying he thought "we was going steady." But she said no, he was mistaken. Nevertheless, he stalked her, following her and her date to the theater, where he was outraged to see her rest her head on the other man's shoulder. He interrogated her about this later, and she said she was just tired. But he told Dr. Welner, hurt and angry, "She never done that to me!"

Kathryn's parents didn't like Clark and refused to speak to him at their first meeting, which he took as a grave affront. In spite of all this, Clark asked Kathryn to marry him. He was 25, she was 24.

Dr. Welner asked him why he had proposed marriage to a woman who he felt was already treating him badly. "Because I felt like I wouldn't have a chance with anybody else," he said. Kathryn later told Mike Anderson that Clark had threatened to kill himself if she didn't marry him.

On November 13, 1973, they took their vows in the Logan temple, but Clark quickly realized he wasn't ready for marriage—its practical responsibilities or its spiritual ones. "I wasn't ready to go through the temple because I was out boozing it up," he said.

His relationship with Kathryn got no better, though they produced four children in quick succession. "She just belittled me, and I couldn't handle it," he said. He responded by initiating an affair with her best friend, who promptly turned up pregnant. "I was hurting, and I needed somebody to give me some attention, and that's what she did."

He and Kathryn separated, then got back together. They got divorced, and then started dating again. "It was a lot better dating that time because we laughed and had a good time," Clark told Dr. Welner. "So we got married again, and it went down the tubes again. If I'd stayed with her, they'd have to have put me in a straightjacket."

They ran a restaurant in Logan that went belly up after a few years, and the family sold their home to pay off their debts. "We lost everything," Kathryn told Mike Anderson. They moved to Arizona but did no better there. "And then he decided it was too hard to support a family." They divorced for good in 1980. "So, he left me with no home, and our car was taken away. He left me with nothing but four little kids, the oldest was five. He was a selfish, selfish man."

Marrying Lloyd Clark, she said, was "the worst mistake of my life, but well, other than I had four kids with him."

CONTENT WARNING:

This chapter contains material that is particularly difficult to read. There are graphic descriptions of grooming and explicit online conversations between a pedophile and someone he believed was a child (but was actually a police detective). There was also an offer of payment made for a visit with the child. This constitutes child trafficking. Please read the chapter with caution.

After the divorce, Lloyd Clark had some trouble holding a job. Shortly after his interview with the FBI about Valarie's assault, he moved to California and stayed with his sister Ruth Ann and eventually got work with a numismatist—a rare coin dealer. He went to California, he told Dr. Welner, "to try to find a new life and start over and get my feet back on the ground." He needed space from family because he felt they underestimated his abilities. "A lot of times when I wanted to start a business or do something like that, [my family would] always put me down and say, 'You can't do that. You don't know how to do it. So just forget about it and go over there and work the nine-to-five job.'" For his part, John Miller scoffs at Clark's explanation for his move to California, believing instead that his hasty departure had everything to do with avoiding Utah's snooping FBI agents.

Clark worked collecting and selling coins in the Golden State until he got in a fight with his boss, who was angry that Clark hadn't warned him that his star salesman was quitting. The boss "hit me and knocked me clear across the room," said Clark. "And told me I was fired." Clark said he "packed up my things and come back home."

He lived in Salt Lake managing a Burger King, but before a year was up, he was back home with his mother in Clarkston, working a nine-to-five at Ritewood Egg Farm. He stumbled through a few more unsatisfying attempts at relationships and at least twice visited a whorehouse in Nevada with a friend. He told Dr. Welner he didn't like it there, because "there's no real feeling in it." The only feeling was, he said, "that you're losing a hundred bucks."

In his 40s, he found his way, with the help of another friend, into a long, destructive relationship with pornography. Chat rooms and sites with webcams "just overwhelmed me and I got too deep," he said. "It took over my life."

While talking about various sexual scenarios, he explained, he and his interlocutors took turns masturbating in front of the camera. His favorite chat room, he told Dr. Welner without shame or pause, was called "Incest." He set up his computer to connect to the site automatically.

It wasn't long before Clark transitioned his sexual urges from fantasy to reality and began to molest his then eight-year-old granddaughter, K. H.

K. H. told investigators decades later that he first touched her vagina in a swimming pool in 2003 in Logan, Utah. The family, unaware of the abuse, moved away because of K. H.'s father's work, but when they returned to Logan during her fifth-grade year, her grandfather's abuse resumed. She remembered that Clark touched her nipples while she was sitting on his lap. He also did so when he was online chatting with women on the internet. He molested her when he was babysitting her and when playing the "tickle game." On a few occasions, Clark also slept in the same bed with her.

The abuse ended when Clark was arrested for soliciting sex with a child over the internet in June 2007. The details of the case against him were outlined in documents prepared by the Cañon City Police Department. The following descriptions of their internet communications are repulsive and disturbing, but they speak directly to the character of Lloyd Clark, his limited intelligence, and his inability to tell the truth.

On January 15, 2007, someone using the screen name of "firtouch" contacted "Sheryl," an undercover police officer posing as a woman with an 11-year-old daughter. "He asked questions about my daughter," the officer wrote in her report, "and told me he had an eleven-year-old granddaughter who had a very nice looking and great body. He said he had rubbed her nipples once and he wanted to do more sexual things with her. He told me that she was just getting her 'titties' and it was so sexy. He wanted to know if my daughter was getting breasts also."[1]

Firtouch, who claimed his name was Thomas, sent Sheryl his phone number, which she then traced to Lloyd Thomas Clark. He asked if Sheryl wanted to see what her daughter thought of him by having her look at his webcam. She agreed and transferred the chat to her daughter, "C.". The officer's report continued:

> Thomas then spoke with my daughter under my adult profile name. He said that he wanted to do fun things with us and that he would like to cuddle with us so we could play with each other. He told her that he wanted to touch her "titties" and kiss them and he wanted to watch her masturbate and have sex with me. He asked my daughter if she wanted to have sex with him. He said he wanted to have sex with her. He told her that he thought her "little pussy" would taste good. He said that he guesses that she was very tight and that guys liked that. He continued by saying that he would love to see her nice sexy "titties." He asked if she liked her nipples sucked and her pussy

licked. He told her that he was getting very excited. He asked her if we had a webcam. She said that he seemed "kewl" and he told her he hoped the rest of him would satisfy her.

Thomas told Sheryl that he got interested in young children because of the internet and had been looking for very young children for about two years. He said he had never "been with" a young girl before. It would be his first time.

He told Sheryl "to give my daughter a kiss for him and to kiss her nipples and 'pussy.'" He asked C if she "had put her finger inside herself." He told her that a "cock" would feel even better.

Thomas told Sheryl that he would "love to help me teach my daughter about men," and he was specific about his desire that she would "suck" on his penis and that he would ultimately penetrate her, but he averred, "he wanted to be careful with her and didn't want to hurt her." He then revealed that he had identified a Quality Inn in Cañon City and had scouted out a room that was "right by an indoor pool." They made plans to meet on June 18, 2007, first without the daughter at a Denny's near the motel. He told Sheryl he would be wearing a "black shirt with stripes and cut-offs."

On June 18, Thomas approached the Denny's, unaware that 12 officers were stationed inside and outside the restaurant. "He appeared to be nervous and quite suspicious," per the arrest report. "He walked around the establishment, eyeing the patrons in a long and careful manner. He then returned to the front, paced around near the entrance, and frequently looked closely again at the patrons, of which there were 10 to 12. After a short time, [he] seemed to relax and then sat down at the bench near the entryway."

Soon, Sheryl arrived. The two entered the restaurant and sat at a booth. Thomas told Sheryl that while at Walmart, he had bought some white shorts and a yellow tank top as a present for her daughter. Thomas said "we could take things as they came," but that there would be "no force." He told Sheryl he could give her $100 in exchange for being with her daughter.

They decided to leave to pick up the daughter, and when Thomas stepped outside, he was tackled, handcuffed, arrested, and placed in a patrol car.

At the Cañon City Police Department, Lloyd Clark waived his rights to an attorney and signed a consent form allowing a search of his hotel room and his vehicle. Later he signed a consent form for officers to search his residence and his computer. He also gave the police the password to his instant messaging account for the screen name that he used while communicating with Sheryl.

In a post-arrest interview, Clark said he "didn't believe there was a real eleven-year-old anyway," but he arranged the meeting because he was "curious." He said he "would not have done anything sexual with her at all because he had grandchildren her age." Although Clark had admitted to Sheryl that he'd touched his granddaughter, the Cañon City Police did nothing to initiate an investigation.

Clark told the police that he had "about 20 child pornography pictures"[2] on his computer. He said he regularly kept a collection of pictures for about a month, then deleted them and got more. He admitted that he spoke with other adults and children about "sexual things of this nature."

When asked about the significance of his "firtouch" screen name, Clark said it stood for "first touch."

Mike Anderson told me: "He's a pedophile. He spends every moment of his miserable life thinking about touching children. We perhaps know 2 percent of what Lloyd has done."

—

Dr. Welner explored Lloyd Clark's life history for several hours on December 1, 2021. He ended that day's conversation by saying, "It sounds from what we've talked about, like there's very little that you're able to add about Bob Dahle."

Clark interrupted him: "Like I said, I don't know, cause he was older than me, and I never did go out, you know, do things with him."

And as far as Gary Thompson was concerned, Clark said, "He's dead."

After the session, Dr. Welner told Richard Lambert, John Miller, and Mike Anderson that he predicted Clark would only reveal what he knew about Valarie when "his back was up against the wall." Dr. Welner believed that only when Clark felt desperate and had nowhere else to turn, would he admit to seeing Valarie's rape.

Although Clark knew he faced additional prison time, his current place of incarceration wasn't dangerous or uncomfortable. His back wasn't yet against the wall.

Dr. Welner returned to the prison early on the morning of December 2, and he asked Clark if he'd had any dreams or new thoughts. Clark said no. Dr. Welner once again reviewed Clark's current predicament with him, trying to get him to focus on the seriousness of his situation and his only way out: to provide the Miller team with what it wanted—a factual description of what had happened to Valarie in the Clarkston barn.

To that end, Dr. Welner reminded him that he was still facing sentencing for the abuse of his granddaughter, whereupon Clark interrupted and, with great emotion, insisted "that he had admitted to the offenses," according to Welner's notes—as if that nullified his guilt and its real-life consequences.

Unimpressed, Dr. Welner told Clark: "I don't think you have a memory problem; you have a denial problem."

Dr. Welner then mentioned something that was bound to make Clark squirm: the ride Van Dell Henderson gave him to Salt Lake City to meet with the FBI agents in 1990. This was a trip Clark had never mentioned to Mike Anderson during their numerous conversations, and something he evidently wanted to keep from him. Dr. Welner recalled in his written notes of the interview, "I reminded him that he had been driven to and from the FBI meeting in Salt Lake City by Van Dell Henderson. He acknowledged that this 'could be.'" Dr. Welner then told Clark that Van Dell Henderson "had spoken to us" and had said that he had mentioned that "there were four people at the scene in which Valarie was attacked, and that [Lloyd] was one of them, as had been Mr. Godfrey."

Suddenly, Dr. Welner recalled, Clark "rose in his chair and declared that he was going to end the interview." He waved his arms, he swore, and he walked away from the camera. He said "screw this" and that he would sue Richard Lambert, Mike Anderson, and Dr. Welner.

Dr. Welner, surprised by Clark's reaction, "tried to reassure him that this was only what Mr. Henderson said, and that this was his opportunity to speak."

But Clark was done. He said, "Fuck you," then waved his arm angrily and dismissively, saying, "Go back to New York," before he stalked off, calling for a guard.

Anderson had earlier observed that Clark "sits there like a church mouse until there's something that really is threatening to him. He becomes physically agitated when you get close to something that he feels really threatened by. And then he starts [moving] his body. It's like a switch is flipped."

But what had threatened him, I wondered to Anderson.

With characteristic bluntness, Anderson said, "Lloyd's got the IQ of a turnip. He is a stupid man, but he is married to this lie, and one of the most important things in his sorry, miserable life is preserving this lie. I can only imagine how much of the limited intellect he's had available to him over the course of his life that he's devoted to cultivating and protecting this lie."

———

On April 11, 2022, Lloyd Clark pled guilty to one count of aggravated sexual abuse of a child, a first-degree felony, in a plea deal. This was for the charges brought by his granddaughter, identified in court documents as K. H. He appeared for sentencing on May 23, 2022, in Cache County District Court. K. H. elected to make a statement to the court against him. Fighting back tears of pain and outrage, she offered a pointed indictment of her grandfather's treatment and its psychic cost to her:

When I was a young girl, I had all of the innocence of childhood taken from me. I was sexually violated and abused by a man I was supposed to trust and look up to—my grandfather. Lloyd Clark came to the absurd conclusion that my body was his to do with as he pleased.

Lloyd's choices to violate and abuse me as a child changed my life forever. . . . As a result of Lloyd's vile choices, I have been left with a lot of emotional damage the last 16 years. I have dealt with a skewed perception of my self-worth because my body was used for someone else's sexual desires.

I thought that that is where my self-worth lies. I have felt a lot of self-hatred because of this. For many years, I thought a woman's role was to be desirable and pleasing for men. It wasn't until I got married that I learned how false that is. My amazing husband showed me the error in my thinking through his love and respect for me. I'm still working on believing that I am more than my body . . . I have dealt with anxiety, including social anxiety and too many panic attacks to count. I have trust issues. I've dealt with immense shame and guilt with myself because of what happened. I also have emotional eating problems stemming from that shame and guilt. One thing I have learned recently is that I am a survivor. I don't give up, and I will not give up on myself in regards to healing. I am seeking counseling to help me heal.

She concluded: "I am incredibly grateful for the justice system and each person that has made it possible for me to stand up for myself today. Thank you for the opportunity to speak my truth and share my story."

And then, her voice breaking, she turned to Clark and said: "And I just want to say that, despite the hell you have put me through, I forgive you."

She later told John Miller she didn't forgive Lloyd because her religion demanded it, nor to ease his guilty conscience. Rather, she did it for herself. "I truly believe forgiveness is about letting go of that control someone has over our mind and heart," she explained. "It doesn't mean we won't ever feel anger or sadness or pain over what they did to us, it simply means it won't control us anymore. Boundaries are also so very important and should still be enforced when we forgive. Boundaries are quite foreign for abuse survivors in my opinion, at least they were for me for a long time."[3]

Lloyd Clark was given a sentence of five years to life, of which he is expected to serve 8 to 10 years, according to the Cache County Attorney's Office. As of this writing, he remains unwilling or unable to tell what he knows about Valarie's rape in the barn. Mike Anderson expects that Clark will die in prison.

CHAPTER SIXTEEN

Last Rites and Wrongs

ON THURSDAY, JUNE 23, 2022, I knocked on the front door of Bob and Ollie Lou Dahle's house in Clarkston. Ollie Lou answered, and I asked if Dahle was home. She told me he was out back, but then he suddenly appeared in the front yard, which he was famous for keeping in immaculate order. He looked dapper in a sport coat, slacks, and aviator sunglasses. He mentioned that he and Ollie Lou were on their way to a funeral. I explained that I was writing a book about Valarie Clark Miller and wanted very much to hear his side of the story. He listened quietly, leaning his back against the garage door for support, and when I finished my pitch, he said, "I don't believe I would want to be involved with it."

I asked him if he knew Valarie, and he smiled. "Oh, yeah, I knew her."

I again explained that I would like to talk to him about her and the town. He said, "I think you probably just need to get ahold of her family."

We spoke for another couple of minutes, and I asked one more time if he'd be willing to tell me his side of the story. Once again, he demurred. "I gotta run," he said. He entered the garage and pulled out the car.

Four weeks later, on Wednesday, July 27, 2021, I learned that Bob Dahle had suffered a stroke and was in the hospital.

The next day, the Clarkston gossip lines were sparking with activity.

Dahle was grievously ill, suffering from cancer of the liver, hip, pelvis, and spine and had only two or three weeks to live.

Dahle was aware of the Millers' filing of the notice of claim the previous November, and he knew that the Utah Department of Public Safety was conducting its own investigation of the supposed 1990 internal affairs probe of Valarie's claim that he had raped, beaten, and abused her. DPS had offered him defense counsel if he wanted it. In the last weeks of his life, he was dodging calls from the attorney general's office, trying to arrange a date to question him; he could hear the hoofbeats of his pursuers thundering up behind him.

Bob Dahle managed to dodge the bullet one more time. He died on August 1.

Ollie Lou said that her husband's final words were, "It's over."

Bob Dahle's funeral took place on Tuesday, August 9, 2022, and he got a fulsome send-off. The church parking lot was packed with cars, and despite the investigation, the Highway Patrol sent 20 uniformed patrolmen in pressed uniforms riding polished motorcycles to escort Dahle's casket to the cemetery. The cover of Dahle's funeral program featured a drawing of the Logan Temple, something that was important to Ollie Lou, and inside there was not one, as was customary, but two different photos of Dahle, one of him in his uniform and a wide-brimmed Highway Patrol hat. "How Great Thou Art" was sung, as was "Homeward Bound."

When Debbie Clark Cooper saw the elaborate funeral procession, she was so upset that her daughter had to take her for a drive out of town.

"I feel like he won again," she told me in despair.

When I told John Miller this, he said, "Not for long. It will be all the more dramatic when the truth comes out very soon." There is a teaching in the LDS church that states: "Whatever is hidden shall be revealed."

The obituary in the local newspaper was a rewrite of the long encomiums

Ollie Lou had offered up on the occasions of his 80th and 85th birthdays, with some extra details. Dahle had started a hog farm with his sons and won ribbons for his prize hogs. He "made large wishing wells for his wife, daughters, and daughters-in-laws." Even his beloved '67 Ford truck made it into the obituary: "The great-grandchildren loved to ride in Grandpa Bob's old green and white truck up to Mike's to feed the cows." Family life was given its due: "Bob enjoyed working in his yard and having family parties. The summer party and the Christmas party were his favorites. At the Christmas party, Grandpa Bob would sit in the rocking chair, read the story of the birth of Jesus as the young ones in costumes would take part. Such a special memory!"[1]

But oddly, the obituary left out one declaration that had been published in both his 80th and 85th birthday announcements. Missing was: "Dad is a man of his word; a great example of love, sacrifice, service and dependability. We couldn't have asked for a better example for us, our kids, and grandkids."[2]

Dahle reserved his own final wish for the back page of his photocopied funeral program. It is expressed in a poem titled "The Fisherman's Creed":

I pray that I may live to fish
Until my dying day.

And when it comes to my last cast,
I then most humbly pray!

When in the Lord's great landing net
And peacefully asleep,

That in His mercy I be judged
Big enough to keep.

Beneath the poem is a photo of Bob Dahle in full fishing regalia, crouching in the mud beside a stream, his mouth open in a jagged facsimile of a smile, a large, glistening rainbow trout dead in his lap.

CHAPTER SEVENTEEN

Justice Delayed

ON DECEMBER 5, 2022, a calm, gray day, I walked into the third-floor meeting room of the Utah State Bar building in Salt Lake City for a press conference called by the Miller family. It was full to bursting with local journalists and television cameras, stands, and wires. In the front row, beside an enlarged photo of a sad but defiant 16-year-old Valarie, Denzel, 92, sat with his daughter Debbie and grandchildren Ryan, Brooke, and Annie. Debbie's husband, Dan Cooper, was present, as was Zane Clark's wife, Annette, and many other family members, including John Miller's brothers Bruce, Ted, and Scott.

Victims' advocate Paul Cassell opened the briefing. "This is really quite a remarkable story," said the slim, soft-spoken law professor. "Really like nothing else I've ever heard of in the crime victims' rights field."

Cassell explained that the Utah Department of Public Safety had proffered the Miller family a letter he described as "unprecedented in the history of Utah, perhaps unprecedented even if you look more broadly around the country."

"Yesterday, we received a letter of apology from the State of Utah for a sexual assault that was committed more than a half-century ago against a woman who tried to get justice from the State of Utah—unsuccessfully," he explained. "The State of Utah apologized to Valarie for what happened." He continued: "Crime victims are on a long and winding road to justice, and all too often, they don't get justice. At least in this case, there's some small measure of justice."

Cassell read from the letter, signed by Commissioner of Public Safety Jess Anderson, who explained that his department, in cooperation with the attorney general's office, had "interviewed scores of witnesses over several months." Based on that "thorough investigation," Anderson wrote, "I have concluded that the factual allegations you raise in your notice of claim and subsequent communications about DPS actions in 1990 rest on a foundation of extensive and disturbing evidence."

Anderson offered the Miller family a personal apology. He wrote that he had "agonized over the events you described and the generational impact on your family." Though there was no legal recourse available to him "to right the wrong that was done to Mr. and Mrs. Miller more than three decades ago," he expressed "my deep regret to John R. Miller and family members of Valarie Clark Miller (now deceased) for the emotional distress suffered by Mrs. Miller, Mr. Miller, and the family as a result of the actions described in your notice of claim."

Cassell noted that Anderson had further promised that the Department of Public Safety would bring in a well-respected outside expert agency to examine its policies and procedures to make sure that what happened to Valarie and her family would never happen to anyone else. "So we have both a retrospective apology and a prospective effort to improve the policies and procedures that are in place here in Utah," Cassell said.

Although no timeline had been established for the study, Cassell later explained to me, "We had a very clear meeting of the minds about what needed to happen—it's the proverbial question: Can you rely on the fox to guard the henhouse?" The answer to that question remains to be seen.

The apology had come after months of negotiations between the DPS and the attorney general's office, with input from the Millers' legal team. It had been a delicate dance, as the relationship between the attorney general's office and DPS was complicated. Formally and legally, the people in the attorney general's office were the lawyers for DPS. But, said Cassell, "practically, they are separate entities." In the end, he said, "fortunately, it appears that the investigations of the AG and DPS, started at separate times, ended up aligning to the same supporting conclusion as ours."

The chances of cooperation, never a sure bet, were made more likely because Cassell was known by the attorney general's office as a principled advocate and sober-minded negotiator. In 2014, he had been hired by newly appointed Attorney General Sean Reyes to investigate corruption allegations against his two predecessors. "I think I was able to help facilitate communication and signal to the attorney general's office the seriousness of what had happened in this particular case," he explained.

Back in March, four months after the notice of claim had been submitted, Cassell wrote a letter to Attorney General Reyes in which he proposed the outlines of a possible settlement. Acknowledging that the Millers' goal was not monetary, but rather "public acknowledgment from the State that Valarie's allegations were never properly investigated," he suggested a way forward.

"One way to achieve that vindication would be through litigation," he wrote in his letter to the attorney general. "But pursuing litigation to a trial and a verdict could be time consuming, expensive, and emotionally draining." Also, the state was well aware of its potential liability, as it had recently borne the cost of a large and emotionally bruising settlement with the family of University of Utah student Lauren McCluskey, who was murdered by an ex-boyfriend after university police failed to respond to more than 20 requests for protection from her in the weeks before her death. Cassell offered the state an alternative: If it issued a satisfactory apology, the family would dismiss its complaint. The state decided this was the best way to move forward.

Back at the press conference, after Cassell's introduction, Richard Lambert and Mike Anderson detailed the Miller investigation as described fully in the pages in this book. When they were done, John Miller took the podium to thank the people who had helped to bring about the outcome, including the family, his own legal team, Attorney General Sean Reyes, Chief Criminal Deputy of the Attorney General's Office Spencer Austin, and Assistant Attorney General and Director of the Litigation Division Joni Jones. Lastly, he thanked DPS Commissioner Jess Anderson, "who had the courage to stand up and say, 'You know what, mistakes were made, and we're gonna admit what they were.'"

But John wanted to bring back into focus the woman at the center of the tragedy. "Valarie was certainly a victim," he began. "But she was also a woman of great courage. If you can imagine having suffered what she went through for a lengthy period of time, the abuse itself and the threats, and then having the courage to go to the state and present to the state in detail what had happened to her. And then for the rest of her life, whenever needed, she was always willing to share the story in hopes that it might help somebody else."

John then read aloud one of Valarie's most tortured recollections as a reminder to the assembled group of the unspeakable cost of child abuse and cruelty, and the pain of mistreatment that time seldom soothes. It was the heartbreaking note Valarie wrote to her doctor at the Menninger Clinic, trying to drag out the feelings she had spent her life denying: "It's hard for me to explain how I felt when Gary and Bobby would not allow me to show my anger or disgust. It makes me feel nauseated and a little dizzy. It's hard because I can feel myself being there, feeling hot, and sweaty, and dirty, inside and out."

He told the assembled group his objectives in bringing his action: "To restore Valarie's good name and repudiate the lies and the distortions told about her for many years. To bring a measure of justice and accountability to the assailants and those who were involved in the cover-up. To enable the Clark family and Miller families to find a measure of closure. And also, to encourage other victims to have the courage to come forward."

And he reminded the group that the damage caused by child abuse is passed from one generation to the next: "It is passed to the children, the grandchildren, and the great-grandchildren, and the only way it's ever stopped is when closure is found and people can find meaning and purpose in life." He encouraged other victims of childhood abuse to "come forward" and "allow healing to replace the pain."

Lastly, he wanted to address a question that had floated over the proceedings but had not been specifically addressed: "Why bring this issue up after so many years?" He remembered that was his own thought when two years earlier, his son, Ryan, suggested they take one last shot at trying to find the truth. And he now understood why it was the right thing to do.

"History is a process of searching for the truth and why things happen," he said. "Honesty makes better history. The truth matters, and the truth sets us free."

In the days following the press conference, 16 TV segments ran about Valarie and the settlement, 10 radio stories and one podcast episode were aired, and 18 print or online articles appeared. John received congratulatory texts and calls from many friends and acquaintances. One moved him particularly. A woman he'd known his whole life wrote him a note saying that after almost two decades of marriage, her husband told her he'd been abused by his brother from age two until seven. The effects had of course touched all aspects of their marriage. The woman told John that at age 65, after much agony and pain, her husband finally decided to go speak to a therapist, and they had chosen one who specialized in adult males who had been sexually abused as children. But on the day of his appointment, her husband was admitted into the hospital with chest pains and was taken off life support two days later. He never got the chance to unburden himself.

John deeply regrets that Bob Dahle died before he was held to account for his savagery against Valarie. He hopes Clarkston will find the courage to face its history, that families will open up about past abuse and try to stop the cycle so that it will no longer allow its children to be attacked and abused for the pleasure of deviant adults.

Ryan is more circumspect. As he puts it, "Even if all we end up doing is stopping Lloyd Clark from sexually abusing one other kid, I will be happy. Because it's not just that one kid, right? It's their kids and their grandkids. And it's the whole cascade. If we can stop that from happening to one more person, I'll be happy."

Debbie called me five days after the press conference and said that while sitting in church that morning, she realized that the feeling of having a stone sitting on her heart—a feeling she'd carried for 30 years—was finally gone.

"After the press conference, I still felt uneasy," she told me, but back in the safety of her familiar church, she realized the feeling was gone. "I feel free, and it is a good feeling."

She said her father was happy for Valarie that the truth had finally been told. He told a reporter for the *Herald Journal*: "It's fulfilled a dream in my heart and a prayer that Valarie would be vindicated from the malicious lies that had been told."[1]

Debbie said that although Mike Dahle, Bob Dahle's younger son, was not a regular churchgoer, she'd seen him in church that morning. I had been tipped off that he'd logged on to the Zoom call for the press conference on December 5. Thinking he might want to say something, I called his home and left a message and my number. He did not call back.

Debbie said that a couple of her friends had called to offer congratulations and their love and support to her and her family. But she had also felt a distinct coolness from others in town. It occurred to her that Clarkston was again dividing, as it had in 1990.

She said her nephew Zach, one of Zane's sons, had noticed something interesting: Every woman in town who was under 50 believed Valarie's story, but the older women didn't.

"It's not that they don't believe it," offered Denzel. "It's that they won't say it."

Shirleen's sister, Venna, told Denzel she approached Ollie Lou Dahle in church and told her she was sorry to have heard the news about the press conference and the difficult information about her husband.

"Don't feel sorry for me," retorted Ollie Lou, who'd just posted a red-and-white "Private Property" sign on her front door. "It's all lies."

APPENDIX

Photos

Aerial photo of Clarkston—town with mountains behind. (From Ben J. Ravsten and Eunice P. Ravsten, *History of Clarkston: The Granary of Cache Valley, 1864–1964* (printed by authors: 1966)); photo credit: Jay Howell.

Valarie Clark with her beloved horse, Leo, in high school.

Valarie Clark, crowned Cache Valley Dairy Princess in 1972.

A photo of a thoughtful Valarie, in high school. When looking at this photo after the truth of her abuse had been revealed, her father Denzel said, "Maybe she wasn't as happy as we thought."

Valarie Clark, daughter of Mr. and Mrs. Denzel R. Clark, Clarkston, a senior at Sky View High.

Valarie is a member of the executive council and of Vistauns. She is active in debate.

Last year she was a member of the Junior Prom royalty. In her sophomore year she was a class officer and queen of the Christmas dance.

She is a member of the acapella choir and a third year Seminary graduate.

In Junior High she was a ninth grade cheerleader and an eighth grade class officer.

Her hobbies are horseback riding, hunting and all sports.

To fight off the shame of her mistreatment, Valarie overcompensated with hard work and many activities. Her accomplishments were highlighted in the local paper.

Valarie Clark and John Miller in 1973, before
his departure for Australia on his LDS mission.

Denzel and Shirleen Clark's home in Clarkston.

Gary Thompson's home directly across the street from the Clarks.

Debbie, Zane, and Valarie Clark, 1980. The Clarkston church brought in a photographer one day for a Boy Scouts fundraiser, and many families sat for photos.

Esther Shirleen Thompson, known as Shirleen,
in her high school graduation photo, May 1948.

Valarie, 4, and Debbie, 7, with their father, Denzel, at Christmas, 1958.
Valarie said Gary Thompson, Denzel's first cousin and their neighbor
across the street, began to molest her on family camping trips
and at home when she was four years old.

Bob Dahle, 18, and Ollie Lou Anderson, 19, on their wedding day, 1955.

Bob Dahle and Gary Thompson, best friends, bag an elk,
as reported in the *Herald Journal*, 1965.

Ricks Cabin, a summer retreat on the road to Steel Canyon,
was still standing in 1991, according to this Ricks family photo.
Valarie said Bob Dahle brought her here to rape her in the 1970s.
Strangely, not a trace of the structure remains.

CLARK, LLOYD T

Name:	CLARK, LLOYD T	DOC Number:	139732
Age:	75	Est. Parole Eligibility Date:	06/14/2009
Ethnicity:	WHITE	Next Parole Hearing Date:	Mar 2024
Gender:	MALE		
Hair Color:	BROWN	This offender is scheduled on the Parole Board agenda for the month and year above. Please contact the facility case manager for the exact date.	
Eye Color:	HAZEL		
Height:	5' 10"		
Weight:	210	Est. Mandatory Release Date:	
		Est. Sentence Discharge Date:	01/20/9999
		Current Facility Assignment:	BENT COUNTY CORRECTIONAL FACILITY

CURRENT CONVICTIONS

Sentence Date	Sentence	County	Case No.
01/08/2008	2Y-LIFE	FREMONT	07CR205

Lloyd Clark, whom Valarie claimed was a witness to her first rape by Bob Dahle and Gary Thompson when she was 13. He is now serving prison terms for soliciting a child for sex over the internet, and for aggravated sex abuse of a child, his granddaughter.

Bob and Ollie Lou Dahle take a break at Big J Burgers in West Richmond, near Clarkston, 2022, months before he died. He knew a new investigation of Valarie Clark's assault claims against him was advancing.

Doug Bodrero (left), commissioner of the Utah Department of Public Safety in 1990, when Mitch Ingersoll (right) was assigned the job of investigating Valarie and John Miller's sexual assault complaints against Bob Dahle.

Utah Highway Patrol Academy, Camp Williams - 1967

With the passage of a Utah Peace Officer Standards & Training bill in 1967, this was the last UHP Academy Class. (kneeling left to right) M. Clair Rasmussen, Jim Yates, Robert Dahle, JDell Sackett. Mel Schiffman, E. Mark Nielsen, Gene Ercanbrack
(standing left to right) Capt. E.M. Pitcher, Lt. Col. Paul M. Christison, Col. Ray Evans, Wayne Rider, Roger G. Taylor, Spencer Thompson, Knewell Knight, Stan Manning, Richard Hull, Paul Mangelson, Comm. Raymond Jackson

Bob Dahle's graduation photo from the Utah Highway Patrol Academy in 1967.

A photo of the Miller family in 1991.
From left, John, Ryan, Valarie, Brooke, Erin, and Annie

Newton Reservoir, where Valarie says Dahle punched her,
knocked her out, and threw her into the water one cold
November day in 1971, leaving her for dead.

What happened to Diana Dahle, Bob and Ollie Lou's youngest child?
She died from esophageal varices, a symptom of
heavy drinking, at home at age 37.

The press conference, held on December 5, 2022, at the Utah State Bar
Association building in Salt Lake City, announcing the state's apology to
the family and acknowledging the claims of the Miller investigation
"rest on a foundation of extensive and disturbing evidence."
In the front row, Denzel, 92, sat with his daughter Debbie,
and grandchildren Brooke, Annie, and Ryan.

Valarie toward the end of her life.

While in therapy at the Menninger Clinic, sometimes Valarie drew pictures of things too difficult to say. Here is a picture of a man with big ears: Bob Dahle's signature feature. She also drew a tent with a dark, forbidding entrance. Denzel Clark said that his cousin, Gary Thompson, had easy access to the youngest children during the family camping trips, when other men were hunting and the women were cooking.

Acknowledgments

I AM GRATEFUL TO KEVIN HELLIKER, Pulitzer Prize–winning reporter for the *Wall Street Journal*, who recommended me for the job of writing this book. Valarie's sister, Debbie Cooper, and father, Denzel Clark, gave selflessly of their time over three years to help me understand Valarie, her childhood, and the town of Clarkston. Valarie's mother, Shirleen Clark, before her passing, offered memories of her own hardscrabble youth in Clarkston. Sue Saunders, Valarie's one true friend and college soulmate, spoke movingly of Valarie and her special gentleness and spiritual qualities. I am indebted to Valarie's surviving children, Annie, Ryan, and Brooke, who probed their own painful memories to bring Valarie alive, as did Valarie's second husband, Gary Martin. Alex Monroe was a thoughtful observer and a fun companion in Salt Lake City. This book would not have been possible without the dogged investigative work of Michael Anderson, retired special agent of the FBI and polygraph expert, who drove thousands of miles across the western United States seeking answers. His careful questioning of Robert Norman Dahle and former Utah Department of Public Safety officials revealed the essential facts of the 1990 DPS cover-up of the criminal investigation Valarie requested against Dahle, a former highway patrolman, for sexual attacks against her as a child. Former Assistant US Attorney Richard Lambert, who helped successfully prosecute Brian David Mitchell and his wife, Wanda Barzee, for the kidnapping of Elizabeth Smart, directed the Miller family's case against Dahle and the Utah Department of Public Safety. His novel legal strategy and his extensive experience in criminal prosecution aided the case throughout. Professor Paul Cassell and Richard Burbidge, top-tier lawyers both, were eminently helpful not only to the case but also to the author. Teri Davis helped me in ways too numerous to describe and impossible not to acknowledge, and she also injected a measure of fun and stimulation into Valarie's later life by relieving her bleak nursing home existence with the occasional outing to the ballet or to therapeutic horse rides. Teri is the behind-the-scenes rock of the Miller operation.

John Miller supported and oversaw the investigation, influencing and directing its shape and scope. If he had not kept private journals throughout his life, neither the legal action against the Utah Department of Public Safety nor this book would have been possible. Quite simply, without his notes, Valarie's story would have disappeared into the mists of time. A traditional Mormon custom, the practice of keeping written contemporaneous journals is a dying but irreplaceable aid to historians, families, investigators, and writers everywhere in the world. One wonders what could possibly take its place. I am gratified that he trusted me, a complete outsider, to take on this searing personal story and write the truth that I found.

Valarie's kind and caring doctor at the Menninger Clinic, whom I refer to as Dr. Brown in these pages because he still maintains an active practice, generously clarified his clinical notes about Valarie with me. His sensitive regard for the fragile woman he cared for so very long ago helped her and helped me. I am grateful to the various Clarkston women who spoke out in spite of their fears of being ostracized from the community for doing so. I am also grateful to the hundreds of other Cache Valley residents, observers, and others who spoke to Mike Anderson and to me for this investigation.

Bob Roe, formerly of *Sports Illustrated* and *Newsweek*, edited this book and wrote the splendid chapter titles. His speedy, deft touch helped me through the most difficult sections detailing Valarie's decline, and his puns kept me smiling when my spirit lagged. Christopher Hodson, professor of history at Brigham Young University, offered up some of his own archival research about both Clarkston and the church's sex education for girls in the 1970s. He smoothed out and deepened the sections summarizing Mormon history, and moreover proved a fascinating interlocutor on matters of chattel slavery, the paintings and life of Élisabeth Louise Vigée Le Brun, and the relationships between France, West Africa, and the Americas. I am honored to call him a friend. F. Ross Peterson, the influential Utah historian and USU faculty member, is a brave and principled man who offered wise and hard-earned insight into the history and culture of his people.

Valarie was a beautiful, intelligent, devout woman and gifted athlete who deserved a happy and fulfilling life but was denied all of that and more by two venal criminals in a clannish town that managed to value, with equal fervor, secrecy and denial. When she was able finally to confront her abusers, she was denied justice by officials in the Utah Department of Public Safety, the very people whose job it was to protect her, who further abused her with self-serving lies. I hope that Valarie's sacrifice, now that her story has been told, will provide the people of Clarkston with the impetus to do whatever is necessary to ensure that no other child will ever again suffer as Valarie did.

Some readers may wonder why I did not include a chapter about the LDS church and its posture with regard to the many cases of child sexual abuse brought against it. Early on, I identified the most likely readers and possible beneficiaries of this story to be Mormons from the Cache Valley area and beyond, and I wanted to make sure the book, in tone, approach, and style, would be accessible and acceptable to them. This was a decision that I have second-guessed many times. I was told that Valarie, in the book she herself dreamed of writing, wanted both to offer understanding and succor to survivors of child sexual abuse, and to do what she could to eradicate the scourge wherever it exists. The entire team has endeavored to honor her wishes.

A good deal more evidence of past abuse against children in Clarkston was uncovered during the reporting of this story but not included in these pages out of concern for how those revelations might affect the reputations and feelings of those children, now adults, if that abuse were made public.

Emily Benedek
March 10, 2024
New York City

Notes

Prologue - A Little Bird, Lying There Broken

1. Some of the descriptions and much of the dialogue in this section come from an unpublished narrative about Annie's accident and recovery that John Miller commissioned from writer Cari Lynn in 2014.

Chapter 2 - "Like a Weird Faulkner Novel"

1. F. Ross Peterson, *A History of Cache County* (Salt Lake City: Utah State Historical Society, Cache County Council, 1997), 46.

2. "Cache County, UT Climate," Best Places, accessed February 14, 2023, https://www.bestplaces.net/climate/county/utah/cache.

3. Kaylene Griffin, "A Brief History of Clarkston," RootsWeb, accessed February 14, 2024, http://freepages.rootsweb.com/~archibald/genealogy/clarkston.htm.

4. Peterson, *A History of Cache Valley*, vii–viii.

5. Ross Peterson interview with author, n.d.

6. Peterson, *A History of Cache Valley*, 78.

7. Kaylene Griffin, "A Brief History of Clarkston," RootsWeb, http://freepages.rootsweb.com/~archibald/genealogy/clarkston.htm.

8. Griffin, "A Brief History of Clarkston."

9. Ben J. Ravsten and Eunice P. Ravsten, *History of Clarkston: The Granary of Cache Valley, 1864–1964* (printed by authors: 1966).

Chapter 3 - "He Never Saw Her Run"

1. Denzel R. Clark, interview by Terrence Durham, James Moyle Oral History Program, Historical Department of the Church of Jesus Christ of Latter-day Saints, October 1992–April 1993.

2. Tad Walch, "Church Finalized Pageant Decision: 4 to End, 3 to Continue," *Deseret News*, December 5, 2018, https://www.deseret.com/2018/12/5/20660498/church-finalizes-pageant-decision-4-to-end-3-to-continue.

3. Hermioni N. Lokko and Theodore A. Stern, "Regression: Diagnosis, Evaluation, and Management," *Primary Care Companion for CNS Disorders* 17, no. 3 (May 2015), https://doi.org/10.4088/PCC.14f01761.

Chapter 4 - Crawling Through Broken Glass

1. Bessel van der Kolk, *The Body Keeps the Score: Brain, Mind, and Body in the Healing of Trauma* (New York: Viking, 2014), 20.
2. van der Kolk, *The Body Keeps the Score*, 20–21.
3. van der Kolk, *The Body Keeps the Score*, 62.
4. Maia Szalavitz, "Opioids Feel Like Love. That's Why They're Deadly in Tough Times," *New York Times*, December 6, 2021, https://www.nytimes.com/2021/12/06/opinion/us-opioid-crisis.html.
5. C. B Nemeroff, et al., "Differential Responses to Psychotherapy Versus Pharmacotherapy in Patients with Chronic Forms of Major Depression and Childhood Trauma," *Proceedings of the National Academy of Sciences of the United States of America* 100, no. 24 (2003):14293–96.
6. van der Kolk, *The Body Keeps the Score*, 43.
7. William Shakespeare, *Macbeth*, act 2, scene 3.
8. van der Kolk, *The Body Keeps the Score*, 43.
9. van der Kolk, *The Body Keeps the Score*, 64.
10. van der Kolk, *The Body Keeps the Score*, 100.
11. van der Kolk, *The Body Keeps the Score*, 21.
12. van der Kolk, *The Body Keeps the Score*, 30.

Chapter 5 - "Dirty, Inside and Out"

1. *The Search for Meaning: Laurel Manual, 1968–9* (Salt Lake City: YWMIA, 1968), 150–151.
2. Aubrey P. Andelin and Helen B. Andelin, *Fascinating Womanhood: Principles Applied to Sex* (Santa Barbara, CA: Andelin Foundation for Education in Family Living, 1974), 6–12.
3. Andelin and Andelin, *Fascinating Womanhood*, 2.
4. Andelin and Andelin, *Fascinating Womanhood*, 2.
5. *The Search for Meaning*, 147–154.
6. Elizabeth Smart said this on many occasions. For example, see Peggy Fletcher Stack, "Elizabeth Smart Reveals She Considered Suicide after She Was Raped," *Salt Lake Tribune*, September 19, 2017, https://www.sltrib.com/religion/local/2017/09/19/elizabeth-smart-reveals-she-considered-suicide-after-she-was-raped/.

7. M. J. Meaney and A. C. Ferguson-Smith, "Epigenetic Regulation of the Neural Transcriptome: The Meaning of the Marks," *Nature Neuroscience* 13, no. 11 (2010): 1313–18.

8. Ross Peterson interview with author, n.d.

9. Dr. Brown interview with author, November 1, 2021.

Chapter 6 - "Her Memory Recall Is Very Painful"

1. Bessel van der Kolk, *The Body Keeps the Score: Brain, Mind, and Body in the Healing of Trauma* (New York: Viking, 2014), 94.

2. Dr. Brown interview with author, November 11, 2021.

3. Dr. Brown interview with author, November 2, 2021.

4. Juliet Macur, "For Years She Said a Coach Abused Her. Now She Has Named a Legend," *New York Times*, March 20, 2023, https://www.nytimes.com/2023/03/20/sports/olympics/jennifer-fox-sexual-abuse-the-tale.html.

Chapter 7 - "Blood on My Boots"

1. M. Russell Ballard, "A Chance to Start Over: Church Disciplinary Councils and the Restoration of Blessings," Church of Jesus Christ of Latter-day Saints, September 1990, https://www.churchofjesuschrist.org/study/ensign/1990/09/a-chance-to-start-over-church-disciplinary-councils-and-the-restoration-of-blessings?lang=eng.

2. Joseph Bauman, "State Settles 3 of 4 Sex Suits against Former UHP Trooper," *Deseret News*, August 31, 1988, https://www.deseret.com/1988/8/31/18776895/state-settles-3-of-4-sex-suits-against-former-uhp-trooper.

3. Chris Jorgensen, "UHP Patrolling for Ways to Mend Image," *Salt Lake Tribune*, December 20, 1991.

4. Letter from Stan Abrams, PhD, to law enforcement officials, Portland, Oregon, June 20, 1990.

5. Roland Summit, "The Child Sexual Abuse Accommodation Syndrome," *Child Abuse & Neglect* 7, no. 2 (1983): 177–93.

Chapter 8 - "All She Had Left Were Her Dreams"

1. Sarah DeWeerdt, "Tracing the Opioid Crisis to Its Roots," *Nature*, September 11, 2019 https://www.nature.com/articles/d41586-019-02686-2.

2. Jesse Hyde and Daphne Chen, "The Untold Story of How Utah Doctors and Big Pharma Helped Drive the National Opioid Epidemic," *Deseret News*, Oct 26, 2017, https://www.deseret.com/2017/10/26/20635281/the-untold-story-of-how-utah-doctors-and-big-pharma-helped-drive-the-national-opioid-epidemic.

3. Ross Peterson interview with author, n.d.

Chapter 9 - "Mayberry, with a Really Deep Evil Streak"

1. "Fay Burke Godfrey," Sims Funeral Home, accessed February 22, 2024, https://www. simsfh.com/obituary/1392827.

2. Scott Montgomery et al., "Concussion in Adolescence and Risk of Multiple Sclerosis," *Annals of Neurology* 82, no. 4 (October 2017): 554–561, https://pubmed.ncbi.nlm.nih. gov/28869671.

3. "Diana Dahle," Allen Mortuaries, accessed March 15, 2024, https://www. allenmortuaries.net/obituaries/diana-dahle-626.

Chapter 10 - "The Big-Eared Bastard"

1. "Voluntary Manslaughter: Verdict in Weston Slaying," *Herald Journal*, January 24, 1954.

2. These details from Lynn Izatt were conveyed to Mike Anderson during interviews he conducted in Alaska. Anderson then detailed them to the author.

3. Ross Peterson interview with author, n.d.

Chapter 11 - An Environment of Hiding Things from Each Other

1. "Plural Marriage in Kirtland and Nauvoo," The Church of Jesus Christ of Latter-day Saints, accessed February 23, 2024, https://www.churchofjesuschrist.org/study/manual/ gospel-topics-essays/plural-marriage-in-kirtland-and-nauvoo?lang=eng.

2. "Plural Marriage in The Church of Jesus Christ of Latter-day Saints," The Church of Jesus Christ of Latter-day Saints, accessed February 23, 2024, https://www. churchofjesuschrist.org/study/manual/gospel-topics-essays/plural-marriage-in-the-church-of-jesus-christ-of-latter-day-saints?lang=eng.

3. John Kincaid, "Extinguishing the Twin Relics of Barbaric Multiculturalism—Slavery and Polygamy—From American Federalism," *Publius: The Journal of Federalism* 33, no. 1 (Winter 2003): 75–92.

4. Grover Cleveland, State of the Union Address, December 8, 1885, https://www. gutenberg.org/files/5029/5029-h/5029-h.htm.

5. *Diary of Ole Anderson Jensen. A Biography and Observations of Ole A. Jensen, Events of his Life and Written from Memory Each Year*, L. Tom Perry Special Collections, Brigham Young University, Mss 619, 10.

6. See, "Doctrine and Covenants Official Declaration I" in church documents, https:// www.churchofjesuschrist.org/study/scriptures/dc-testament/od/1?lang=eng.

7. Jessie L. Embry, "The History of Polygamy," History to Go, Utah Department of Cultural & Community Engagement, updated April 19, 2016, https://historytogo. utah.gov/history-polygamy.

8. Brendan Case, "From 'WEIRD' Monogamy to Informal Polygamy," Institute for Family Studies, March 10, 2021, https://ifstudies.org/blog/from-weird-monogamy-to-informal-polygamy.

9. James Keller, "Polygamy Produces a Host of Social Ills, Court Told," *Globe and Mail*, December 9, 2010, https://www.theglobeandmail.com/news/british-columbia/polygamy-produces-a-host-of-social-ills-court-told/article1319012.

10. Michael Hicks, "Minding Business: A Note on the 'Mormon Creed,'" *BYU Studies Quarterly* 36, no. 4 (1986): 125.

11. Hicks, "Minding Business," 128.

12. Hicks, "Minding Business," 129.

13. John Taylor, "The Gathering," in G. D. Watt, et al., eds., *Journal of Discourses* (London: Latter-Day Saints Book Depot, 1854–188), vol. 25, 355.

14. Benjamin J. Ravsten and Eunice P. Ravsten, *History of Clarkston: The Granary of Cache Valley, 1864–1964* (Town of Clarkston, n.d.).

15. Ezra Taft Benson, "Civic Standards for Faithful Saints," Church of Jesus Christ of Latter-day Saints, April 1972, https://www.churchofjesuschrist.org/study/general-conference/1972/04/civic-standards-for-the-faithful-saints?lang=eng.

16. See, "Jack and Polygamy" audio file (1:49) at FamilySearch, https://www.familysearch.org/photos/artifacts/43955238?p=51583872.

17. Ross Peterson interview with author, n.d.

18. Ross Peterson interview with author, n.d.

19. "Emma Smith's Path through Polygamy," Joseph Smith's Polygamy, accessed February 23, 2024, https://josephsmithspolygamy.org/common-questions/emma-smith-plural-marriage/#RevelationonCelestialandPluralMarriage.

20. Rod Boam, "Unraveling the History of Preston's Bloody Bucket," *Cash Valley Daily*, June 1, 2022, https://www.cachevalleydaily.com/news/archive/2022/06/01/unraveling-the-history-of-prestons-bloody-bucket/#.YpkGbi1h1bU.

21. Charles McCollum, "Did Willie Nelson Really Do a Long-Ago Gig Near Preston, Idaho?," *Herald Journal*, October 2, 2011, https://www.hjnews.com/opinion/editors-corner-did-willie-nelson-really-do-a-long-ago-gig-near-preston-idaho/article_4adb1e80-eca3-11e0-9de5-001cc4c002e0.html.

22. Rod Boam, "Unraveling the History."

23. Rod Boam, "Unraveling the History."

Chapter 14 - Denial and Slander

1. GRAMA is short for the Government Records Access and Management Act of Utah, which establishes the right for public access to state records (Utah Code Section 63G-2-201(1)).

Chapter 15 - "My Memory Is on My Mind"

1. Cañon City Police Department, "CIRT Operation to Arrest Lloyd Clark," narrative for case number 07-10317a29, June 26, 2007.

2. Advocates for survivors of child sexual abuse recommend referring to child pornography as "child sexual abuse material." See: https://www.justice.gov/d9/2023-06/child_sexual_abuse_material_2.pdf.

3. K. H. conversation with John Miller, March 26, 2024.

Chapter 16 - Last Rites and Wrongs

1. "Robert Norman Dahle," Legacy.com, August 4, 2022, https://www.legacy.com/us/obituaries/hjnews/name/robert-dahle-obituary?id=36136201.

2. "Robert Norman Dahle's 85th Birthday," *Herald Journal*, March 12, 2022, https://www.hjnews.com/announcements/birthdays/robert-norman-dahles-85th-birthday/article_b4381839-710f-533d-a150-68f6715781da.html.

Chapter 17 - Justice Delayed

1. Jackson Wilde, "'Extensive and Disturbing Evidence': Utah Expresses 'Deep Regret' Regarding Clarkston Woman's Rape Complaint Against Former-UHP Trooper," *Herald Journal*, December 9, 2022, https://www.hjnews.com/news/crime_courts/extensive-and-disturbing-evidence-utah-expresses-deep-regret-regarding-clarkston-woman-s-rape-complaint

About the Author

EMILY BENEDEK grew up in Belmont, Massachusetts, and graduated from Harvard College. Her stories and essays have appeared in the *New York Times*, the *Washington Post*, *Newsweek*, *Rolling Stone*, *Vogue*, *Mosaic*, *Tablet*, and on NPR, among others. She is the author of three nonfiction books: *The Wind Won't Know Me: A History of the Navajo-Hopi Land Dispute* (Alfred A. Knopf, Inc., 1992), *Beyond the Four Corners of the World: A Navajo Woman's Journey* (Alfred A. Knopf, Inc., 1996), *Through the Unknown, Remembered Gate: A Spiritual Journey* (Schocken, 2001), and two thrillers: *Red Sea* (St. Martin's Press, 2007) and *Iranian Rhapsody* (Goldmann Verlag, 2014). She lives in New York City.